HEAR ME ROAR

HEAR ME ROAR

WOMEN,

MOTORCYCLES,

AND THE

RAPTURE

OF THE ROAD

ANN FERRAR
With Photographs by the Author

Crown Trade Paperbacks
New York

Copyright © 1996 by Ann Ferrar

Published by Crown Publishers, Inc., 201 East 50th Street, New York, New York 10022.
Member of the Crown Publishing Group.

Random House, Inc. New York, Toronto, London, Sydney, Auckland

http://www.randomhouse.com/

CROWN TRADE PAPERBACKS and colophon are trademarks of Crown Publishers, Inc.

Printed in the United States of America

Design by Kay Schuckhart

Library of Congress Cataloging-in-Publication Data
is available upon request.

ISBN 0-517-88172-1
10   9   8   7   6   5   4   3   2

For my mother, Marie

To my sweetheart, Frank

And in memory of my beloved father, Anthony . . .

Dad, wish you could see me now.

C O N T E N T S

"*Ginger Rogers did everything Fred Astaire did. She just did it backward in high heels.*"

—Ann Richards, motorcyclist, former governor of Texas

INTRODUCTION

I was riding along a deserted highway in Florida when the Great Nor'easter of March 1993 struck the whole eastern seaboard. I was on my way home to New York. My mount at the time was a sporty, 650cc Hawk GT with no wind protection other than a small, bubble-shaped shield.

Suddenly, the storm rocked the sky. On came the lightning, the wind, and the rain. My bike was precariously top-heavy with camping gear. Leaning against the wind, I struggled to stay on course but some gusts were so violent, at times I was blown across my lane. Just minutes before the power lines went out, I pulled safely into the garage of Teri and Harold, a couple I'd met the week before at my campground.

Farther north, along almost every state on my route, a blizzard was blowing. I couldn't wait for long—I had to get back to my job as a writer for a voluntary health organization. And so I rode into freshly fallen snow and ice along I-95 and sub-zero windchills from North Carolina to Manhattan.

What was I doing on my motorcycle in the dead of winter so far from home? Bike Week, the enormous, yearly convergence of motorcyclists in Daytona Beach, had lured me south. During that trip, I had a variety of experiences that would later enrich this book.

I met the legendary Dot Robinson, an octogenarian astride a Harley who had been a champion sidecar endurance racer. I met a contingent of her Motor Maids, the first

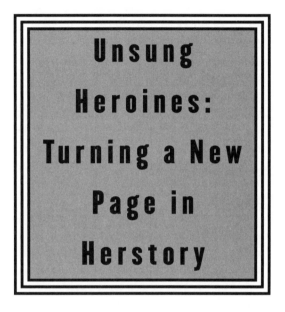

Unsung Heroines: Turning a New Page in Herstory

nationwide club for women riders. I flicked my bike through the winding roads of a state park where oak trees formed a canopy and the only sound was my engine. In town, I cruised Main Street amid the rumble of thousands of Harleys, many ridden by women. At the speedway, I watched the Daytona 200. Every morning I had a breakfast of pancakes and friendly conversation at a campsite where a local BMW club served as hosts. There, I met Teri and Harold.

That's how it is in the world of motorcycling. During my travels, I encountered its various subcultures. People from all walks of life—from yuppies to outlaws—were drawn together in a diverse but definite *community*.

Daytona '93 was the midway point in an

intense six-year odyssey throughout which I interviewed women, shot photographs, and wrote this book. My travels took me and my motorcycles (I've owned four) intermittently from Laconia, New Hampshire, to California, and from Ontario to Key West. My journey started in 1990 en route to the Black Hills Motor Classic in Sturgis, South Dakota, the *other* mega-rally of bikers. In those days, I earned my living as a freelance writer, and I went to Sturgis to write a magazine article about the first all-women Harley drag races.

I was a passenger on a friend's motorcycle, because I hadn't learned to ride yet. Having grown up in New York City taking mass transit, I'd reached my early thirties with little *car* driving experience. The thought of operating a motorcycle was something I couldn't fathom. So I rode on the back because I just loved being on a bike. But the lack of control and dependency on someone else were frustrating.

At Sturgis, I saw more women riding their own motorcycles than I'd ever imagined. My life changed when I met members of a club called Women in the Wind. There was an exuberance and an audacity about them. They were rule breakers and different from any other women I'd known. Their spirited honesty, and their stories of their many adventures and travails on the road, were the initial inspirations for this book.

These women encouraged me to take the bull by the handlebars and learn how to ride. Immediately, I learned the basics at a Motorcycle Safety Foundation course. After that, it took all my nerve to ride in New York City, with its crater-potholes, killer cabs, maniacal bicycle messengers, and hit-me-if-you-dare pedestrians. I survived, and then a sea change occurred in my psyche. The other hassles of life in that difficult city seemed eas-

ier compared to the gauntlet of two-wheeled urban combat, which I'd faced and overcome.

As I spoke to more and more women, I saw similar emotional tread patterns. In so many cases, a woman's mastery of a motorcycle was metaphoric for her ability to surmount other obstacles. I also found that women, as well as men, have played a vital role in the evolution of motorcycling as a slice of American history. Take Adeline and Augusta Van Buren. In 1916, these sisters became the first women to complete a transcontinental trip on two solo motorcycles. They did it to show Uncle Sam that women could serve as motorcycle dispatch carriers during World War I. The Van Burens are gone now, but I had the pleasure of meeting Adeline's daughter, Anne Tully Ruderman, who wrote this tribute to her mother:

> *Adeline Van Buren's name is not in the Guinness Book of World Records, nor is it in a Women's Hall of Fame. It ought to be, for she rode and wrote a unique chapter in the story of women's independence. The newspapers called my mother and aunt the gentle sex, but made much of the fact that they had done something no women had ever done, in a manner that no man in his right mind would attempt. They tackled a "daring test," riding into the wilderness, over mountains, and across deserts, without benefits of arms or man.[1]*

About three-quarters of a century later, as I roared off on one of my cushy, three-thousand-mile trips on paved roads, I met Bessie B. Stringfield, who had made her mark during World War II. Imagine how many jaws dropped at the sight of this lone black woman riding a Harley for the army!

The author on the road in 1993 with the Honda Hawk GT, Westerville, Ohio

Joanna Strohn

Stringfield, now deceased, was a one-woman civil rights movement.

Today's women motorcyclists are iconoclasts who are doing something totally unexpected of women, yet they are largely unrecognized outside of the motorcycling community. The women in this book include a hair stylist who became the fastest woman on a Harley-Davidson drag bike, a grandmother who rode through the mud and frost heaves of the Canadian Yukon, and a computer programmer and remedial reading teacher who spearheaded a "Pony Express" motorcycle ride around the nation to raise money for breast cancer research.

This book is about diehards who live and breathe their motorcycles, who view their bikes as extensions of their personalities, and who steep themselves in a milieu—be it a disciplined life riveted to racing or a free-spirited lifestyle centered on the Harley "mystique." These women are nonconformists. Each one is doing something that only the tiniest fraction of the United States population is doing. There are, at the highest estimate, only about seven hundred fifty thousand women who ride motorcycles.

When a woman decides to ride, often the act is more than it appears. Ever since the late nineteenth century, when women bucked tra-

Joanne Flaster

On Long Island, New York, with my current bike, a BMW R65

dition to ride bicycles, the sight of a woman awheel has been tied to a slew of conflicting messages about her femininity, competency, power, and liberation. Suffragist Susan B. Anthony was quoted as saying that riding bicycles "did more to emancipate woman than anything else in the world" and that a woman moving forth on two wheels was "the picture of free, untrammelled womanhood."

Today, women bikers are still scrutinized in a way that our male counterparts are not. We're controlling these huge, mechanical beasts, getting them to do our bidding. A few people don't know what to make of the girl-next-door taking charge, breaking free.

Fortunately, for every observer who just doesn't get it, there are two enthusiasts saluting the woman biker with a "thumbs-up."

There were a couple of days in the summer of 1993, when I was humbled to be in the presence of eighty-year-old Vera Griffin, one of the Motor Maids' first officers. For decades, Vera had ridden motorcycles that had to be cranked (kick-started). Most roads she traveled were unpaved. "I called all my motorcycles my magic carpets," she said, "because they took me to wondrous places I could not have gone any other way."

Vera gave me a pile of original vintage photographs and period clippings that helped shape the section about women in the 1930s through the 1950s. I promised to take good care of the photos and return them. But I think Vera sensed something. "Keep them," she said. "What you're doing is very important. I have no one to leave them to."

Vera Griffin passed away seven months later, in the winter of 1994. She had knowingly prepared me to carry on the legacy of an unusual group of women whose contributions to "herstory"—and history—have remained largely hidden.

I now live on eastern Long Island near the beach and great roads, with my other half, Frank Dusek, and our three sets of twins: my 1987 BMW R65 and his 1973 Harley-Davidson Sportster and 1950 Indian Scout. It is eighty years since the Van Burens made their trailblazing journey on machines so primitive, the headlights were lit with matches. I will never be half the rider that they were, or that Vera was. But in my own way, through the gift of story, I hope I have done them proud.

ANN FERRAR

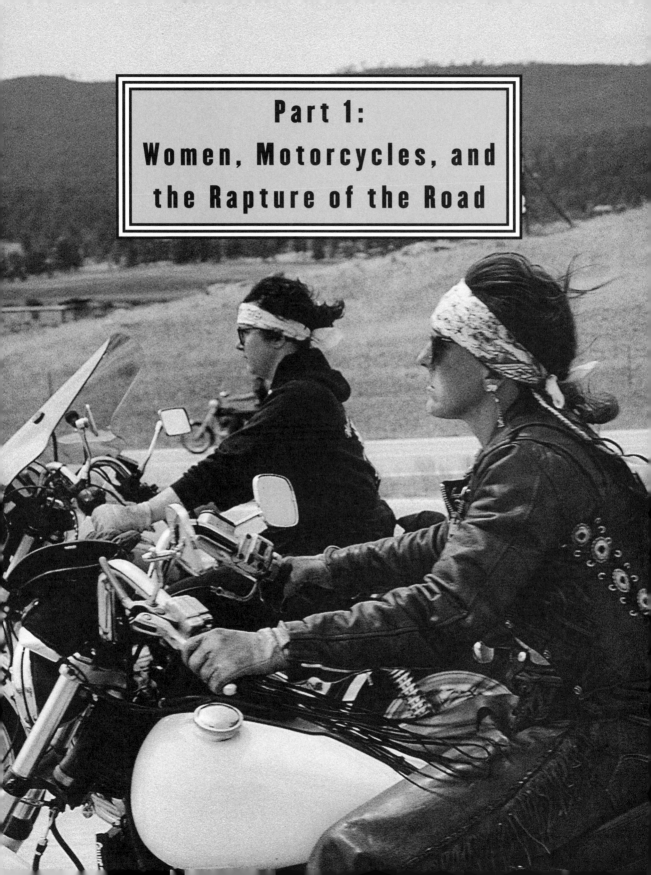

Part 1:
Women, Motorcycles, and the Rapture of the Road

"I like the speed, the competition. And I love the motorcycle. There's something about this machine that thrills me and I just can't seem to get enough."

—Fran Crane, Scotts Valley, California

"Everywoman" as a Rebel: The Voices of Women Who Ride

"I've always been a rebel, your basic tomboy type. Something happens when you put on that black leather jacket and boots. It's like you could kick ass, even though you wouldn't. A certain amount of power comes with it."

—Judy Jackson, Toledo, Ohio

"Riding has given me a lifestyle of my own and a place where I belong. The motorcycle is a stress reliever that helps me block out the corporate bull at work. When I'm eating too big a slice of the system pie, I think about that bike and that part of myself, and it helps me get through the sludge."

—Sandy Couture, Toledo, Ohio

"I felt like that song, 'I am woman, hear me roar!' I can do anything! I can have grandchildren! I can cook! I can ford rivers on a motorcycle!"

—Catharine Rambeau, Lantana, Florida

"I was asked to speak at a fundraiser and was introduced as a woman who wears many hats. I said, 'One of my hats is a motorcycle helmet.' People take that as an expression of power and self-confidence. You have to be secure to be a professional woman with a certain standing, and ride a motorcycle."

—Ana Dumois, New York City

OPPOSITE: Cindy Earle with her BMW K75S

> **"I**'m not a 'biker.' I don't wear black leather with studs. I ski and ride horses. There are parallels. It's the flirting with danger, the idea of pushing my limits within safety factors I can control. Riding a motorcycle is a little more challenging than most people are willing to tackle. Something prevents them from doing it, but I'm *doing it.*"
>
> **—Jenny Alexander,**
> **Santa Barbara, California**

These are the voices of motorcycling women—a little-known breed of gutsy, independent mavericks who explode convention every time they start their engines. The women above are in their thirties, forties, fifties, and sixties. They ride all types of motorcycles, from a powerful 1000cc BMW sport-tourer, to a raucous 883cc Harley-Davidson Sportster, to a small, springy 250cc Honda dirt bike.

Many of these women have taken physical and emotional risks to get on the front seat. They have challenged personal limits and defied social stereotypes. They have raised eyebrows among family, friends, and coworkers. In so doing, they have carved niches in a male-dominated lifestyle and broken records in a male-dominated sport. They have ridden to the far reaches of the globe and reinvented themselves on motorcycles.

Fran Crane is a parking enforcement officer who is obsessed with bikes and the road. She earned a Guinness Book world record for marathon-riding a BMW K100 from New York to San Francisco in forty-four hours and twenty minutes. Judy Jackson is a nursing student and mother who started riding twenty years ago after a serious lung operation. For Jackson, it was therapy, "a way to get back among the living." Catharine Rambeau is a magazine editor and grandmother who rode the little dirt bike on a solo, 14,300-mile trip from the United States to the southern tip of Argentina—to Ushuaia, a village on the island of Tierra del Fuego known as the end of the world. She was the first woman ever to do so. Sandy Couture escapes from her office on the Sportster. She is a "lifestyle biker" in a subculture where the world revolves around Harleys, leather, and chrome.

Jenny Alexander is an educational psychologist who sees herself as "fairly traditional,

Fran Crane on her K100RS, similar to the bike she rode into the record books

W.G. Allen/BlackRiders Magazine

A moment of female pride: Members of the Lady Hawks Motorcycle Club of Maryland show off their trophies for participation in various events.

and yet I ride a motorcycle. It's unexpected. That's part of the kick." Cindy Earle is a schoolteacher who spends summers on her bike. Cuban émigré Ana Dumois is a Ph.D. who heads an agency that provides health care to underprivileged women. She rides to poor communities astride a weathered, 450cc Honda Rebel because "we are not in a box. We are open, accessible. We are about people taking their destinies into their own hands and taking risks to promote change. My riding a motorcycle represents all that."

Indeed, it does. Today's motorcycling women are a legion well over half a million strong—roughly a tenfold increase from the 1960s. And yet they are still just a fraction of the nation's 7.5 million motorcycle riders.

Who are these women?

They are wives, mothers, grandmothers, white-collar professionals, athletes, and blue-collar workers. About a third have a college background or degree. They are lawyers, secretaries, corporate vice presidents, small-business owners, and homemakers. They range in age from teenagers to octogenarians. A few are celebrities—actresses Ann-Margret and Kirstie Alley, tennis greats Martina Navratilova and Gabriela Sabatini, and singers k. d. lang, Wynonna Judd, Tanya Tucker, and Queen Latifa are among the glitterati-on-wheels. Others are dignitaries, such as former Texas governor Ann Richards, who learned to ride a Harley in celebration of her sixtieth birthday. While the majority of women motorcyclists are caucasian and heterosexual, women of color and lesbian riders are more visible than in decades past.

Like their male peers, women riders of all backgrounds have a passion for two wheels that is fueled by many factors: the exhilaration of the motorcycle's wind-in-the-face freedom, coupled with a strong sense of independence and control; the allure of adventure and the closeness with nature; the kinesthetic relationship with a responsive machine that is straddled and ridden like a horse; the camaraderie of the motorcycle community; and the mystique, the romanticism, the challenges around every bend in the road.

> "It's the blump-blump-blump of the engine. It goes with your heartbeat. Then there's the sound of the pipes. On one level, it gets down to real primitive stuff. On a conscious level, I have freedom waiting in my garage."
>
> **—Sandy Couture**

> "I feel a cowgirl spirit. On a bike, you're one with the elements like the old cowboys were. That's part of what our country was founded on. It's a real closeness with life."
>
> **—Jacquie Bonney, rancher, dirt bike and rodeo rider, Pueblo, Colorado**

For many women, the bike represents all of these things. Often, it becomes a vehicle of self-discovery. For some, it conveys rebellion.

To sixty-four-year-old Ana Dumois, rebellion isn't new—her motorcycle is merely an extension of her nature. In the 1950s, Dumois was involved in the Cuban revolution. She said, "When Castro betrayed democracy, I left Cuba. I chose my current profession because I knew it would be tough and I love a good fight!"

In her quest to help underprivileged women, Dumois chose a motorcycle to overthrow the image of the stodgy executive. "When I ride to one of our clinics, I don't show up in a fancy dress in a big car," she explained. "I am the director, but the staff and clients can relate to me. You have to be different to promote change."

Rebels come in all shapes and sizes. They can be found among the conservative Motor Maids, the nation's first club for women riders, founded in 1940. At their conventions, many gray-haired members still parade in their matching uniforms through small-town America. And there are rebels among a group of leather-bustiered, thigh-high-booted women who cruise Main Street during Daytona Bike Week, a motorcycle Mardi Gras. Their club patch screams, CUNTILEROS. And there are rebels among the quiet individualists who are seriously obsessed with bikes, like endurance rider Fran Crane. "My mother threatened to disown me if she so much as caught me on the *back* of a motorcycle," said Crane. "So I started riding because she didn't want me to. Today, I don't go anywhere in four-wheeled vehicles." Crane, now forty-nine, has owned twenty-

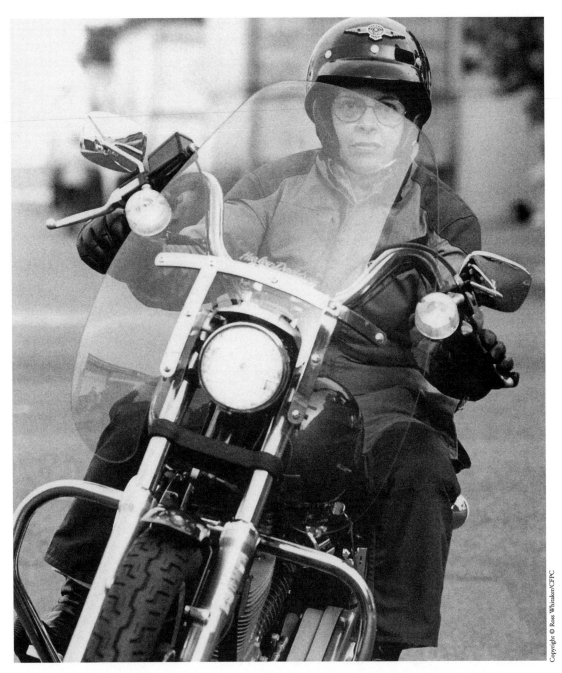

Copyright © Ross Whitaker/CFPC

Ana Dumois on her 1991 Harley-Davidson FXR, one of three bikes she owns. In the boardroom of her agency is a wall of plaques: her diplomas, citations, distinguished service awards . . . and in the middle, "Long Distance Female, Big Country Moto Guzzi Rally, 1986."

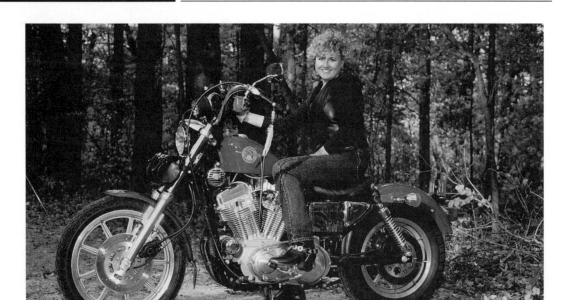

Becky Brown

Sandy Couture on her 1990 Sportster, an 883cc Hugger. Drag pipes let the neighbors know she's coming home. She says, "I believe in the cliche 'Loud pipes save lives.' Plus I like having a macho bike!"

eight bikes and logged many hundreds of thousands of miles.

METAMORPHOSIS

When a woman masters a motorcycle, often she undergoes a change that spreads to other aspects of her life. This growth doesn't come from merely donning a leather jacket and boots. Some women take a long look at themselves, accept self-imposed challenges, and make changes with great resolve. When they learn to control a motorcycle, they do likewise with their fate.

Sandy Couture, a divorcée from Toledo, Ohio, moved to the front seat when she was thirty-four. "Riding my own bike has changed my life forever and I love every bit of it," she declared. "Before I bought my own bike, I'd been a passenger on Harleys for fifteen years. I was proud to be a biker, but I always had problems with the thinking that a biker woman 'belonged' to her man. I was no militant women's libber, but I couldn't live with the double standards."

She couldn't live with the local biker scene, either: "It seemed like every time my husband would say, 'Let's go for a ride,' he'd get in the wind five yards to the nearest bar and talk about what a biker he was."

After her divorce, Couture said, "I was frustrated on the back of a guy's bike, praying I'd get home okay because he'd had too much to drink. They took you for a ride and then expected you to put out. I refused to go through it."

In 1990, when she bought her Harley Sportster, she found freedom and a new circle of friends. A year later she was elected Toledo chapter president of the motorcycle club Women in the Wind.

Like many beginners, Couture had early doubts. "At first I wondered, Hey, can you really do this? It had been a long time since I'd had to work so hard to overcome the fear

"When I turned forty-two, my husband decided to leave and 'find himself.' For twenty-four years, he was all I had. In an effort to claim my independence, I decided to ride my own bike. Because I'm only five feet one and ninety-five pounds, some people thought I would never be able do it. My dream of being in control of this machine made me even more determined. My life has gotten better for all the self-worth and perseverance riding has taught me. My work, too, has reflected my strong sense of accomplishment."

—Nikki Mongaraz, former secretary promoted to computer software trainer, Frankfort, Illinois[1]

"When I was younger, I did the domestic part of my life. Now I can be proud of what I accomplish on my own. A lot of women never experience this because they don't get the opportunity to go on the road alone. I didn't when traveling with my husband; he used to take care of me. But now, on the road by myself, it's me, the motorcycle, and that's it."

—Cindy Earle, fifty-something, Baton Rouge, Louisiana

of something. But once I mastered it, I knew I could do anything I put my mind to."

Couture's path to self-realization followed a familiar pattern. Dagmar O'Connor, Ph.D., a New York psychologist and author, commented: "If you take a physical or emotional risk, you break through a barrier. This usually has a ripple effect into other areas. Especially if a woman sees the motorcycle as a dare— something she was afraid of—overcoming it can provide the confidence to tackle things she might fear emotionally. Physical risks often become symbols and practice grounds for emotional risks."

Vicki Randle, singer-percussionist for the band on *The Tonight Show with Jay Leno*, rode dirt bikes as a West Coast teenager. Today, at forty-one, she says, "I spend a lot of time commuting on the freeways. When I arrive at the studio after being on my Harley, I feel so good."

"*Riding is intuitive. On a bike, you're invisible to cars, so you have to be aware of your surroundings at all times. You're aware of your speed, how you lean, the condition of the bike—you become part of that machine and it becomes a part of you. It's total involvement.*"

—Vicki Randle, musician, Venice, California

THE REVERIE OF THE ROAD

The road calls. The bike beckons, like a stabled horse that needs to be taken out. Whether it's the deep, loud rumble of a Harley, the clickety-clack of a BMW twin, or the turbinelike drone of a high-revving Japanese sport bike, the speed, motion, and machinery orchestrate their own mellifluous song. With the wind rushing past her body and the steady roar of the machine below, all of the rider's senses are engaged in a hyper-receptive mode. She is alert yet relaxed, absorbed in a moving meditation. On the road, at speed, the mind is cleared of rubble. Her concentration is so focused, she is nothing but the sum of her experience and her awareness of the present.

The view from the saddle is panoramic, unobstructed by the TV-tube frame of a car windshield. She marvels at the scenery . . . and may be simultaneously splattered with it. She is undeniably alive, connected at once to her own humanity, to the earth, and to the powerful bike that carries her faster and farther than she could go on her own. On top of her two-wheeled flying machine, the rider downshifts and banks into curves with authority. She upshifts to fifth on a straightaway . . . and with a twist of the throttle, she's as free as a woman can be on the ground.

In her autobiography, *On the Perimeter,*[2] the late Hazel Kolb wrote, "The bike is strapping like a bull, sleek like a running horse, and

has the kind of power that, when you yank on it, makes your eyes slide to the horizon and your imagination fly beyond." Kolb was a Motor Maid and grandmother who swapped her leisure suit for a leather jacket. She left small-town Missouri in 1979 to circumnavigate the United States on a Harley. With those words, Kolb captured the exuberance of a woman rider soaring above the rote of daily existence. A woman riding a motorcycle is buoyant, both metaphorically and in a very tangible way. On her bike, she is whole, not fragmented as so many women are when catering to children, husbands, lovers, and bosses. When she's riding, the constantly changing ground beneath her wheels is her own private space. She is mobile—no one can catch her. She can't be squished into any of the compartments that women are forced to inhabit.

Karen Signell, Ph.D., author of *Wisdom of the Heart: Working with Women's Dreams,* observed: "Women have been held back so much. We are grounded in careful realities. We do these unending tasks. We do the dishes and then we do them again. We cook meals and then we cook them again. Riding a motorcycle provides the thrill of moving forward. A lone woman breaking through barriers and showing what she can do is inspiring. It's also true for a great skier or a woman who can fly a plane or race a horse. She captures our imagination."

The woman who gets on a motorcycle has to *really want* to

Courtesy *American Woman Motorscene*

Courtney Caldwell of *American Woman Motorscene*

ride. She knows that on the bike, she may bake in the dry heat of a desert highway . . . or shiver from the chill of a thunderstorm that dumps buckets of hail and fogs her helmet visor so badly, the road becomes a blur. In city traffic, her mind revs as fast as the engine. She maneuvers the bike aggressively yet defensively, making hundreds of split-second decisions per mile, upon which her safety—her life—depends. Sometimes the machine breaks down. She is vulnerable. She is not surrounded by four doors and a roof. She resorts to her own devices and, sometimes, the helpfulness of other bikers who miraculously appear on the side of the road. The Everywoman who gets on a motorcycle drinks in all these experiences, which just don't happen in a four-wheeled "cage."

A CROSSROADS AT THIRTY-SOMETHING

Courtney Caldwell, publisher of *American Woman Motorscene* magazine, noted that many women are ready to embrace the challenges of the road on two wheels when they reach their mid-thirties—when they've matured, when their careers are established and the children are in school. Said Caldwell, "By the age of thirty-five, women are more secure about who they are and they're looking for ways to vent their adventurous side." Caldwell views the recent surge in women riding motorcycles as an extension of the fact that more women are enjoying action-adventure sports, from skydiving to rock climbing.

"More women are in management positions, where there's risk and stress," she pointed out. "As men do, they're seeking ways to relieve stress and they believe, 'If I can do this in my career, then I can ride a motorcycle.' Adventurous and challenging sports are a new frontier."

For some gay women, the motorcycle can be a visible symbol that tells the world, "This is who I am."

"I'm a thirty-nine-year-old woman who happens to be gay. I joined Women on Wheels and had the good fortune to meet some great straight women who accept me and my partner just the way we are. You might want to know it works both ways. It does get a bit tiresome when you married women get too long-winded about your husbands. Some of us have survived on our own. Some of us have worked hard to buy our own motorcycles, which feels pretty darn good."

—Shelly Beeson, Seattle, Washington[3]

> "I prefer to be around women who are like me. I'd rather not hear straight women say they have to get home from a ride, pick up the kids, and do the dishes because Bob has been out all day and he doesn't want to do it. I perceive that generally, dyke bikers are more self-sufficient. They'll say, 'My bike broke and I've got to fix it.' A lot of straight women say, 'Honey, my bike is leaking oil.'"

—L. B. Gunn, thirty-four, Women's Motorcycle Contingent organizer, San Francisco, California

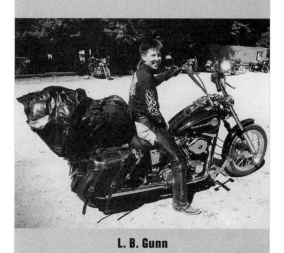

L. B. Gunn

AN INVASION OF WANNA-BES

"Riding a motorcycle is like an Annie Oakley thing," said Sandy Couture. "When they first settled the West, women had to have guts and not be prissy little frail things. That is what it takes to ride a bike. You have to get your manicure dirty."

That's the difference between real women motorcyclists and the cadre of fashion models and movie and TV stars who began decking themselves in studded leather in the early to mid-1990s. Women riders spawned a motorcycle fashion and image craze that invaded popular culture. Trend watchers called it biker chic.

"Motorcycle mania brought black leather as much into the fashion vernacular as the little black dress," tolled *Harper's Bazaar* as designers put models ("prissy little frail things") on motorcycles in TV and print ads. The Council of Fashion Designers of America presented an award to Harley-Davidson MotorClothes for what *Newsweek* dubbed "decades of style influence on everyone from club kids to Chanel." Stars dressed like bikers to prove they still "had it." Marking her sixtieth birthday in a 1992 issue of *Life*, a leathered-up Liz Taylor straddled her purple Harley named Passion. Comedienne Roseanne, sporting a new tattoo and a biker jacket, vamped for the cover of *Us*.

More and more images of attractive, independent women at the controls have appeared continuously throughout the media. And yet, despite all the hype, a real woman riding a motorcycle down Main Street, USA, is still a curiosity. She triggers reactions that range from awe and smiles of approval to frowns of disdain or even fear.

> **"I** see expressions of awe in little girls. But some adults don't know what to think. One time, a friend and I pulled up next to a pair of seniors at a stoplight. As soon as they heard our bikes, we heard their door locks go click, click! We just laughed."
>
> **—Becky Brown, factory worker and mother, Toledo, Ohio**

At rest stops, complete strangers are drawn to the woman who's just pulled in on a motorcycle. People wonder what kind of person she is. On the road, with her dark sunglasses, leather jacket, and boots, a weekday careerwoman/weekend biker may be perceived as anything from a goddess on wheels or a sex fantasy, to a tomboy or an outlaw biker "mama." B movies like *Chopper Chicks in Zombietown* and *She-Devils on Wheels* have perpetuated such myths.

As this book will show, motorcycling women have been doing something bold and unconventional for nearly a hundred years—long before the fashion mavens, the celebrity wanna-bes, and the Madison Avenue media barrage. Women riders are doers, not followers. They are a little-known sorority that has defied gender stereotypes ever since the first motorcycles were rolled out at the turn of the century. Women riders blasted through the mores of Victorianism. They exploded the boundaries of female containment in the 1950s. They predated the modern women's movement. And they have ridden roads less traveled ever since.

So. Who are these two-wheeling women? Some view themselves as *bikers* and partake of a lifestyle where Harleys reign amid leather and chrome.

Others never use the word *biker,* but think of themselves as "motorcyclists" or just people who like to ride. For these women, any brand of bike will do because they each have their own appeal.

Some ride through male resistance; most ride with male encouragement.

Some ride with clubs, attend motorcycle rallies and races, and become involved in motorcycle events to benefit charities and political causes.

> **"I**n Brooklyn, I faced a couple in a car waiting to make a left turn. The woman seemed oppressed or emotionally distraught. As I rode by, she smiled and blew me a kiss. She probably thought, Power to you, you're free. Many times while riding I see in women a look of longing. Perhaps they feel that they, too, might do it someday."
>
> **—Ana Dumois**

Judy Jackson with her Honda Shadow 500

Others ride great distances alone, using their motorcycles as vehicles to explore the world and the limits of their own endurance.

Some ride street bikes on paved roads. Others are dual-sport or off-road jockeys, kicking up dust on desert and mountain trails.

Some are athletes who thrive on speed and competition, while others are weekend cruisers seeking relaxation and camaraderie.

Yet no matter how diverse their backgrounds, and no matter how entrenched they are or aren't in any of motorcycling's subcultures, strong running threads unite women riders. They have invented their own brand of feminism and redefined what is feminine. Like their counterparts in other action-adventure sports, these audacious women have rejected the notion that feminine strength is a contradiction in terms.

"Most women riders are a breed in themselves," said Judy Jackson. "We share a lot of the same views. It's been real good for me, the camaraderie. I don't know if it's that we're tomboys or just terribly independent."

Becky Brown, who founded Women in the Wind, a nationwide club with six hundred members, put it even more simply: "It's part of the whole progression of women. Voting, working, riding motorcycles. More freedom."

"The motorcycle girl is a twentieth-century phenomenon, but the spirit that moves her is as old as Eve. It was the spirit of the motorcycle girl that sent the pioneer mothers out over the prairies. . . . But it has almost nothing to do with being a perfect lady."

—from *Listen, World!*, a 1925 Hearst newspaper essay

Incredible Women and Their Freedom Machines: A Chronicle, from the Turn of the Century to the Fifties

Today's motorcycling women come from a long line of mavericks who thumbed their noses at convention, hitched up their Victorian skirts, and shocked society by riding bicycles. To ride "the wheel," women dumped their corsets and curfews. They reveled in mobility—and the freedom that comes with it.

Even temperance leader Frances E. Willard, one of the most influential women of the Victorian era, saw bicycling as a symbol of liberation. In 1895, she wrote: "That which made me succeed with the bicycle was precisely what had gained me a measure of success in life—it was the hardihood of Spirit that led me to begin, the persistence of will that held me to my task, and the patience that was willing to begin again when the last stroke had failed."[1]

Six years later, Willard's sentiments would

OPPOSITE: **Motor Maid Vera Griffin of Indiana**
(Vera Griffin Collection)

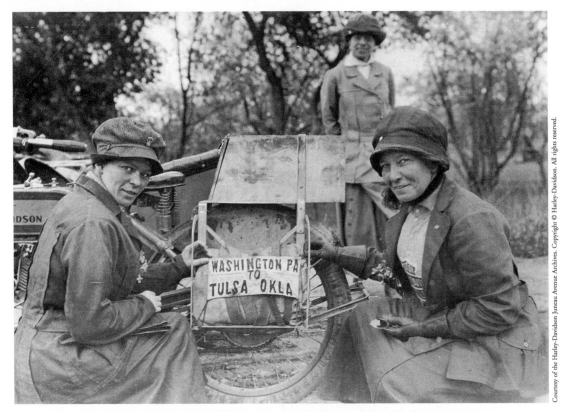

Two women prepare to hit the road in 1914 on a two-speed Harley-Davidson Model 10-F with a sidecar.

apply to the women who rode the first American-made motorcycles, really gasoline-powered bicycles. Though the motorcycle had been invented in Germany in 1885, it wasn't until 1901 that E. R. Thomas sold the first ones in the United States, followed soon after by Indian, Harley-Davidson, Henderson, Excelsior, and many others.

To appreciate the hardiness of early women riders, one must realize that in the decades before World War II, motorcycles were primitive, persnickety machines, and that our nation was barely strung together by mudways and dirtways. In 1906, the transconti-

nental ride of W. C. Chadeayne, a male biker, was chronicled by a reporter who wrote:

As one penetrates the interior of the American continent, well-made roads give place to almost indistinguishable tracks, often impassable. The desert gives way to mountains, their narrow paths strewn with boulders, over which it is necessary to pick one's way laboriously. Streams and torrents must be plunged through boldly, for bridges are unknown. Such is a brief description of the difficulties that must be faced by the man who is sufficiently intrepid to cross the American continent in this way.[2]

Or the *women* who were sufficiently intrepid—and there were many. In fact, women not only rode motorcycles, they raced and won in competition.

In October 1910, an eighteen-year-old named Clara Wagner rode a four-horsepower motorcycle in a 365-mile endurance race from Chicago to Indianapolis. Even plagued by inclement weather and roads buried in mud, Wagner achieved a perfect score, defeating most of the men. The Federation of American Motorcyclists (the predecessor of today's American Motorcyclist Association) declared Wagner's victory "unofficial" and denied her a trophy.[3]

Five years later, the daughter-mother duo of Effie and Avis Hotchkiss achieved a per-

In 1915, Avis Hotchkiss watched her daughter Effie christen the Pacific with Atlantic Ocean water they carried in the sidecar from New York.

Courtesy Adeline's daughter, Anne Tully Ruderman

Adeline and Augusta Van Buren made a stop at the Akron, Ohio, headquarters of the Firestone Tire Company in 1916.

sonal victory over the continent. It was 1915, a year after the outbreak of World War I. Effie had been working on Wall Street. According to the *New York Sun,* the "rush and clatter and monotony and tension" began to wear on her nerves, so she bought a Harley. She learned to repair it and attached a sidecar. With her mother, Avis, she embarked on a circuitous, five-thousand-mile journey to see the Panama-Pacific International Exposition in San Francisco. Three months later, the Hotchkisses rode the sidecar rig onto the beach and christened the Pacific with a jar of

Atlantic Ocean water they'd carried with them. They rode back to New York and were the first known women to make a round-trip, transcontinental motorcycle journey alone.

The following year, America was still in the midst of a national preparedness movement for the war. Two sisters in their twenties from Brooklyn, New York, left home on Independence Day 1916, each riding her own Indian Power Plus motorcycle. Augusta and Adeline Van Buren were descendants of former president Martin Van Buren. Like the Hotchkisses, their destination was California,

**Adeline (left) and Augusta had mudguards installed on their three-speed Indians.
Like gaslamps, the headlights were lit with matches.**

Courtesy Anne Tully Ruderman

The Van Burens went to Mexico before riding to California. They were never called to military service. Adeline went to NYU law school and earned her juris doctor. Augusta became an aviatrix and flew well into her sixties.

but they had a larger mission: to prove that women were fit to serve as dispatch riders for the military. Adeline, an English teacher, and Augusta, a business school correspondent, were well prepared for the challenge. They were small-boned "society girls," but they were also award-winning athletes who swam, skated, wrestled, sprinted, and rode horses. Adeline designed their red leather coats, worn with leather caps, breeches, and leggings. Their "masculine uniforms" attracted reporters—and the police, who arrested them several times in small towns between Chicago and the Rockies. In each case, they were released with a

reprimand and shooed out of town.

None of this dampened their enthusiasm. In Colorado, they rode their cycles up the treacherous paths to the summit of Pikes Peak, becoming the first women to drive motorized vehicles up the 14,109-foot mountain. According to one account, in the desert between Denver and Salt Lake, "the deep sands, washes, and rocky trails caused repeated spills, and great physical and mental stamina in rescuing the machines from sink holes and ruts." With their canteens nearly dry, the Van Burens got lost for seven hours in the desert, described as "the most inhospitable and difficult stretch of country in the North American continent."

Nevertheless, for much of the trek during stopovers they had a "bully time." After sixty days and fifty-five hundred meandering miles, the sisters arrived in California, entering history as the first women to make a transcontinental journey on two solo motorcycles. Augusta wrote:

That preparedness pays is demonstrated in the fact that we arrived in San Francisco without having encountered any serious trouble, and with New York air still in our tires. The whole trip was a perilous one for two girls alone. It had its hazards, but it had its pleasures, too, and it all goes to prove that woman "can if she will."

That same year, the Harley-Davidson Motor Company began publication of its *Enthusiast* magazine. It was peppered with the feats of motorcycling women, including the Van Burens, the Hotchkisses, and many others. It was clear that motorcycling women were an independent lot. They broke gender barriers and scored magnificent firsts alongside and, in some cases, well before women in other walks of life. The Hotchkisses had made their extraordinary journey seven years before

Amelia Earhart took her first solo, domestic airplane flight, and five years before women in all states could vote. Curiously, there is no evidence in feminist "herstory" books about the achievements of these unusual iconoclasts, motorcycling women.

THE TWENTIES: HEAR THEM ROAR

In motorcycle terms, never was a nickname for a decade so apt as the Roaring Twenties. The not-for-profit American Motorcyclist Association (AMA) was founded in 1924 to organize social and competitive events, including "Gypsy Tours," large group rides from which most other organized motorcycle rides have

Vivian Bales, "The Enthusiast Girl"

Courtesy Dot Robinson

Sidecar endurance champion Dot Robinson. "It was hard for some men to accept a woman beating them at their own sport," she said. But when they tried to bar her from racing in the thirties, "no man would say he was afraid of a woman, so they had to let me in."

evolved. The AMA chartered riding clubs. As Henry Ford's automobiles became the nation's preferred means of practical transport, motorcycling became a sport and a pastime. But it wasn't for everyone—even at this early stage, because of a few bad apples, the sport had an image problem. One newspaper huffed over "motorcycle speed artists" who "chase up hills at reckless speed, kick up dirt, run over dogs, and make themselves obnoxious."

Beyond motorcycling, the decade conjures up images of social abandon and the unblushing flapper. It was in the twenties that the first Miss America was crowned. But the larger reality was much less glamorous for most women. According to *Second to None: A Documentary History of American Women*:

Neither the war nor the much-vaunted revolution in manners and morals altered the societal expectation that after marriage, the normal American woman would devote herself to domesticity, living a life not far removed from that of her mother. . . . Modern young women increasingly rebelled against the view that marriage was incompatible with a career, though in the absence of an active feminist movement, few met with success in attempting to live out that credo.[4]

In the summer of 1929, right before the stock market crash, a young woman named Vivian Bales (later Faison) defined her own personal credo as "wanderlust or something." She wrote to Harley-Davidson, detailing her dream of riding a five-thousand-mile loop from her home in Georgia, up through the Midwest, and on to the Harley factory in Milwaukee, Wisconsin. Harley officials recognized the public-relations value of putting a woman on a motorcycle. They sponsored Bales, while local dealers provided meals and lodging, over the occasional protests of some disapproving wives. A newsreel company picked up the story of this flapper-on-wheels who sang Betty Boop songs at civic halls along her route. Upon her much-trumpeted arrival in Milwaukee, Bales was awarded a loving cup and dubbed "The Enthusiast Girl." She was the personification of Miss America on a motorcycle.

It was also in the late 1920s that two distinguished women—an Australian-American in Saginaw, Michigan, and an African-American in Boston, Massachusetts—climbed aboard their first motorcycles. Though they were contemporaries, their paths rarely, if ever, crossed. These two women, as much as any prominent male peer, would define the sport of motorcycling for generations to come. Their names, respectively, were Dorothy "Dot" Goulding Robinson and Bessie B. Stringfield.

Dot Robinson and Bessie Stringfield, arguably more than any other riders of their gender, served as inspirations for thousands of women who would follow in their tire tracks. They both loved Harleys, and they both rode great distances under adverse conditions. But their personal styles were very different, as were the obstacles they faced and overcame.

Dot Robinson: A Rebel in (a Pink) Disguise

If Norman Rockwell had depicted a multigenerational motorcycling family, it might

Courtesy Dot Robinson

Dot (right) with her daughter, Betty Robinson Fauls, out for a spin in their Motor Maids uniforms, circa 1940s.

have been the extended clan of Dot Robinson. She was practically born in a side-car made by her father, Jim Goulding. She was sixteen and working as a bookkeeper in Goulding's Saginaw Harley franchise when a motorcyclist named Earl Robinson came in for a quart of oil and was smitten by the spunky, red-haired Dot. They married in 1931, bought the franchise from her father, and moved it to Detroit.

Dot's views may have been influenced by this nuclear family milieu, but she has always been a paradox. While she painted her Harleys pink, wore pink outfits, and attached a lipstick holder to her bike, this woman was tough—yet always in her own relentlessly polite way. She made a religion out of projecting a "lady-like" image, but beneath the perfectly powdered nose and hair-sprayed coif, she was far from a traditional wife and mother.

Beginning in the Depression years, when motorcycles were a "hard-times alternative" to cars, Robinson spent countless weekends competing with men in endurance races throughout the Great Lakes area backcountry. At five feet two, she couldn't touch both feet to the uneven ground in the woods, so she raced in the sidecar classes, carrying a male passenger. She won her first trophy in a hundred-mile race with a perfect score. But the truest test of her skill and perseverance was the arduous, two-day Jack Pine Enduro.

The Enthusiast gave a blow-by-blow account of the 1937 Jack Pine, and concluded: "It was indeed a survival of the fittest and proved beyond any doubt the courage of the riders. Out of 88 entries, only 41 finished the nightmare of sand, swamp, fire lanes and river crossings along the grueling, 500-mile course."

Dot Robinson not only finished, she placed *second* in her class. In 1940, she won. Robinson triumphed over the difficult course and over men who felt she'd invaded their turf. In the late thirties, when former AMA secretary E. C. Smith tried to bar women

from competing in the Jack Pine, everyone knew the rule was aimed at Dot. Undaunted, she got AMA members to sign petitions disallowing Smith's rule. Robinson broke this gender barrier three decades before Shirley Muldowney convinced the National Hot Rod Association to let her drag-race a car in 1966. Up until her retirement from competition in 1971, Robinson collected hundreds of trophies for first-place and top-three finishes in various types of endurance events.

Away from the competitive arena, Robinson was ahead of her time as well. From Day One, she managed the books of the Harley franchise, of which she was part owner. In 1940, she became an equal business partner with her husband, Earl, when she bought out their third partner. During World War II, when millions of civilian women

Motor Maids founder Linda Allen Dugeau (left) met Dot in Yosemite for a "girls only" camping trip in 1946.

Courtesy Dot Robinson

Dot in 1991 at age seventy-nine. She still drives her husband around in a sidecar. "On a bike," she said, "you're a master of whatever you do. I found that out very young."

worked on war-plant assembly lines, to stay on her bike, Dot took a job as a motorcycle courier for a private defense contractor.

In the late 1930s, Robinson became involved with the Motor Maids, the first nationwide club for women riders. The Motor Maids were the brainchild of a Wellesley College graduate named Linda Allen Dugeau, who envisioned the group as motorcycling's version of the 99s, Amelia Earhart's elite club for women pilots. In search of members who were "neat, clean and above reproach," Dugeau wrote to dealerships around the country. She met Robinson and, together, the pair took three years to locate fifty women. The Motor Maids received their

AMA charter in 1940 and were dedicated to volunteerism and to promoting a positive image of the sport. Robinson was elected their first president and held the position for a quarter century.

While Earl stayed home, Dot hit the road, sometimes clocking as many as fifty thousand miles a year traveling to Motor Maids events and drumming up publicity. Her daughter, Betty, and her mother, Mary, were her frequent companions on the road. Mary rode tandem or in the sidecar. When Betty was very young, Dot strapped the tot behind her with a belt.

When she was sixteen and riding her own bike, Betty accompanied her mother on an eleven-thousand-mile trip around the United States. Said Dot: "I knew that soon, Betty would be old enough to get married and we'd lose her. I wanted her to see the country." She added: "I've had a unique relationship with my daughter all her life. We've had the same thing in common, which means I never had one minute of trouble with her." Over the years, as they rode from state to state in their impeccably pressed Motor Maids uniforms— gray serge with blue trim, matching caps, white boots, and gloves—they became motor-cycling's most famous mother-daughter duo.

Even while wiping Jack Pine mud off her cheeks, Dot took great pride in being the near-perfect lady. "I've always tried to project the best image from a motorcycle," she said. "I made people realize that not all of us are like the bearded, black-leather-jacketed hoods that the media tars us with. Probably my best con-tribution to motorcycling has been my image."

As an octogenarian, Dot has continued to ride. Having totaled more than one and a half million miles on thirty-five Harleys, Robinson has often been called the First Lady of Motorcycling. But she was never called a rabble-rouser. "I didn't go against tradition," she explained. "I got my way with finesse. We have our own ideas, and when somebody tries to force you to do something, and you don't, they say you're rebellious. But you're not, really. You're just being an individual."

Bessie B. Stringfield: The Color Blue

A woman who could have written a book on individualism was Bessie B. Stringfield. She was a legend who embodied what it means to

Bessie B. Stringfield on one of the twenty-seven Harleys she owned in her lifetime.

Bessie B. Stringfield Collection

Bessie B. Stringfield Collection

**"I just crank up a Harley and it talks to me," Stringfield said.
"In my mind, it was the only motorcycle ever made."**

live and breathe a lifetime in the saddle of a motorcycle. Accessible, vulnerable, Stringfield personified the strength and resiliency of a woman who refused to let barriers—either gender based or racial—keep her down. She rode, alone, through an era and through areas where it was considered not just "unladylike" for a woman to ride a bike, but even shocking, perhaps, for a black woman.

Stringfield's beginnings were far less idyllic than Robinson's. Bessie's Dutch caucasian mother died while she was still an infant. Her father, a Jamaican of African descent, abandoned her when she was only five. Although she was adopted by a wealthy Irish couple in Boston, as a young wife and mother, Stringfield was devastated when three children by her first husband died of illness. This tragic loss contributed to Bessie's resolve to lead an independent life. She married and divorced six times.

Even as a girl, Stringfield was fiercely independent. Her adoptive parents gave their blessing to her desire to see the country in her own determined way. When she was sixteen, she said, "I wanted a motorcycle, and I got it." She had no idea how to ride.

"I wrote letters to the Man Upstairs, Jesus Christ," Stringfield recalled. "I put the letters under my pillow and He taught me. One night in my sleep, I saw myself shifting gears and riding around the block. When I got out on the street, that's just what I did!"

Her first bike was a 1928 Indian Scout. It wasn't long before she was riding in situations where most of us wouldn't dare—in stunt shows, for instance. She once rode the Indian around the walls of a carnival motordrome, a huge wooden sphere where the rider uses body language, speed, momentum, and centrifugal force to keep the bike from crashing to the bottom.

In 1930, she replaced the Indian with her first Harley, a Sixty-One. When she was just nineteen, she set out on the first of her solo, cross-country tours, which typically lasted from April to October. "I'd toss a penny over a map, and wherever it landed, I'd go," she said. "I was never afraid on the road because I had the Man Upstairs with me."

Throughout her journeys, Stringfield continued stunt riding whenever opportunities arose. She lay down on the bike and drove, rode sidesaddle, stood on one footpeg, and hoisted herself from one side of the bike to the other.

Her lone adventures were a far cry from "The Enthusiast Girl's" police-escorted, factory-sponsored tour, and the reception she received was hardly on a par with Dot Robinson's experiences. Stringfield traveled with only a leather jacket, a money belt, and whatever spare clothes fit in her saddlebags. "I'd sleep on my Harley at gas stations at night," she recalled. "When I found black folks, I'd sleep next to their children because no one would rent me a motel room."

Stringfield had many positive and happy encounters as well. "All along the way, wherever I rode, the people were overwhelmed to see a Negro woman riding a motorcycle," she said. One time, a Southern white gas station owner was so impressed with her audacity, he filled her fuel tanks, wished her luck, and refused to take any money, saying, "You can just have that little bit of gas!"

After her adoptive parents died in the late 1930s, Stringfield made Miami, Florida, her home base—and promptly raised eyebrows by tooling around the streets standing on the saddle of her Harley. Sometimes she had "co-riders"—her poodles, Sabu and Rodney, perched atop each knee, their front paws on the handlebars. "They thought they were driving," she chuckled.

Some neighborhood people had trouble adjusting to this outspoken woman, her motorcycle, and her dogs, so Stringfield sought the help of a local police captain, Robert Jackson, whom she affectionately called Captain Jack.

He doubted her abilities at first, saying, "If you want to ride a motorcycle in Miami, do exactly as I tell you." He told her to get her bike up to speed, slide off the back, run and catch it, and get back on. Bessie laughed and replied, "That's all?" She completed the maneuver, earning Captain Jack's respect and friendship.

After the outbreak of World War II, while thousands of women joined the WACS (Women's Army Corp), WAVES (Women Accepted for Volunteer Emergency Service), WASPs (Women's Air Force Service Pilots), and WAFS (Women's Auxiliary Ferrying Squadron), Stringfield joined a little-known branch of the army: the motorcycle dispatch unit. Captain Jack was her instructor.

Stringfield was the only woman in a unit of six other black riders. She had to climb her then-current Harley, a Seventy-Four, up a sandy, ninety-foot hill and make an immediate hairpin turn at the crest. To get the bike across a canal, Stringfield learned to weave a bridge with tree limbs. After training, she took to the courier job with gusto. Between 1941 and 1945, she traversed America's primitive back roads and even swamps with classified documents in her saddlebags.

In the late 1950s, Stringfield attended nursing school and earned a license to become a practical nurse. She started the Iron Horse Motorcycle Club in the Miami suburb of Opa Locka, and bought a house "for motorcycle riders to have fun." Her home became the clubhouse, and her escapades ("I was raisin' the devil on a motorcycle") were popular fodder for the newspapers. The local press dubbed her the Motorcycle Queen of Miami.

Decades after the Iron Horse Motorcycle Club disbanded, Stringfield still wore their blue and white colors. Her home was filled with motorcycling memories. There were five AMA trophies in the living room and den,

and dozens of photographs and other memorabilia throughout the house.

The only thing missing was her most recent, beloved Harley, a blue 1978 FLH. In the late 1980s, the bike was badly vandalized in a robbery attempt, and Stringfield could not afford to repair it. She sold it and took short rides on borrowed or rented Harleys. She even considered selling her house to buy a new FLHTC. "It's got to be blue and it's got to be new," she said, adding: "I never bought anything used—except husbands!"

In 1990, when she was seventy-nine, the AMA honored Stringfield at the opening of its Heritage Museum in Ohio. Tiny at less than five feet tall, Stringfield peered up at an exhibit that featured her name and likeness. She had twenty-seven Harleys, sixty-three years of riding, and eight solo, cross-country gypsy tours of the United States under her belt. Shortly before her death in 1993, Stringfield said, "I spent most of my life alone, lookin' for a family. I found my family in motorcycling."

LEADERS OF THE PACK

What Dot Robinson and Bessie B. Stringfield accomplished from the 1930s through the 1960s is so profound, it transcends motorcycling.

For starters, Robinson and Stringfield rode their Harleys around the country during an era when the only machinery deemed suitable for women were contraptions built for "women's work"—that is, cooking and scrubbing. Prior to, during, and after World War II, home appliances proliferated like a virus, confining women to indoor labor. While lawn mowers and other gadgets had men toiling *outside* the house, men also had toys that provided an escape. They had motorcycles, cars, even airplanes—machines geared toward freedom, adventure, and leisure. Most women had no such toys that belonged to them alone. The few motorcycle ads that included women usually had them all gussied up, sitting in the sidecar, with condescending text that said things like "Your girl does not have to be an acrobat to get in or out of your sidecar with this new windshield."

And yet, despite this cultural oppression, Dot Robinson and Bessie Stringfield turned motorcycles into their personal freedom machines. And after the war, unlike thousands of Rosie the Riveters, Robinson and Stringfield didn't go back to the kitchen, because they'd never been confined there in the first place.

Robinson was winning endurance contests and she was a partner in a successful, male-dominated business during the decades when women were told not to "steal" jobs from men. While Dot Robinson toured the country alone on two wheels, Betty Friedan (who *later* wrote *The Feminine Mystique* and then became a feminist leader) was taking cooking courses and looking at suburban real-estate ads.[5]

Bessie Stringfield's horizons were so wide, and her career so astounding, during an era when opportunities for most black women were limited to servile roles such as cook, laundress, or maid. What's more, Stringfield broke down color barriers well before Jackie Robinson broke baseball's color barrier in 1947, and well before Rosa Parks ignited the Civil Rights Movement by refusing to give up her seat on an Alabama bus in 1955.

Robinson and Stringfield were two of the boldest and bravest in their day, but they weren't the only women who found freedom, exuberance, and a sense of accomplishment on motorcycles.

In 1938, a woman named Genevieve "Gyp" Baker won the five-hundred-mile Denver Endurance Run in the Colorado Rockies. On New Year's Eve of that year, she rode to the top of Pikes Peak, despite ice and two- and three-foot snowdrifts.[6]

During the Depression, Louise Scherbyn of Waterloo, New York, climbed aboard an Indian Scout; thus began her thirty-year career as a stunt rider and endurance racer. Scherbyn rode her Indian in carnival motordromes, and, in 1940, she performed in what was billed as "America's First All-Girl Motorcycle Show." In 1950, she founded the Women's International Motorcycle Association (WIMA), a correspondence club for riders and passengers.

At around the same time that Scherbyn

Louise Scherbyn on her Indian in 1940.

Vera Griffin Collection

Vera Griffin Collection

**The Motor Maids at their 1947 convention. On the bikes,
left to right, are Dot Robinson, Vera Griffin, and Helen Kiss Main.**

was getting started in the States, in Wembley, England, a young woman named Theresa Wallach upset her parents by repairing and racing motorcycles. Even though Wallach's mentors included factory designers and racers from British manufacturers like Norton, BSA, and Triumph, male bias shut her out of a local riding club. At school, she hid her activities for fear of being expelled. Yet in 1935, while still a teenager, Wallach and a female roommate decided to take a little trip—*to Africa.* Riding a single-cylinder, 600cc Panther pulling a sidecar and a trailer, they became the first known women to motorcycle across the Sahara Desert alone. Back in England, her riding prowess finally earned her renown. Wallach circled the Brooklands Racetrack on a Norton 350 single, averaging a hundred miles per hour. For this feat, she won the British Motorcycle Club's elite Gold Star award in 1939.

During World War II, she served in the British Army Transport Corps, first as a mechanic, then as a dispatch rider guiding military convoys across a blacked-out England.[7] After the war, Wallach settled in the United States. When novices flocked to the sport on inexpensive Japanese bikes during the seventies, she opened her own teaching facility, the Easy Riding Academy, in Phoenix, Arizona. Wallach summed up her passion for the sport in a 1977 *Road Rider* magazine interview:

> *When I first saw a motorcycle, I got a message from it. It was a feeling—the kind of thing that makes a person burst*

Linda Dugeau lead a cow-trailing run with about fifty water crossings through the San Fernando Valley of California.

> *into tears hearing a piece of music, or stand awestruck in front of a painting. That is what I believe I can teach—that motorcycling is a tool with which you can go about accomplishing something meaningful in your life. It is an art.*[8]

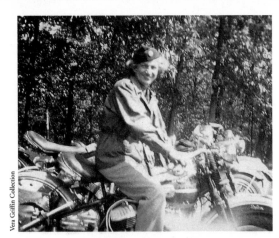

Vera Griffin Collection

Nelle Jo Gill in 1945

During the war years and beyond, the AMA's monthly magazine had pages devoted to "Our Girl Riders." The pages were filled with the adventures of the Motor Maids, considered a ladies' auxiliary of the AMA. The Motor Maids and other groups spearheaded social and competitive events to raise funds for the war effort and various charities. There were photos of the club's founder, Linda Dugeau, who was a motorcycle courier in Los Angeles. On weekends, she

Vera Griffin Collection

Helen Kiss Main on her Indian at Daytona Beach, circa 1947.

"cow-trailed"—rode her heavy bike through rock-strewn cow trails in the mountains, forded the iron horse across streams, and made it look easy.

Enthusiast readers were treated to the chronicles of many women, including Nelle Jo Gill, a Motor Maid from Columbus, Indiana. Just months before the bombing of Pearl Harbor in 1941, Gill and her friend Eleanor Stanton rode cross-country on Gill's red and chrome Harley named Lotus Blossom. Their destination was Hollywood; the occasion, a star-studded bowling tournament. The women were decked out in matching black breeches, black satin shirts, and black boots. They must have been a glamorous sight in the eyes of small-town America. During a stop in Salome, Arizona, Gill recalled, "We believe the entire population of 250 came over to our Harley-Davidson and inspected us."[9]

In spite of the pre-wartime tension gripping the nation, Gill and Stanton were free spirits. "It was so simple when we got these unpredictable urges to leave suddenly," wrote Gill in *The Enthusiast*. "Just grab our things, kick over Lotus Blossom and away we'd go—instant transportation—as comfortable and convenient as a magic carpet." Hardly a common sentiment to come from women in those days! The following year, with the United States entrenched in World War II, Gill joined the WAFS. She repaired airplanes, chauffeured generals (including Eisenhower), and was promoted to sergeant.

Another darling of the motorcycle press was Helen Kiss Main of Pottstown, Pennsylvania, the Motor Maids' first treasurer. Her pink

Vera Griffin in 1993.

Indian and matching outfits outdid Dot Robinson's getup, and earned Main the nickname Pink Lady. In 1941, Main won the Typical American Girl Motorcyclist trophy at the Laconia, New Hampshire, rally (the granddaddy of all the big national rallies, dating back to the 1920s). Variations of this award were the National Motorcycle Queen and Most Popular and Typical Girl Rider. Robinson and other Motor Maids were winners, too.

A Motor Maid from Columbus, Indiana, stood out in quiet contrast to Robinson and Main. She was the chubby-cheeked Vera Griffin, who endeared herself to the motorcycle community with her soft-spoken manner and dry humor. Marveling at the pastel outfits worn by her snazzier friends, she once quipped, "In those days, we didn't have blacktop. Dirt roads were sprayed with oil to keep the dust down. Lord knows, I would'a been a mess!"

In 1939, Griffin took a trip with her buddy Ruth as a passenger. "We had cloth helmets, no windshields, and we were filthy," she declared. When they came upon a hill

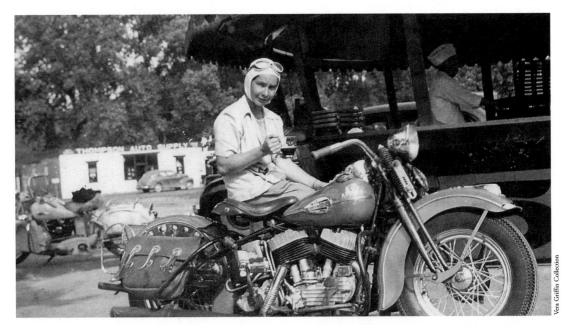

Vera on her 80-cubic-inch Harley in 1947. That's Louise Scherbyn's Indian in the background.

Vera Griffin Collection

with oil at the crest, she said, "we slid right down, fell off the bike, and it landed on top of us. We were covered in grimy oil." At a rest stop, they rubbed the slime off their skin with gasoline. Griffin chuckled, "The attendant said he didn't see too many women on motorcycles. Then he peered in my face and asked, 'You *are* women, aren't you?' "

In 1940, while working as a toolmaker for an engine company, Griffin and her husband founded the Stoney Lonesome Motorcycle Club. Often she outscored the men at motorcycle field games. She competed in one-thousand-mile, twenty-four-hour marathons and "all-girl reliability trials," in which the women were timed to arrive at checkpoints along a rough course.

In a few short years, Griffin was widowed when her husband lost his life in a trucking accident. She never remarried but maintained a love affair with Harleys, Triumphs, and the road. During a ten-thousand-mile

trip in 1948, when road crews were starting to tame the Wyoming wilderness, Griffin navigated a construction zone laden with live rattlesnakes. Her technique: "I rode with my feet up on the handlebars!" Mind you, the bike was a hardtail—no rear shock absorber—and safety helmets were not yet available.

Over a sixty-year span, Griffin logged more than a million miles throughout the forty-eight contiguous states, Canada, and Mexico. Back home, so beloved was this local matriarch, her cronies named an event for her, Indiana's Own Vera Griffin Meet. Upon her death in 1994 at the age of eighty-one, she was laid to rest in a coffin draped in an orange and black Harley-Davidson banner.

Alice Meyer of Seattle, Washington, in the height of fifties fashion.

From their rolling perches, Griffin and her contemporaries literally rode through time as well as physical space. They putted along the historic Route 66 from Chicago to Los Angeles, once known as "America's Main Street." They rode through a rapidly changing postwar America, whose ideology was reflected in the way that roads and travel changed to accommodate the automobile. As cars became faster and more efficient, winding dirt and gravel back roads gave way to straight, predictable asphalt ribbons. When superhighways tamed the continent, the original meaning of travel—*travail*—was lost on most people. By the 1950s, cars had grown fins and were named for explorers—DeSoto, Hudson, Cadillac—to create the illusion of adventure. As the nation suffocated under Cold War conformity, men controlled the steering wheel, and most women sat passively on the right side of the family sedan.

But not motorcycling women. Like their male peers, they were bored by the idea of driving past the country in a cubicle. Mainstream America hopped in cars for comfort and security, but motorcyclists preferred the risks, the challenges, and the closeness with nature inherent to two-wheeled travel. On a deeper level, for many bikers, the one-on-one experience of riding a motorcycle on an open road was—and still is—a harkening back to archetypal American concepts: freedom, individualism. In this context, the motorcycle is nothing short of a twentieth-century replacement for the horses that pioneers once rode across the frontier. And in the cookie-cutter mentality of the era that produced *Father Knows Best* and *Ozzie and Harriet,* women riders were nothing short of rebels.

Woman on a Harley Hummer

In the early 1960s, even as JFK passed the torch to "a new generation of Americans," and *Feminine Mystique* author Betty Friedan identified "the problem that had no name," hysterical teenagers

We've Ridden a Long Way: A Chronicle, from the Sixties to the Present

fainted over the Beatles, and girl groups sang about boys, boys, boys. Women's liberation was hardly a mass movement. Media scholar Susan J. Douglas, in *Where the Girls Are: Growing Up Female with the Mass Media,* wondered:

Was I supposed to be an American—individualistic, achievement-oriented, independent? Or was I supposed to be a girl—nurturing, passive, dependent? These warring messages—"be an American; no, no, be a girl"—were amplified and dramatized in the electronic hothouse. . . . We were the first TV generation, [which] gave us psychological mutations all our own.[1]

Beginning in the 1960s, the decade of "free love," advertisements in the motorcycle press changed to reflect loosening sexual mores. Women who had once been buttoned up in sidecars were replaced by girls in bikinis and boots, straddling the backseat or splayed across bikes in Playboy Bunnyesque poses. In the thirties, forties, and fifties, motorcycling had been marketed as a family

OPPOSITE: Becky Brown, founder of Women in the Wind, on her Harley-Davidson Heritage Softail Classic.

pastime that husbands could share with their wives; in the sixties and seventies, bikes were (and sometimes still are) marketed to young men as a way to get girls.

Honda's ubiquitous ad campaign, "You Meet the Nicest People on a Honda," did it with a little finesse. Some people believed those ads, with their smiling preppy couples on small, nonthreatening bikes, "redeemed" motorcycling from the headline-grabbing Hell's Angels. But for women riders in those days—women living on the brink of one of the greatest social movements of the twentieth century—it did nothing.

Although it was the era when MEN WORKING signs were replaced with PEOPLE WORKING signs, the media was still leery of strong women. In 1972, during construction of the Eisenhower Memorial Tunnel in the Colorado Rockies, *Life* magazine profiled an engineer and motorcyclist named Janet Bonnema. She was a world traveler and rock climber who rode her only vehicle, a Honda CL350 motorcycle, to work every day. Bonnema was assigned to plot data from instruments in the tunnel, but, unlike the men, she was not allowed *in* the tunnel. Bonnema filed a sex discrimination suit and won. *Life* trivialized her accomplishments by calling her "a rugged superwoman who can bat her eyelashes," adding, "for all her devotion to the cause of women's rights, Janet would rather stay home and make split-pea soup." Even Harley-Davidson's *Enthusiast,* pro-woman for the past sixty years, bowed to prevailing attitudes. In 1976, *The Enthusiast* ran a story about a woman who rode a Harley to her job as a service assistant for Indiana

Bell. The headline blared, NOT LIBERATED—JUST ENJOYING HER MOTORCYCLE.

The now-defunct *Cycle* magazine, looking back at the gender gap, moaned that the "army of New Women" had more passion for their careers than for men. Satirically, *Cycle* said:

Mr. Cheap Tour would welcome women into the sport, if only to keep him company. . . . But, a lot of women hanging around might muss up [guys'] macho image. There is something about a leggy chickster looking fast on a [bike] that sets my blood boiling.[2]

Well, Mr. Cheap Tour be damned, a handful of "leggy chicksters" were already racing. In 1960, Californian Mary McGee was the first woman to compete on a modern asphalt road-racing track. But the few women in cycle sports faced heavy bias. In 1971, dirt track racer Kerry Kleid of Rye, New York, had her license confiscated in the field because "AMA rules did not provide that women could race professionally." A federal district court judge put her back on the dirt track.[3]

On the asphalt, Wendy Epstein of San Francisco recalled: "I was the first woman to gain recognition as a serious racer, but I was also left out of publicity." In 1978, Epstein and Jill Keenan may have been the first all-female team to complete an American Federation of Motorcyclists (AFM) endurance race. Said Epstein: "We raced a 650 Kawasaki for six hours with no pit crew and took second place. We were written up as Keenan and Epstein. No one knew we were women." A year later, Epstein was the fastest privateer (self-supported rider) to qualify for an AMA national superbike race, clocking 163 miles per hour on the straightaway.

"Everyone who beat me was factory sponsored," she said. "As a woman, it was harder for me to get a factory ride." In the early eighties, it was rumored that one company sponsored a slower female rider, probably because the male teammate didn't want to risk being beaten by a woman.

Meanwhile, Tammy Jo Kirk of Dalton, Georgia, was to dirt track racing what Epstein had been to asphalt road racing. Kirk told *Harley Women* magazine: "Most folks don't realize how hard it is for a non-corporate sponsored privateer. We pay our own way, don't always have fresh motors stacked in the van, and often we arrive bone-weary from driving all night to get to the track." Not to mention that privateers do their own wrenching (bike repair and maintenance).

Out on the highways, women comprised a mere 1 percent of registered motorcycle owners in the 1970s; old-timers say this was a sharp drop from the number of women riding in the thirties and forties, when bikes were a viable alternative to cars.

Beginning in 1969, a street bike that made a splash in the motorcycle press was Honda's four-cylinder CB750. Technologically advanced for its time, the bike was considered a forerunner of today's superbikes. The CB750

ushered in an era where racetrack speeds would be attainable on the nation's new superhighways. For Jhonneen-Lee Finnegan, an African-American and former U.S. Air Force technician with a degree in mechanical technology, the CB750 was an escape from the tightly packed houses that lined her block in Queens, a New York City borough.

Finnegan, then in her twenties, rode her CB750 on a solo, cross-country trip in the early 1970s, when the transcontinental Interstate Route 80 was still under construction. As a young woman enraptured by the speed of the bike, she remembered soaring along I-80 during a pitch-dark night—and suddenly running out of road. Lost in a Midwestern prairie, she said, "I found my way back to civilization by following a flower-painted psychedelic bus filled with friendly hippies."

She recalled: "It was a time when the country had been going through political unrest. I thought, being black, perhaps I should bring a weapon. My mom said, 'If you take it, you might need it; if you don't take it, you won't need it. Just trust in God and everything will be okay.' And it was. People on the road were all so helpful and kind."

Twenty years later, Finnegan attributed that formative journey with shaping the rest of her motorcycling life. Using her technical background, she drew up specifications for state-of-the-art components that turned her six-cylinder Honda GL1500 Gold Wing into a two-wheeled equivalent of a high-performance luxury car. Now working as a psychiatric rehabilitation therapist, Finnegan still enjoys testing her skills by muscling her eight-

Jhonneen-Lee Finnegan with her performance-enhanced 1500cc Honda Gold Wing

hundred-pound "Super Wing" through serpentine roads far from the crowded metropolis.

In 1977, Police Officer Betsy Kreiter made history when she strode across a previously all-male threshold at the Maryland National Capital Park Police Department. Kreiter was the first policewoman in America to become a motorcycle patrol officer. Three years later, Ramona Murray Prieto became the first female motorcycle cop on the California Highway Patrol, where the training regimen was so tough—one cone-weave maneuver was dubbed "The Eliminator"—nearly half of cadets didn't make it.

In another few years, Joanna Needham, a former AMA desert racing champion, broke through the gender barrier in the motorcycle unit of the Los Angeles Police Department. Some days on the job unfolded like the script of a TV cop show. Needham chased criminals on freeways at speeds up to 110 miles per hour and pursued them into twisting canyon roads at night. One time, upon dismounting, she saw her Kawasaki 1000 smashed when a perpetrator floored his car backward and rammed into her bike.

Male reaction to policewomen on wheels was mixed. Needham's colleagues christened her "Puss'n'Boots." Others were treated with suspicion. Recalled Prieto: "When I started riding, people asked me what I was trying to prove, and if I liked girls. 'No!' I said. I just liked riding a motorcycle. I didn't come with any baggage."

In 1978, Debbie Evans, a petite Hollywood stuntwoman, packed her bags for Scotland. At age twenty, Evans rode a motorcycle where few women had ridden before—in the grueling Scottish Six Days observed trials competition.

Observed trials riders must navigate dirt bikes across unforgiving terrain with bike-sucking bogs, sandy hills, boulders, felled trees, and waterfalls. Riders must do wheelies, jump their bikes, change direction in midair, and balance stopped motorcycles without putting a foot to the ground.

Said Evans: "When I got there, people laughed at me because I was a small girl." She rode a 175cc Yamaha, underpowered compared to most of her rivals on 250s and 325s. "People made bets on me in front of my face as to whether I'd last the first day. That just motivated me even more—that made me so mad!"

At the end of the sixth day—after she'd ridden through rain and snow, had her hands frozen to the handlebars and her calves locked in muscle spasms—Evans placed fourth in her class. One observer marveled: "American Debbie Evans put many men to shame. She

In 1988, Officer Kelcy Stefansson became the first woman in the motorcycle patrol of the United States Park Police in Washington, D.C. Astride an 880-pound Harley, she did everything from escort the president's motorcades to the occasional criminal chase.

Lynn Oldenburg

SAFETY AND RIGHTS: "EDUCATE, DON'T LEGISLATE"

"After I started my job as a telephone installer, I realized the importance of the Equal Rights Amendment because there was still harassment. In 1978, I volunteered for the National Organization for Women and helped work on passage of the ERA. We lobbied, passed out flyers, asked people to sign petitions, made phone calls, and wrote letters to legislators. I was a single mother at the time and took my daughter to meetings. . . . I started riding my own motorcycle in the early 1980s and got involved with motorcycle rights because I didn't like anybody telling me what to do. I'm an eighth-generation descendant of Daniel Boone—independence runs strong in my family! I merely transferred my experience with women's rights to activism for motorcyclists."

So said forty-three-year-old Lynn Oldenburg of Highland, Maryland. Oldenburg was one of many women in the seventies and eighties who helped spearhead two grassroots movements that sprung up in the motorcycle community: rider education and safety, and motorcyclists' rights. Oldenburg was both a legislative adviser to American Bikers Aimed Toward Education (ABATE) and a riding instructor for the Motorcycle Safety Foundation (MSF). When the senate threatened to withhold state funds from Maryland's rider education program, Oldenburg and others worked tirelessly to ignite a coalition of motorcyclists who struggled to save the program.

She said, "We took out an ad in the *Washington Post*. We stood in front of the sen-

was the first lady rider in four years and showed remarkable ability in coping with the tough sections. The fact that she can stand on her head in the saddle might help her balance."[4]

Back in Hollywood, the young duchess of hazard went on to a prolific career in stunt work. She successfully rode a motorcycle through explosions and jumped a bike across a sixty-foot ravine. On the other hand, riding through a wall of fire left her with second- and third-degree burns when the flaming wall came with her. A missed landing from a jump off a ninety-four-foot hill left her with a mild concussion. But, said Evans, "I'm not a daredevil, really—I don't ride much on the street."

ate office building with signs that said, 'Save or educate, don't legislate! Save the motorcycle safety program!' We had people going all over the building to see their legislators. They were receptive. It wound up being a compromise bill, but we saved the program."

The motorcyclists' rights movement swelled in the wake of negative media coverage of gangs like the Hell's Angels and the ensuing police crackdowns that occurred in certain pockets of the country. It also occurred in the wake of the rabble-rousing sixties and the civil rights consciousness that pervaded the country.

ABATE, a loosely knit network of statewide organizations, was one of several bikers' rights groups. ABATE originated in the hard-

Wanda Hummel-Schultz

core pages of *Easyriders* magazine and originally stood for A Brotherhood Against Totalitarian Enactments. The group appealed to rough-edged types, including some "outlaw bikers" and anti-establishment crusaders who protested anything that smacked of "Big Brother Government." To this vociferous group, Big Brother was most intrusive when he *ordered* bikers to wear helmets (instead of giving them the choice). The paramount issue —safety—was sometimes lost in all the yelling. Though ABATE changed the meaning behind the acronym and many chapters toned down their act, ABATE as a whole hasn't really shed its hardcore image. Some factions still hold "helmet roasts," a tactic that turns off bikers who believe in wearing helmets.

Beginning in the mid-seventies, an Indiana homemaker named Wanda Hummel-Schultz was, amazingly, able to lead this group. Schultz, a longtime Harley lifestyle biker with a no-nonsense attitude, was the first woman to launch a statewide ABATE organization. Between 1975 and 1982, she became a near-legendary figure and was, in a sense, the personification of ABATE. "I was always telling somebody off while doing good," she chuckled.

Schultz became involved after reading in *Easyriders* "about legislators wanting to put beacons on helmets and seat belts on bikes. I did *not* like it!" She poured herself into a fight to repeal the state's helmet law. "I became a figure," she recalled. "It was seven days a week. There was nothing in my life except ABATE, bikes, riding, and taking care of business. I was always going to meetings, but I had to be home to have supper on the table. My marriage went down the tubes."

Fran Crane made history as an endurance rider but her other passion is sprint racing. Here she is with one of her race bikes.

She added, "I had to work five times harder than a guy to be taken seriously. I sat up all night writing the newsletter, mailed it, and took care of memberships. I was *it* in Indiana. But if I was going to do all the work, I was going to do it my way." They called her the Dictator.

Schultz's legacy was a personal victory. "I did something for *me*," she said. "I was the only woman to start an ABATE organization and make it work. We got the state's helmet law repealed with just 350 members. We proved a point. I made a difference."

Today, the bikers' rights movement fights

A SISTERHOOD IN THE WIND

Becky Brown

"One day in 1979 I was riding my Harley around Toledo and stopped at a light next to a family with a carload of kids. One kid yelled, 'Look, Mom, it's a *girl!*' They'd never *seen* a woman on a motorcycle."

The rider, a twenty-four-year-old factory worker named Becky Brown, had never seen one either, so she placed a tiny newspaper ad seeking other women riders. The initial handful of responses snowballed into a club called Women in the Wind (WITW), which now has six hundred members in twenty American states, four Canadian provinces, and chapters in England and New Zealand.

The members favor Harleys, call one another sisters, and have a sticker that says, "I'm proud to be a lady biker." Their rambunctious humor jumps off the pages of *Shootin' the Breeze,* their newsletter. In one mid-nineties issue, "Reverend Mims" declared, "Being able to conduct weddings, baptisms and funerals is an awesome responsibility. I may not be able to save our souls (or mine). . . . Just one question remains: Do I wear a Dog or a Bitch collar?" Male partners help out at many WITW events.

Today, with so many sisters, Becky Brown can hardly find the time to answer all her mail. She finds herself writing when she'd rather be out riding.

That situation once applied to Californian Arleen Ruby, who founded Women on Wheels (WOW) in 1982. When this club became too large for her to handle, it was shepherded by a string of energetic women. Now, with eighteen hundred members in forty-eight states and five Canadian provinces, WOW is the largest of the all-brand women's clubs. In essence, it is a giant cheerleading squad for motorcycling, with husbands, boyfriends, and fathers doing some cheering, too. Patty Mills of Topeka, Kansas, the club's national director from the late eighties through the early nineties, was the consummate WOW member: mild-mannered and Midwestern . . . yet beneath the genteel exterior was a woman who'd been riding for more than fifteen years throughout North America, Mexico, the United Kingdom, and Europe. Mills, who runs a blueprint business, was elected to the AMA's board of trustees in 1989. Currently, WOW is led by Sue Frish, Susan Konopka, Kathy Heller, and Linda Stone.

Patty Mills

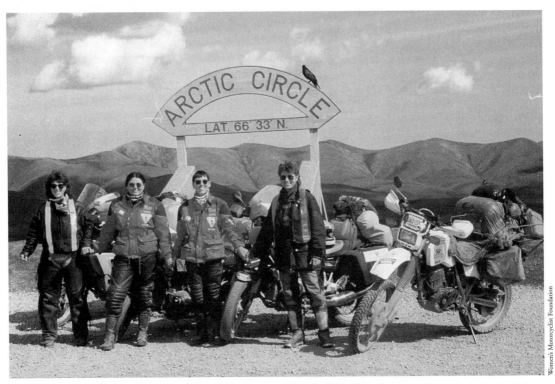

Women's Motorcyclist Foundation

From left, Leenie Bachman, Gin Shear, Sue Slate, and Doris "Book" Buksa are literally on top of the world on the Dempster Highway, Northwest Territory, Canada.

policies that single out or exclude motorcyclists. Besides mandatory helmet laws, activists battle land closures to recreational vehicles, health insurance discrimination, harassment of bikers in groups, and other issues.

WOMEN'S BOOM:
THE GREAT 1980s AND '90s

In her classic, *Passages: Predictable Crises of Adult Life,* Gail Sheehy wrote:

Women are much more likely to see a

realm of unimagined opportunities

opening up in the middle years. An

initial sense of danger and timidity may

give way to invigoration. For most of

them, there are still so many firsts ahead.[5]

Indeed, for the many middle-class, thirty-something and over-forty women of the baby-boom generation who got on motorcycles for the first time in the mid-1980s, realms of opportunities did open up—for the independence and self-realization that comes with mastering a motorcycle. What a stroke of luck for bike makers! Professional women with disposable income flexed their muscles and a new market fell into the industry's lap. Sales to women soared.

Foreign motorcycle makers shipped over small cruisers styled to look like Harleys. Honda's 250cc and 450cc Rebels, Yamaha's 250cc Route 66, and Suzuki's 650cc Savage were lighter and much cheaper than Harley's smallest model, the 883cc Hugger. Women bought roughly a third of some entry-level models; with experience, they bought larger bikes. Ads for the smaller imports were targeted to beginners, not women—imagine the droves of men who would've taken up *golf* rather than be seen on "a girl's bike." Harley-Davidson was the only company to court women. Their "I Am Woman, Hear Me Roar" recruitment ads for the club Ladies of Harley became fixtures in some magazines.

By the mid-nineties, industry analysts estimated that seven hundred fifty thousand women were riding motorcycles. Of these, more than five hundred thousand were registered motorcycle owners—a dramatic increase from the seventies. The boom wasn't just fueled by yuppie women. Many working-class readers of *Harley Women* magazine wrote letters on how they scrimped to get on the front seat. Many did so with encouragement from the men in their lives, such as this man, who wrote:

I'm the father of three girls. Raising independent, self-sufficient women was my goal. It takes a special woman to ride a motorcycle, much less THE motorcycle. It takes an independent woman to put up with flack from the lesser females and bros whose own security is a little shakey. Harley Women *is an "Atta Girl" affirmation for these unique women.*[6]

THE EXISTENTIAL MOTORCYCLIST

One unique woman was Fran Crane, who started riding motorcycles in her teens to rebel against her mother. Crane, now forty-nine, got on a bike, started riding in a straight line, and has hardly put a foot to the ground ever since.

By the late 1980s, this soft-spoken but driven woman had evolved into one of the world's most awesome endurance riders. Crane was an existential motorcyclist, like Jack Kerouac's drivers in *On the Road,* who drove for the sake of pure driving without a destination. Yet for this woman it went deeper. Her numerous marathon riding sessions were self-imposed gauntlets—Crane vs. Crane, Crane vs. machine, Crane vs. the weather and the endless white lines of the interstate.

What was it about Crane that drove her to such literal lengths? She said, "My parents both worked ever since I can remember. I raised my two brothers and cooked meals when I was so small, I had to stand on a chair to reach the stove. Now I don't want any responsibility except for myself."

British émigré Jacqui Sturgess is a founding member of New York City's Sirens, a club with a predominantly lesbian membership. Dating back to 1986, the Sirens are still regarded as one of the nation's leading clubs for gay women, along with Boston's Moving Violations. Sturgess is an advertising executive and just as likely to appear on her bike in a blouse and blazer as in leather. She is terminally ladylike, but turns into a tigress of sorts when defending her turf.

Jacqui Sturgess

Sturgess has helped to give lesbians—whose voices have long been suppressed beneath those of gay men—their proper place. For the Sirens, no other place would do except the very head of New York City's annual gay pride march. "Out Loud, Outrageous, Out Everything!" (an understatement, to say the least) was how one flyer described the event.

With one hundred forty riders in their wake, the Sirens lead the parade. The riders range from prim, feminine corporate types to women with Mohawk haircuts and buttons that scream, "Dyke Bitch from Birth." On that boisterous day, this diverse group of women are united by their pride and their motorcycles.

Crane became the undisputed queen of the elite, long-distance road rally circuit. In 1988, she set a Guinness Book world record for riding her BMW K100 from New York to San Francisco in forty-four hours and twenty minutes. Two years prior, Crane became the first woman to finish in the top ranks of the Iron Butt Rally, riding roughly eleven thousand miles in eleven straight days through horrific levels of sleep denial. She did this two years in a row, placing second and third in a contest so grueling, about half of the entrants drop out.

She said, "You're either too cold, too hot, too tired, too hungry, or a combination of the above to consider the Iron Butt 'fun.' I did it for the challenge. It takes a great deal of physical and mental stamina."

Crane stuck to the helm no matter what. She recalled, "One night on the way to Jacksonville, Florida, I rode into the worst storm I'd ever been in. The water was so high on the pavement, it knocked my feet off the footpegs. I couldn't pull off because I couldn't see. Then lightning struck in front of me. It came so close I thought I'd been hit and had died. I touched myself to see if I was alive."

Crane started motorcycle sprint racing— six to eight laps on a high-speed track—with the same intensity. While working as a parking enforcement officer in Santa Cruz, California, she moonlighted to pay off debts racked up from her passion. Crane has lived with her boyfriend for twenty years but they are not married. She said, "Walter knows this is what I want to do and he will not stop me. That's one reason we're still together."

FANTASTIC VOYAGERS

While Crane was testing her endurance on the rally circuit, New Yorker Tabitha Estabrook, a recent graduate of Amherst College, tested her endurance in what some say was the ultimate motorcycle ride: a twenty-month voyage around the world. Her companions were her then-boyfriend, Jim Rogers, a self-made Wall Street millionaire, and a stream of motorcyclists from different countries who shared the journey with them.

Estabrook was twenty-four and fresh out of the MSF beginning rider course. She learned to tear down and rebuild their BMW twins, said good-bye to her family, and in March 1990 set off on a journey that was as profoundly internal as it was outward and physical. For every one of the 57,354 miles she rode, challenges were flung her way. In between the exotic cultures and spectacular sights, Estabrook dealt with broken roads, broken bikes, bad weather, bureaucratic bumblings, illness, relationship rifts, and self-doubt.

"For the first six months, I was wretched," she admitted. "Early in the trip on horrible Yugoslavian roads, Jim was leading, pressing to make time, trying to get me to pass with him. I was a novice on a 1967 600cc bike. He was an experienced rider on a 1989 1000cc bike. There was oncoming traffic and I couldn't complete the pass. I put on too much rear brake and the motorcycle fishtailed. I lost control, the bike flew into a ditch, and I slid hard on the pavement. Fortunately, I had my helmet and full leathers on, so I really didn't get hurt."

In Siberia, she said, "we rode our heavy street bikes over roads that were piled with grapefruit-sized rocks or mired in mud. There, Jim fell and his bike broke down. I was the mechanic, so now I was an asset and an old dynamic between us changed. My confidence, and thus my abilities, went up." In a remote Siberian village, Estabrook helped hand-machine steel parts from a truck engine, to replace the parts on Rogers's bike that had failed.

From there, she rode through everything from the shifting sands of the Sahara Desert to monstrous thunderstorms in the Australian outback before returning to Manhattan in November 1991.

"People tell me how brave I was," she said. "I was just stubborn. This trip was about stretching myself beyond what I was and trying on something new. Up till then, it was the most important thing I'd done. But at age thirty, I hope it's not the greatest thing. Children will be just as great."

In July 1993, four weary, mud-caked women rode into the village of Inuvik in the Arctic Circle. It was one-thirty in the morning. Under the glare of a twenty-four-hour sun, the women dismounted from three weather-beaten BMWs and a patched-up Yamaha. After riding 4,500 miles across the top of the United States and into Canada, they had just conquered the Dempster Highway—all 480 rutted, gravelly, kidney-jarring miles of it. The women hugged and jumped up and down triumphantly. They

Gloria "Gee Gee" Green

inspired thousands of North Americans to contribute more than thirty thousand dollars to the Susan G. Komen Breast Cancer Foundation. Said Slate, "No matter how many hardships we dealt with on this journey, there was nothing we did that could compare to the courage of a person fighting breast cancer."

Empowered by their achievement, Slate and Shear launched another campaign— Pony Express Tour '96, National Ride for Breast Cancer Research. The plan called for at least ninety teams of women to gather donations, then ride legs around the nation's perimeter. In the spirit of the old Pony Express, at the end of every leg, the lead "cowgirl" would pass to the next leader a medallion and scroll containing the names of people affected by the disease.

With grace and determination, and by blending with the sport's various factions, Slate and Shear have done what few in society have done. They have rallied a broad spectrum of people—straight, gay, female, and male—behind a common cause, the fight against breast cancer.

WE'VE RIDDEN A LONG WAY

"There's nothing women can't do. We can even stand up and pee." This was the attitude that put African-American Gloria "Gee Gee" Green at the head of the Five-Borough Motorcycle Association, a male-dominated coalition of black and Latino clubs in New York City and Long Island. Green, fifty-one, has six foster children and works with mentally disabled youngsters. Clubs in her coalition do charity work and deliver toys to children's hospitals.

had just reached a frontier that few humans ever see: the northernmost town accessible by land on the continent.

The lead riders were Gin Shear, a forty-three-year-old computer programmer, and Sue Slate, forty-six, a remedial-reading teacher. These women had been riding together and sharing a household in upstate New York since the mid-1970s. With them were their friends, Bostonian Leenie Bachman and Canadian Doris Buksa.

On their bug-splattered, gravel-scratched windshields were decals that read, "Women Riding for Research, Arctic Tour '93." Slate and Shear had publicized the ride through the Women's Motorcyclist Foundation, their not-for-profit networking group. In so doing, they

Across the nation, there are more than half a million women of varied backgrounds who are like Gloria Green. They are united by a bond, a love of two-wheeled travel. As Green exuberantly demonstrates, women represent the full spectrum of motorcycling—as a passion, a lifestyle, a sport, a platform to advance larger causes, and a statement of personal independence. As motorcycling has grown into a facet of American life with its own subcultures, folklore, and history, in every way, women, just like men, have played an integral role in its evolution. And for many women, motorcycling has played an integral role in their lives, often becoming inseparable from their self-image. A rider named Billye Nipper, in a recent issue of *Women on Wheels* magazine, put it like this:

> *I have an identity crisis. I am a professional contracting officer for the federal government. I hold a master's degree in Criminal Justice Administration. I have a husband, a house and a garden. I sell cosmetics part-time and I ride a motorcycle! I am proud of me. I have tried many things, such as downhill skiing, golf and distance running, but nothing has challenged me more or has been more exciting than riding a motorcycle. . . . I learned you get instant respect when you're wearing a black leather jacket and riding boots. When you go to the Dairy Queen in Tishomingo, Oklahoma, on Sunday after church, people stare at you and are fascinated. Kids in passing vehicles point you out to their parents. You are something out of the norm. You are defying society's rules. You are a woman on a motorcycle.*[7]

WILD AT HEART

Marlon Brando meets Madonna as black leather combines with fishnet, rap jewelry, pearls, and soft skirts for a sexy new look

"That's *the woman who wears my jeans—* she's independent, she's hot, and she knows how to ride that Harley-Davidson."

—Calvin Klein on *20/20*, referring to biker-model Carré Otis

"Yo! Put your collars on! You're the Sluts! Try 'n' act like it!"

—Dialogue from *Chopper Chicks in Zombietown*, a 1991 B movie about an all-girl motorcycle gang

"I'm a mom, a wife, and a crazy performer who likes to drive a motorcycle and kick up her heels."

—Ann-Margret, writing in her 1994 autobiography[1]

"Straight chicks, take notes! I'm property. I'm possessed. I'm a biker's ol' lady."

—Anonymous, *Outlaw Biker* magazine, 1990

From Biker Chic to B Movies: The Motorcycle Woman as an Icon to Glamorize— and to Trash

Beginning in the early to mid-1990s, as part of a pop culture phenomenon dubbed "biker chic," women on motorcycles pervaded the media. Motorcycling women became icons for trend watchers and trendsetters to glamorize—and to trash. Everyone from Geraldo Rivera to *Vogue* editor Anna Wintour had something to say about motorcycling women, or, more precisely, something to

OPPOSITE: ***Vogue*'s version of biker chic. The idea was to conjure up the gang scenes of *The Wild One*. Not an easy task with those skirts.**
(Peter Lindbergh/Originally appeared in *Vogue*, Sept. 1991)

gain from exploiting real and imagined women on bikes.

Fashion designers, women's magazines, "trash TV" hosts, B movie directors, sitcom writers, music video producers, comic book artists, celebrities in the worlds of entertainment, sports, and politics, and advertisers of a range of goods—from perfume and jeans to hair- and nail-care products—have cast the motorcycling woman as a creature with multiple personalities. As the opening quotes suggest, the media's portrayal of motorcycling women has been nothing short of schizoid.

Depending on the eye of the beholder (or, rather, the media purveyor), a woman on a motorcycle must be a vampiress on wheels, as in DC Comics' *Vamps;* a swaggering broad, as

in the B flick *Chopper Chicks in Zombietown;* or a jiggle-TV bimbo, as in an episode of *Married with Children,* in which teen tramp Kelly crashes a bike.

If a motorcycling woman is gay—some lesbians are just as good at reinforcing "dykes on bikes" stereotypes—then she must be an Amazon, as in "Hog Heaven,"[2] an erotic short story in which the sex object is a bull dyke named Sam. Just Sam, thank you, ma'am. On the other hand, the motorcycling woman may even turn up as the latest incarnation of that perpetually heterosexual, but eternally frustrated, Cosmo Girl. In 1994, *Cosmopolitan* magazine gave us a photo of a stunning, leather-clad woman astride a Harley, raising her arms in a V-for-victory

LLOYD KAUFMAN AND
MICHAEL HERZ PRESENT
A TROMA TEAM RELEASE

CHOPPER CHICKS
IN ZOMBIETOWN
"JOE BOB SAYS CHECK IT OUT" —JOE BOB BRIGGS, Dallas Observer

TROMA INC.

In *Vamps*, "Whipsnake" hunts for "men who would be meals."

salute. The photo illustrated an article titled "You Can Be Single and Live a Rich, *Full* Life." Obviously, this Cosmo Girl no longer needs a husband—and who needs that teeny vibrator when she can straddle a Big Twin?

The message purveyed by each of these images is that it's not quite normal for a woman to ride a motorcycle. That is, unless she's a star, a model, or a "rubbie," a rich urban biker. Then—about-face!—she's chic.

In the early nineties, it became fashionable to be a rebel, or at least look the part. The year 1989 had seen the launch of Harley-

Davidson MotorClothes, with motorcycle fashions that were functional and attractive. Soon after, the alluring mix of women, motorcycles, and leather exploded from the runways of Paris and New York to chic magazines like *Vogue* and *Harper's Bazaar,* and to retail stores from Saks Fifth Avenue to Sears.

Calvin Klein was among the first designers outside the motorcycle industry to note that female riders had the look that many non-riding women would imitate. In October 1991, Klein published an unprecedented, 116-page fashion ad supplement to *Vanity Fair*

Pamela Lee of TV's *Baywatch* stars as the motorcycling "superbabe" in the film version of *Barb Wire.*

Courtesy Harley-Davidson MotorClothes

Harley-Davidson MotorClothes set the standard for biker chic.

mechanic named Ross Langlitz. He designed it strictly for function, yet four decades after Marlon Brando wore it in 1954's *The Wild One,* the biker jacket and what it symbolizes —rebellion—had been vaulted to the status of an American classic.

The fixation with biker fashions ranged from the all-too-serious to the ridiculous. *Vogue* published a dreamy photo essay with models in motorcycle jackets over taffeta dresses and hip-hop jewelry. The models posed with Triumphs and Harleys, similar to the bikes in *The Wild One.* A couple of the portraits were included in *On the Edge: Images from 100 Years of Vogue* (Random House, 1992), a milestone hardcover anthology and

Patrice Stable/Courtesy Thierry Mugler

Thierry Mugler's motorcycle bustier

magazine; its theme was a woman, tattooed biker-model Carré Otis, on a motorcycle. During a *20/20* television interview, Klein told Barbara Walters: "*That's* the woman who wears my jeans—she's independent, she's hot, and she knows how to ride that Harley-Davidson."

Chanel, Donna Karan, Anne Klein, and other top designers usurped the biker look, prompting *Vogue* to sniff: "Redesigning the ubiquitous motorcycle jacket seems to be the fashion challenge of the nineties." Indeed, the street—actually, the road—had come to couture. The black leather biker jacket, with its asymmetrical zipper, wind flap, epaulets, belt, and longer waistline in back, was reputedly invented in the early forties by a Harley museum exhibit. The nation's foremost pur-veyor of chic had elevated to landmark status images of women bikers who were feminine to the nth degree.

Subscribing to the theory that fashions are a reflection of a culture, even *The New York Times* pontificated: "Women have long bor-rowed key phrases from the fashion vocabu-lary of men. The process seems to involve some kind of appropriation of the symbols of independence, toughness and power . . . the motorcycle look allows women to be tough and feminine at the same time."[3]

It also allowed them to spend saddlebags of money. In 1992, Harley-Davidson Motor-Clothes reportedly raked in about $49 mil-

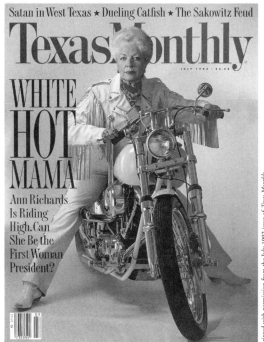

Satan in West Texas ★ Dueling Catfish ★ The Sakowitz Feud

Texas Monthly

WHITE HOT MAMA

Ann Richards Is Riding High. Can She Be the First Woman President?

Reprinted with permission from the July 1992 issue of *Texas Monthly*

Ann Richards learned to ride at age sixty.

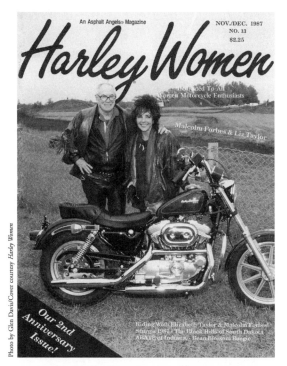

Photo by Glen Davis/Cover courtesy *Harley Women*

Malcolm Forbes, Elizabeth Taylor, and "Passion," the Sportster he gave her in 1987.

lion, much of it from urbanites who didn't ride.[4] Harley put its bar and shield logo on practically everything, even a swimwear line with studded bikinis! Biker chic went truly berserk when French designer Thierry Mugler built a metal and Plexiglas bustier with a head-light, handlebars, and rearview mirrors. Then, all those *Vogue* models who couldn't actually ride a motorcycle could at least wear one.

At the same time, it was an era when femi-nist themes had pervaded advertising. The motorcycling woman was a logical icon of the times: She was independent and free—a modern-day Annie Oakley on wheels. In a prime-time commercial for Lady Stetson per-fume, a cowgirl astride a motorcycle roared off into the sunset—with her cowboy on the *back*

Lance Stadler/Bonaish Group

k.d. lang on her Harley Springer

seat. Revlon even put Cindy Crawford on the front seat of a cycle to sell hair conditioner.

Clinging to the coattails of chic, a gaggle of VIP wanna-be bikers began using, and continue to use, motorcycles and bikerwear to boost their image as sex symbols, rebels, or powerful dudettes. A leather-clad Elizabeth Taylor, celebrating her sixtieth birthday in the February 1992 issue of *Life,* proved she was one sexy sexagenarian. Taylor lounged on Passion, the purple Sportster given to her by Malcolm Forbes, the late billionaire biker and patron saint of rubbies.

Six months later, when political hypesters had former Texas governor Ann Richards poised for national office, Richards appeared on the cover of *Texas Monthly.* A commanding figure in white fringed leather, she straddled a Harley next to the headline WHITE HOT MAMA: ANN RICHARDS IS RIDING HIGH. CAN SHE BE THE FIRST WOMAN PRESIDENT? Well, no. But as a sixtieth birthday present to herself, Richards did learn to ride that bike.

Then, genuine longtime motorcyclists who happened to be celebrities posed on their bikes for paparazzi. Wynonna Judd, who rode while touring, told *People* magazine: "The Harley gives me a chance to pull up beside fans just long enough for them to recognize me, and then I pull away. If you lose the child within yourself, you might as well give up."

k. d. lang, riding motorcycles since childhood, told *Vanity Fair:* "I love the feel of them. I love the wind. I love the aloneness. I like the romance of being on a motorcycle."

Ann-Margret, who has ridden Triumphs and Harleys for about thirty years, has often used bikes during her kitschy Las Vegas stage shows. In her autobiography, she wrote: "People who saw [me as] the performer astride a motorcycle on stage, hair wild, body contorting, could not have envisioned the shy woman inside. By now I had reconciled myself to the two Ann-Margrets."[5]

HOW HARLEY'S MYSTIQUE BEGAT BIKER CHIC

Why all the hoopla over motorcycles and bikers? Much symbolism is attached to the motorcycle. It is an emotionally charged object. Many bikers view the motorcycle as an extension of their personality, a way to stand out, make a statement, and, in some cases, it is a vehicle by which they have reinvented themselves.

Clyde Earl Collection

Ann-Margret years ago on her Triumph T100. In her autobiography, A-M said she wasn't heavy enough to easily kickstart her bikes. Amused fellow actors once strapped a lead belt to her waist. It helped.

"On stage, I talk to my audiences about my love of riding," says country singer Tanya Tucker. "I tell them I have a hot pink Harley. Then I go into a song about independence." Tucker, now thirty-seven, started riding at age nine on a Honda 150.

The motorcycle—specifically, the Harley-Davidson motorcycle—has been elevated to the status of an American pop culture icon. Harleys are right up there with Elvis, rock 'n' roll, and baseball. When an object attains that hallowed status, enter the trend watchers and exploitation artists. They take what is timeless and classic in American life, stylize it to make it seem exclusive, and then sell it back to the masses. That was the essence of "biker chic," which was an aberration of its predecessor, the Harley-Davidson "mystique."

The Harley-Davidson mystique is a nebu-lous concept that has riveted the media for decades and taken root in the hearts and minds of Harley lovers around this entire planet.

The word *mystique* has been defined by Webster's as "a complex of transcendental or somewhat mystical beliefs and attitudes developing around an object." The Harley mystique as we know it today combines patri-otism, rebel-heroism, and Yankee ingenuity with Hollywood schmaltz and commercial-ism. It's very American.

The *seed* of the mystique lies in the fact that the Harley-Davidson Motor Company,

Gene Tierney, 1940s bombshell, was said to have tooled around Hollywood on a Harley.

aerodynamic plastic, chrome-laden Harleys are built to cruise boulevards, to be admired as the rolling pieces of artwork that they are.

And yet there were times when Harley struggled to survive, especially in the 1970s. The Japanese had flooded the market with cheap, reliable bikes, while Harley, then owned by AMF (a bowling ball maker), churned out leaky, persnickety dinosaurs. This, along with economic and other factors, nearly shut the Motor Company down. Senior management employees saved the day when, in 1981, they bought it from AMF.

In 1983, Harley engineers unveiled the Evolution engine, a revamped version of the

Motor Maid Bernice Miles tooled around Peoria, Illinois, on the same bike as Tierney's.

founded in Milwaukee, Wisconsin, in 1903, is the only American motorcycle maker remaining from a field that once had 150 domestic competitors. (Indian, the penultimate survivor, ceased production in 1953.) The *soul* of the mystique is Harley's primitive, pushrod V-twin engine. It may be technologically outdated, yet its deep, rumbling vibration, and the thundering roar of the pipes, can make any person astride Milwaukee iron feel larger than life. Harleys, or "hogs," as they are nicknamed, are also distinctive for their nostalgic, "retro" look—some models closely resemble Harleys of the fifties. Unlike streamlined foreign bikes that are covered in

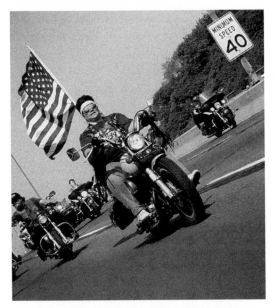

A parade of 68,000 motorcycles shook the highway to celebrate Harley's ninetieth anniversary.

pushrod V-twin, along with other improvements. Just as important, Harley's marketeers gave the mystique a face-lift. In the era of Ronald Reagan and the newly minted "yuppies," Harley courted this new, upscale bunch by forming the Harley Owners Group (HOG). By providing a family-oriented network of clubs, riders had a new weekend pastime, instant camaraderie, and a reason to stick with the product. The company was also the first motorcycle maker to recognize the sea changes occurring among women. They courted *this* new market with Ladies of Harley, an offshoot of HOG. With the introduction of the Hugger, an 883cc Sportster with a twenty-seven-inch seat height, Harleys became accessible to even the most inseam-challenged women. By 1994, women bought

twenty-four percent of all Sportsters. Times had certainly changed; in the old days, one popular magazine called the Sportster "the man's machine of men's machines."

In 1993, the Motor Company celebrated its ninetieth anniversary with much media fanfare. A Harley ad declared: "We've survived four wars, a depression, a few recessions, 16 U.S. presidents, foreign and domestic competition . . . and one Marlon Brando movie." That movie, *The Wild One,* became an unlikely cornerstone of the mystique and forever changed the public's perception of motorcyclists. Brando played the leader of a cycle gang that terrorized a town. The film, released in the mid-fifties, was based on an actual incident that occurred in 1947 in Hollister, California. The rumble made the cover of *Life* magazine; on the coffee tables of America sat a drunken biker on a stripped-down Harley amid a pile of beer cans. A horrified public gaped at a new breed of youth gangs, "outlaw bikers," whom *Wild One* director Stanley Kramer called "the first big divorcement of youth from society."

Although Brando rode a British Triumph in *The Wild One,* the movie had enough bad guys on Harleys to cement the image of the Harley rider as a hoodlum. Harley was stuck with the outlaw image, which Hollywood perpetuated in dozens of bad-biker flicks that invaded drive-ins, mainly throughout the 1960s and '70s.

Meanwhile, a small but real outlaw biker subculture had spread from its California roots. The Harley-loving Hell's Angels, formed in the late 1940s by rowdy, ex–World War II airmen, were fascinating fodder for countless reporters and scholars. The most sensational account of the Angels' raw, tribal subculture was Hunter Thompson's 1967 best-seller, *Hell's Angels: A Strange and Terrible Saga.*

The legendary Angels begat other gangs or "clubs" of dubious distinction. Like Kerouac's beat generation, or the rebel-hero personified by James Dean, the first outlaw bikers sprung from disillusionment with the nation's conformist society during the Cold War era. But a few clubs evolved beyond youthful rebellion to become organized criminal entities.

The dominant players in outlaw tribes have always been men who are, for the most part, misogynists. Their women have been relegated to backseat status in every respect. Some outlaw women have been victims of the subculture's more sordid aspects, but others have been willing participants. Some outlaw women were runaways from abusive families; gang life was preferable to the conditions that had driven them from home.[6]

Among these women, from the earliest days there had been social strata. An outlaw biker's "old lady" was his wife or significant other. On her vest, she sometimes wore a patch indicating she was the "property of" her man. The sorry person at the bottom of this society was the outlaw biker "mama," who was the sexual property of the whole gang. Labels such as "biker chick" and "biker babe" loosely referred to outlaw women but did not confer any rank.

The American Motorcyclist Association had a public-relations nightmare on its hands. An AMA spokesman declared that outlaws comprised a mere 1 percent of all motorcyclists. The statement backfired when outlaws defiantly adopted the label. Adding a "1%er" patch to

their vests, they perpetuated their own myth.

In 1969, hippies hit the road in *Easy Rider.* The Harley-riding drifters portrayed by Peter Fonda and Dennis Hopper nearly sanctified outlaws and enshrined yet another facet of the mystique—the lone, latter-day "cowboy"—in contemporary American folklore. The motorcycle had reached near-mythical proportions, or at least that is what the entertainment industry, and not necessarily motorcycle makers, had the public believing.

Meanwhile, Harley franchises were reluctant to service the more unshaven, beer-bellied, and tattooed devotees of the marque, so outlaws turned to chop shops. There, backyard mechanics spawned the cult of Harley customizing. The steed of the latter-day cowboy was not a stock Harley, but a "chopper," a lean, stripped-down machine. The hallmarks of choppers were their radically extended front forks, high handlebars, and low, laid-back seats.

Before long, the custom cult spread beyond the outlaw community, and the minimalist ethic gave way to the American penchant for chrome. The business of customizing Harleys (and other bikes) blossomed into a full-fledged aftermarket industry chock-full of specialty parts. Custom Harleys became personalized statements. Hand-painted murals and flame motifs graced gas tanks and fenders, chromed parts gleamed, and exhaust pipes turned into fishtails and bell tips. The custom cult grew into a flamboyant, worldwide phenomenon and nowadays, the price of entry ain't cheap—people who can afford biker chic fashions may spend thirty thousand dollars to create a boutique bike. Nearly three-fourths of today's Harley owners are college-educated, and their

KITTEN ON WHEELS
WITH HER BIKE...
HER BOOTS and BIKINI

Out for kicks...in for
trouble! She's going
to Join the...

BORN LOSERS

FROM *AMERICAN INTERNATIONAL* IN COLOR

RECOMMENDED
FOR MATURE
AUDIENCES

median income has shot up to forty-three thousand dollars. Designer-store dealerships now hang MotorClothes next to the motor oil.

HOG and Ladies of Harley, still going strong with two hundred eighty thousand members, continue to offer riders a pleasant alternative to "hardcore" biker gatherings, where the clientele can be pretty rough. At HOG rallies, doctors, lawyers, and executives mingle comfortably with working-class "lifestyle bikers." Bearded men in black T-shirts and women in leather boots, vests, and chaps are the hallmarks of the "lifestyle." Since yuppies have adopted these costumes, bank presidents are indistinguishable from bartenders. The mystique has been gentrified—the toupeed and the toothless are now equally chic.

CYCLE SLUTS AND BITCHES: HOW WOMEN ARE PORTRAYED IN B BIKER FLICKS

Far, far from the rubbie rallies and the fashionable pages of *Vogue* are the girl gangs in the B biker flicks. And when you look at how women have been portrayed in these films, you have to wonder how biker chic could have sprung from the same leather-jacketed seed.

"Remember this, Mama! We ain't no bunch of daisy-pullin' broads. We are the Maneaters, and we live up to the rules or we pay! Now get on that cycle and ride!"

So seethed Queen, the raven-haired, chain-wielding lead villainess of *She-Devils on Wheels.* This B movie had the Maneaters, a vicious, bisexual girl gang, drag-racing for "meat" (sex with wimpy, captive guys). But when one girl developed a crush on her wimp, Queen forced her to tie him to her rear fender and drag him across the asphalt. The

gang's motto: "Sex, guts, blood, and all men are mothers!" That was back in 1968, reflecting, perhaps, the angrier side of the women's movement and a crude attempt at revenge for film violence against women.

"I know I'm a bitch, but, fuckin' A, I gotta be to keep these little pussies together."

So barked Rox, the raven-haired, bullwhip-wielding, lesbian leader of the pack in *Chopper Chicks in Zombietown.* This *1991* B flick had the Cycle Sluts, a girl gang of misfits, stopping in sleepy towns for "meat" (sex with any available penis or penile surrogate). Not much had changed in a couple of decades. Dede was the straight chick who punched her husband and sighed, "Homes and husbands and families are for normal people. I just don't hack it as normal."

Hellcats, Angels Wild Women, Hell's Belles, The Miniskirt Mob, and *Bury Me an Angel* were among the slew of B biker movies of the sixties and seventies. In these and other films, women were almost exclusively portrayed in the context of the outlaw strata. They were generally depicted as domineering shrews, social outcasts, drug-crazed hippies, whores, lesbian bull dykes, or cloying, submissive pieces of property who were verbally abused, slapped, or raped. In most cases, they were shown riding on the backseat.

In the few films where women had the upper hand, or when they rode their own bikes, they were sociopathic man-haters wielding whips, guns, knives, and chains (much like the men). In the final scene of the awful *She-Devils,* they decapitated a man. The women in the bizarre *Easy Wheels,* a throwback released in 1986, were radicals who

EXPLOITATION

SET IT ON YOUR STAGE OR IN YOUR LOBBY

LOCAL WEDDING
MOTOR-FASHION SHOW

Film companies gave promotional material like this to movie houses to exploit the sexy "biker babes" in B movies of the 1960s and '70s.

hated everything in the universe—they stole girl babies to be raised by wolves. In the rare cases where female characters had brains or integrity, they were punished. In 1967's *Born Losers,* a college student who had the audacity to ride her own bike was beaten and raped by a male cycle gang. In *Stone Cold,* another throwback released in 1991, the sole biker chick with a speaking part had a moral conscience; for that, she was shot in the head.

And yet while female characters were frequently raped (usually off-camera), the films rarely delivered the sex touted in the ludicrous publicity copy. The lobby poster for 1971's *Angels Hard as They Come* promised "Big Men with Throbbing Machines and the Girls Who Take Them On!" The one for *Bury Me an Angel* blared about "A howling hellcat humping a hot steel hog on a roaring rampage of revenge." Ads for 1969's *Hell's Belles* leered "Meet the debutante in a leather skirt. Too young, too tough, too itching for action to look for it—she'll make it where she is!"

Rarely in the movies have there been portrayals of heroines or even just regular women (or men) on motorcycles. While 1985's *Mask* had Cher glamorizing the life of Rusty Dennis, a true-life 1%er woman, she was

Mary Hart, cohost of TV's *Entertainment Tonight,* is a regular at the annual Love Ride in Glendale, California. The event, which benefits the Muscular Dystrophy Association, brings out Hollywood's celebrity motorcyclists.

UPGRADING THE IMAGE

Beyond motorcycling, there are few other pastimes, few other lifestyles, that have been exploited so relentlessly by B movie makers. And there are few other pastimes, few other lifestyles, that are as controversial among *non*participants. This is why the majority of honest, law-abiding motorcyclists are obsessed with projecting a positive image. What the nonriding public thinks has real safety ramifications to every rider in traffic.

What the biker chic phenomenon did for motorcyclists was foster a media blip of positive coverage. Human-interest articles appeared with titles like "Boomer Bikers," "Heck's Angels," and "The Mild Ones." The names of Malcolm Forbes and others in his riding club, the Capitalist Tools, were bandied about. Harley-Davidson gave a New York entrepreneur permission to use its logo and re-creations of its V-twin engine to decorate the Harley-Davidson Cafe, a theme restaurant where tourists can pose on a bike in front of a "Harleywood" sign. Visa filmed a TV commerical at Cleveland's Southeast Harley-Davidson dealership, which the owners had turned into a mini-mall with a diner and a kiddie carousel. Yet biker chic had little impact for women riders beyond expanding their wardrobe choices—though not by much, as butter-soft pastel leather doesn't cut it for serious riding.

shown as a chemically dependent victim, not really a heroine, nor did she ride her own bike. Perhaps the only *Thelma and Louise*–type biker heroines appeared in two recent, obscure TV movies. *Shame* was a remake of an Australian film about a motorcycling lawyer who helped rape victims. In *The Stranger,* a foxy vigilante turned out to be a ghost who violently avenged her own rape and murder. In both films, the heroines were icy and unsympathetic.

For forty years, actually, the American Motorcyclist Association had been trying to downplay the fallout from *The Wild One* and the few real biker gangs whose doings became fodder for movies like *Wild Angels*

Courtesy Hardly Angels

VIPs who are genuine bikers have joined the "positive image" campaign. Linda Nighthorse Campbell (seated, second from left), a math teacher and wife of U.S. senator Ben Nighthorse Campbell, helped form what may be the first all-women motorcycle drill team in 1995. Called Hardly Angels, the team is "a chorus line on cruisers" that does figure-eights, V-formations, and other precision maneuvers. Lynell Corbett (standing, far right), a real-estate manager and former dance instructor, choreographs the drills. The women are mostly in their forties and fifties and are based in Durango, Colorado. Says Campbell, "At parades, people's reactions to us are amazing. First they see the bikes coming. Then they realize we're all women and they just go crazy."

In 1994, innocent motorcyclists at a Red Cross benefit ride in South Carolina were allegedly harassed, searched, and videotaped by police. This bizarre incident prompted the American Civil Liberties Union to file a class-action civil rights lawsuit against the South Carolina authorities. All this, in spite of biker chic.

In the 1980s, "Discover Today's Motorcycling" (DTM), a public-relations effort of the trade's Motor-cycle Industry Council, found that 89 percent of media coverage of real motorcyclists was negative. DTM and the AMA knew that women could "soften" the sport's image. In 1987, four yuppie women were given new bikes to ride across the country, a gimmick to commemorate the 1916 transcontinental ride of Adeline and Augusta Van Buren. The media bit, including *The New York Times,* which marveled, "Yes, Real Women Do Ride Motorcycles."

Jo Giovannoni of *Harley Women*

and *Satan's Sadists.* As a result of these nega-tive imprints, even today, it is not uncommon for law-abiding riders, male and female, on any brand of bike, and no matter how well dressed, to be targets of misplaced hostility. A misinformed public thinks that anyone who rides a motorcycle must be out for trouble. Motorcyclists have been deliberately run off the road by car and truck drivers. Bikers have faced discrimination in housing and have been prohibited from bringing their vehicles into recreational areas where cars are allowed.

Jo Giovannoni, a lifestyle biker from a Chicago suburb, took a different, more homespun approach. With her friend Chris Sommer, Giovannoni cofounded *Harley Women* magazine as a clean, family-oriented alternative to the biker skin rags that catered to the hardcore crowd. Many *Harley Women* articles are straight-from-the-heart readers' letters. They consider themselves independ-ent, but since husbands and boyfriends read the magazine also, they choose words carefully to avoid treading on the egos of "the menfolk." Until recently, the *other* F word— feminism—was almost as taboo as owning a "rice burner" (Japanese bike). This prompted a reader nicknamed T-Bone to react:

> *You seem anxious to show you do not endorse women's lib. It's true there are militant types in all groups who give it a bad name. True feminists don't want to be like men, they just want to be free to be the best women they can be. If that means being a wife and mother, or an engineer, cop or waitress, or riding motorcycles, it isn't important. . . . Please don't put feminism in the category of militant women. None of us would like it much if we were told we couldn't ride because of our sex!*

To which Giovannoni replied, "Guess we are true feminists after all. We just don't feel we have to prove anything to anyone about the fact that we like to ride motorcycles. Right, ladies?"

WOMEN IN THE DUAL-AUDIENCE MOTORCYCLE PRESS

As for the sophisticated, slick motorcycle magazines targeted to sport and touring riders of (mainly imported) bikes: You'd think they would be a safe haven for serious women riders. Think again. A small but growing percentage of articles are written by women. And a handful of female editors appear on the mastheads of fine magazines. Yet *advertisers,* especially in the sport magazines geared to the young, male, raging-hormone crowd, still use women's bodies to sell bikes and accessories. With the exception of a few periodicals, ads with scantily clad bimbos far outnumber images of real women motorcyclists at the controls, attired in riding leathers.

Biker chic, B movies, biker rags—just where *do* real women motorcyclists fit in?

According to Women in the Wind founder Becky Brown, "There's a patch that says, 'Real women ride motorcycles.' The real woman who rides is independent, daring, confident, nontraditional. She's a tomboy, yet she can also be feminine. We're like women who ride horses. We can't do it in a dress."

The mere act of riding a motorcycle isn't enough for some women. They like to do it faster than most humans and on a very grand scale. The place they go to indulge themselves is that great American proving ground, the drag strip.

Zoom and the Art of Motorcycle Madness: Women Who Drag-Race Harleys

Women who love Harleys compete in the "all-Harley drags." Their bikes are highly modified for the sole purpose of straight-line, gut-wrenching acceleration. Women who earn professional and semipro licenses can eat up a quarter-mile in half the time it takes to read this sentence, at speeds ranging from 125 to 180 miles per hour.

The all-Harley drags are motorcycling's hot-rod subculture—a world where rubber is burned, fuel is consumed, and engines are strained to their limits for the sake of an adrenaline rush that lasts six to twelve seconds.

The earth rumbles with vibrations that would easily tickle a Richter scale. The ears are assaulted by a deafening roar when carbureted V-twin engines are jolted with electrical charges and flooded with fuel and air, triggering a cycle that has barely changed in a hundred years: Suck in oxygen, dump in fuel, compress the mixture, explode it with sparks, and shoot the waste out the exhaust. And with the crankshaft spinning and pistons stroking, repeat the

OPPOSITE: **A spectacular burnout. Lori Volmert Francis shows the boys how it's done.**

cycle many thousands of times per minute. Nostrils sting, eyeballs burn. Rippling waves of heat rise from the asphalt.

This colorful world is nothing short of a spectacle. Back in the paddock, or "pits," scores of long, low, modified Harleys (FL Big Twins and XL Sportsters) sit under canopies. All the mechanisms of this world are BIG— BIG cylinders, BIG pistons, BIG, fat tires. High hopes ride on high dollars invested in the professional and semipro machines. They are custom-built, often by backyard mechanics, the collective products of thousands of hours of labor and love.

The women who advance to the semipro and professional ranks are Nervy with a capital N, Audacious with a capital A, Competitive

Linda Jackson of Columbia, Missouri

with a capital C. They gotta be. These women wrap their torsos around giant Roman candles, hang on for dear life as they bullet into the void, and push-push-push in pursuit of the win. There's nothing subtle about what they do. In drag-racing jargon, they drop it or dump it (the clutch, that is), then gas it, slam it, hammer it, or gun it. It's WFO—wide friggin' open—on that throttle.

To do this, they gotta have a "dead man's switch"—a breakable tether connecting one wrist to the engine's kill switch. If they fall off and go flyin' and the bike goes flyin', they want that high-revving motor to shut off FAST. They gotta have a wheelie bar—metal rods attached to the chassis that extend five or six feet behind the bike. Wheelie bars keep these rockets earthbound upon their violent launch.

There are different competitive levels or classes. To go really fast—above 150 miles per hour—they gotta have a professional fuel bike, a motorcycle with an engine that drinks nitromethane cut with methyl alcohol. If this sounds like scarey stuff, it is; methane is a type of rocket fuel used by NASA. To go really, *really* fast—above 170 miles per hour, maybe close to 200—they gotta have a fuel bike with a motor that is injected with the stuff; the age-old sucking and mixing of carburetion is too *sloooow*. The 120- to 140-octane gasoline that feeds bikes in the pro and semipro gas classes is for fillies content to trot down the strip at 125 to 155 miles per hour. Amateurs peaking at 100 to 115 in the sportsman or bracket divisions might as well walk.

But everybody's gotta start somewhere, and years ago it was in the sportsman classes that four women—Doris Wiggins, Pam

Cathy "Cat-Lou" West was the first woman to compete in the AMRA in the mid-1980s and has been a fixture at the Harley drags ever since. With a chain from her nose to her ear, West has as much of a "custom" look as her Top Gas machine.

Cummings, Lori Volmert Francis, and Linda Jackson—cut their teeth before climbing the ranks. In this world of overkill, each woman had one of three things: a nickname, a name for her bike, or a name for her race team.

Baby Doris was forty-two-year-old Doris Wiggins, a hairstylist from Clayton, North Carolina. Wiggins became the fastest woman on a Harley when, in August 1992, she soared down the strip on a nitro-injected Super Pro Fueler. Hellraiser was the name of Pam Cummings's race team. Cummings, thirty-seven, a police records supervisor from Waukeegan, Illinois, raised hell a few months

earlier among the "good ol' boys" when she became the first woman to race a carbureted nitro bike. Lady Thunder was what *Harley Women* magazine dubbed Lori Volmert Francis, a thirty-five-year-old homemaker and mother from St. Louis, Missouri. Beginning in the late 1980s, Francis became one of the sport's most formidable, repeat national champions in the Pro Stock class, astride a simple, gasoline-fed Sportster. Quarter Queen was the gas-fed Sportster that helped make Linda Jackson a queen of the quarter-mile in the Modified semipro ranks. Jackson, forty-nine, a graphic arts supervisor from Columbia, Missouri, was a rookie at the start of the 1991 season and a national champ by its end.

What kept these women coming back was the euphoric but visceral thrill of acceleration and the idea that they, mere humans, could harness this power and seemingly defy the laws of physics. The faster they went, the stronger those feelings.

Said Doris Wiggins, "The nitro bike is such an awesome piece of machinery, I get such a rush to think I'm gonna ride it."

"I get butterflies in my stomach before every race," said Pam Cummings. "When you're in a jet plane speeding on a runway and the ground becomes a blur, that's what it feels like on a nitro bike. You're going so fast, just a little more and you'd be flying."

With all its noise and huffing, puffing machinery, drag racing may seem full of

Pam Cummings

machismo, but the motorcycle is truly an equalizer. For all the sport's swagger, you don't have to be a Schwarzenegger to ride a rocket.

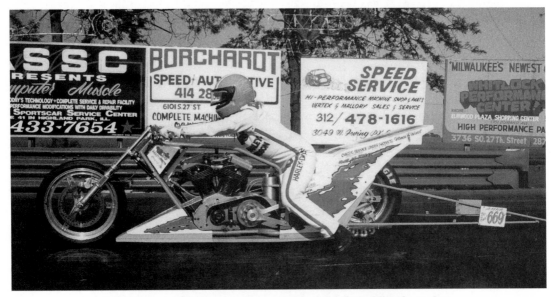

Cummings on the starting line atop her carbureted V-twin rocket; photos of dragster cars inspired the bodywork.

Even the mildest Lois Lane can transform herself into Superwoman, and Pam Cummings was living proof. "I used to be so meek," she said. "I was fat from age five until I was twenty-one. Other kids, including my four brothers, made fun of me. In school, no one wanted me on their team."

In her late twenties, Cummings was introduced to drag racing by her (now ex) husband, a motorcycle mechanic. She said, "At first, I asked myself, 'Are you just seeing how far you can go, or are you trying to prove something?' It felt good to push myself to my limits, beat other people at a sport, and do something better and faster than my brothers."

Sometimes, being better and faster had a price. In a decade of drag racing, Cummings sustained her share of broken bike parts and fractured bones. "Not only was I the first female to get on a nitro bike, I was the first one to explode a nitro motor, in May 1993," she said.

With such tremendous forces placed upon the engines, various mishaps—due to mechanical failure or, occasionally, pilot error—can explode a motor or destroy other vital systems. Metal parts may shoot right through the engine cases like shrapnel.

Cummings explained, "My stock [original factory] engine cases couldn't withstand the pressure. I was about a hundred feet into my run when the cylinders blew and ripped the fuel line off the tank. Nitro sprayed out and a piston shot sixty-five feet in the air. What a mess! I was covered with nitro and oil—good thing there was nothing around to ignite me." Unlike race car drivers, motorcycle racers do not wear fireproof suits because they are not

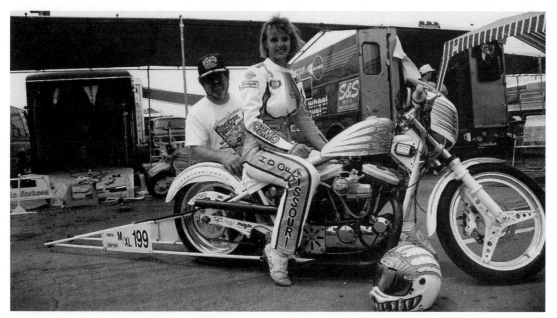

Linda Jackson with John, her husband and crew chief, and the Quarter Queen, their Sportster propelled by a 74-cubic-inch powerplant. They later upgraded the engine.

Jackson on the line

enclosed. Cummings escaped injury that time because the bike simply glided to a halt.

The gentle Linda Jackson had thrown herself into the sport as a means of coping with a devastating loss, the death of her only child. Jackson's daughter had multiple birth defects, including blindness and cerebral palsy. A former Special Olympics wheelchair racer, the girl died in 1991 at the age of nineteen.

Jackson used to exude an aura of melancholy. She recalled, "For nineteen years, I devoted my life and all of my energy to my daughter. When she was taken from me, I felt very alone. I asked myself, How do I socialize with people when all I've known is my relationship with my child and my husband? Drag racing was healthy because I could absorb myself in it. The tension of the competition, the attention paid to me, the curiosity of people in the pits—all of it was new. The sport got me in front of people and turned a lot of things around."

But Jackson, too, paid a price, in the form of a freak accident in 1992. While she was going 115 miles per hour, a bolt on her bike's swingarm (the arm attaching the rear wheel to the chassis) broke. The bike slid on its side. Jackson hung on for a second—long enough for the clutch lever to gouge a couple of fingers before she let go and tumbled for 240 feet. Yet she was back on the track in eight weeks to defend her number-one plate.

The women insisted their sport was safe compared to other forms of motorcycle competition—they were in their own lane, going straight, and done in seconds. They shrugged off the risks, saying they "come with the territory."

Much has been documented on the physiological effects of speed on the human mind and body. Extreme acceleration produces an intense state of arousal, which some people experience as terror, a throwback, perhaps, to a primordial "fight or flight" response. But others get a pleasurable thrill. Either way, the crux is adrenaline.

Richard Wegner, president of the American Motorcycle Racing Association (AMRA), a ten-year-old organization that sanctions all-Harley drags in the central United States, has seen thousands of people in the grips of the fever. He put it this way: "The feeling produced by acceleration gets into your blood. The pursuit of it causes people to give up their jobs, mates, social lives, and anything else that stands in the way of feeling it again."

Fortunately for our intrepid women, the all-Harley drags *were* their social life, sponging up all of their vacation time and most of their disposable income. But they hadn't forsaken their mates. Having a husband (in some cases, a father) for a crew chief was almost *required* in order to advance in this fraternity.

Many women in the professional and semipro ranks grew up in families where the smells of gasoline and motor oil were as common at the supper table as Ma's home cookin'. Many were their "father's daughters." Doris Wiggins's dad pumped gas. Pam Cummings's father owned a gas station/repair shop where she and her brothers worked. Lori Volmert Francis grew up racing dirt bikes on a flat track with her father, brother, and cousins. Linda Jackson's dad, who raced stock cars, "had a little bit of gas in his blood."

The women tended to marry motorheads. These men loved building bikes and experimenting with their creations while their wives served as test pilots. The husbands were usually dyed-in-the-wool Harley men—members of what was perhaps the most "macho" subculture in motorcycling. And yet, like any male racer and his (sometimes female) crew chief, these couples were symbiotic.

Said Doris Wiggins, "When I fly down the strip on that bike that Johnny's worked so hard to perfect, it's his shining glory moment."

"If Ken makes a tuning error, we lose," said Lori Francis. "If he tunes it right, we win when I do my part right. We are a team."

The reactions of less enlightened men were of little consequence to Wiggins and Francis. These women were there to compete, in the dictionary definition of the word: "to seek or strive for something in opposition to others."

Doris and Johnny Wiggins with their Super Pro Fueler, a nitro-injected Big Twin with 300 horsepower.

Lori Volmert Francis (foreground) and Cathy West.

In opposition, certainly, to anyone who dared to ask, "What's a nice girl like you doing on a drag bike instead of doing the dishes?" Both worked at "female" occupations—hairdresser and homemaker—but after that, they parted with tradition.

With her genuine Southern twang, Wiggins declared: "I'm not a woman who likes to shop at malls. It tortures me to go to a grocery store. Motorcycles are my life." Wiggins's clients knew it—she wore Harley T-shirts to the beauty shop, kept a picture of her drag bike on the counter, and readily proclaimed to anyone who'd listen, "I'm the fastest woman on a Harley. When people pick at me for getting on a nitro bike, I just tell 'em I'm a go-for-the-gusto girl." One of seven children, she grew up competing for attention from the minute she opened her eyes each morning until she closed them at night.

At the drag strip, Wiggins quickly learned to ignore naysayers. "In the beginning, the boys in the gas classes had all kinds of attitudes toward me and my husband. No matter what they said, we weren't leaving. The fuel pilots respect me because they know what it takes to ride a nitro bike."

Lori Francis started drag racing twelve years ago on a dare from a girlfriend and won her first event. Her name has repeatedly cropped up on annual lists of national champions—as often as any of the top men.

"When I started, some guys got their feelings hurt," she said. "It wasn't a female/male thing. I'm a good pilot. I tried to make them feel better by congratulating them on positive things they did, even if I'd done it better. It's not like that anymore. Most of them look at me as a competitor, not as a woman."

Not just *anyone* is invited to run with the big boys. Established pilots and track officials observe an up-and-comer, then endorse her professional license. Drag racing may look easy—just gun the throttle and go hell-bent-for-leather, right? It ain't so simple. If it wasn't a constant challenge, the pros wouldn't keep coming back in search of the perfect pass.

Drag racers compete head-to-head in pairs on an eighth-mile or quarter-mile strip. They start with qualifying rounds or passes. Then, in elimination rounds, slower riders are weeded out until the top guns are left to shoot it out in the finals. Performance is measured by speed (MPH) and elapsed time (ET).

At the starting line is a "Christmas tree," colored bulbs that flash for ready, set, go. The racer has to watch the bulbs in her peripheral vision and "cut a light"—that is, drop the clutch and launch on the yellow, four-tenths of a second *before* the green. If she snoozes, she loses. She must ignore a rival who delays staging (getting ready). This ploy forces her to keep her brain and engine revved in anticipation of the go. Tension runs high at the starting line.

On a gas bike, she must shift at the right

Alabama's Sharon Garrison set eight national records on a Sportster.

RPM or kiss the transmission good-bye. Nitro bikes zoom instantly from idle to top gear. The launch is so violent, they may fly down the track solely on the rear wheel. The pilot, atop a 180-MPH unicycle, has a choice: Keep it straight or crash into a guardrail.

Lori Francis has never tired of the chase: "It's not the speed that gets my stomach twisted, it's the competition. If the other guy's ahead of me, I want more. '*C'mon, c'mon, gimme more, gimme more,*' I say to myself. And when it's over, I'm out of breath. Everybody's huffing and puffing like they ran all the way down the strip. There's no other feeling like it, whether you win or lose."

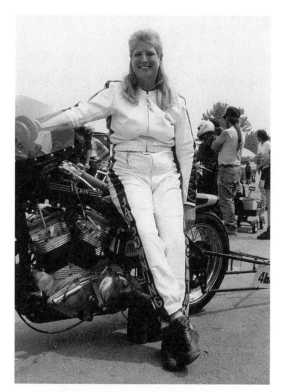

Florida's Jan Downing. Her drag bike was custom-built at Tampa V-Twin, her shop.

More Power! A Brief History of Drag Racing

Courtesy K. Becker

Kristine Becker, the first woman to win a nitro class event in the AHDRA.

The concept of drag racing is as American as apple pie. The sport reflects our national obsession with size, power, competition, and the internal combustion engine. Mine's bigger, mine's faster, mine's better than yours. It's loud, boisterous, and crude. It's American.

While humans have probably gone head-to-head in straight-line competition ever since the wheel was invented, more formalized drag racing got popular at least as far back as the 1940s, when World War II veterans took their hot rods to the dry lake beds of California. Bikers who *really* had something to prove went to the Bonneville Salt Flats near Wendover, Utah. There, they lay down in the cramped cockpits of two-wheeled, cigar-shaped vehicles called streamliners. In 1978, stuntwoman Marcia Holly became the first woman to break into Bonneville's 200 MPH Club. Piloting a Kawasaki-based streamliner, Holly set a land-speed record of 229.361 MPH. (In 1985, she set a record in a car of 272.014 MPH.)

Today, motorcycle drag racing takes place at facilities built specifically for that purpose. The American Motorcycle Racing Association sanctions all-Harley drags in the country's midsection. There are about fifteen hundred licensed AMRA pilots. Of these, about two dozen are women, most in the amateur classes. Roughly the same numbers apply to the All-Harley Drag Racing Association (AHDRA), which holds races on both coasts. The East Coast Racing Association (ECRA) is an all-Harley venue in the Northeast.

Harley lovers like to be amongst their own, partially because Harley "lifestyle" bikers share a unique camaraderie. But it's also so that the push-rod V-twins don't have to be measured against other engines.

If you don't ride a Harley, there are drags for all brands of bikes, such as those held under the banner of AMA ProStar. The National Hot Rod Association (NHRA) also has a motorcycle division. At all-brand events, some of the nitro-injected beasts, running on Japanese-based motors, take about six seconds to rocket through the quarter-mile at well over 200 MPH.

Courtesy K. Hopkins

In 1995, at age 16, Kersten Hopkins became the youngest female nitro pilot ever.

If you're interested in getting your feet wet, consider ET handicap or bracket racing. Basically, you tell the starter how many seconds you'll need to reach the timing lights, then try to match that time. See the appendix for addresses of drag race organizations.

ROCKET WOMEN: SHOOTING STARS OF THE ALL-HARLEY DRAGS

Saturday, June 12, 1993, was the day that Doris Wiggins—fastest woman on a Harley—set her personal best. She did it at a drag strip in Union Grove, Wisconsin, at an AMRA meet in front of thousands of spectators. It was much more than a typical drag-racing weekend. Just twenty miles north, roughly a hundred thousand motorcyclists had converged in Milwaukee to celebrate the ninetieth anniversary of the Harley-Davidson Motor Company. To race Milwaukee Iron that weekend was to be a part of history. The all-Harley drags had a gritty, down-home feeling. The bleachers were filled with Harley "lifestyle bikers"—lots of bearded men in black T-shirts and leather vests, some with club colors (insignias).

About 250 drag racers—whom AMRA head Rich Wegner dubbed "the most awesome Harley racers on the planet Earth"—had come to test their mettle. Of these, at least eight professional and semipro pilots were women. The list read like a Who's Who of the best in the sport. Besides Wiggins, there were Pam Cummings, Linda Jackson, and Lori Francis. Top contenders Sharon Garrison of Alabama, Jan Downing of Florida, and Vicki Johnston of Tennessee had made the trip. So had Indiana's Cathy "Cat-Lou" West, the first woman to compete in the AMRA. And there were several amateurs in the "run whatcha brung" classes.

On Saturday, when the call sounded for the injected fuelers' qualifying rounds, Wiggins pulled on her leathers, tucked her red hair inside her helmet, and climbed aboard her King Kong of a motorcycle. She joined the line of pounding hearts awaiting their turn to fly down the quarter-mile strip. Her Super Pro Fueler looked like a giant praying mantis sculpted from purple metal. The chassis was made of chrome moly, an alloy lighter but stronger than steel. It was eighty-four inches long from axle to axle, and with a six-foot wheelie bar extending from the rear, the whole contraption was almost as long as a dragster car. On the frame above the engine, her nickname, "Baby Doris," was delicately scripted.

But there was nothing delicate about this thirty-thousand-dollar machine, built by her husband and their friend, legendary pilot Bill "Godfather of Fuel" Furr. The bike was an ultimate power tool: 113 cubic inches of Harley's Evolution motor, doctored to churn out more than 300 horsepower. (In its original factory state, it had 60 hp.) A nine-inch-wide rear tire, treadless or "slick" for maximum grip, would carry this rocket down the dragstrip.

But not before the burnout, a critical step that the racers took to get that tire hot and sticky. The burnout doubled as a ritual display of power that transfixed the crowd perhaps more than the racing. And nobody enjoyed it more than Doris Wiggins, the queen of overkill, the self-proclaimed "go-for-the-gusto girl." At the signal from a track official, Wiggins told herself, *"It's showtime!"*

She straddle-walked the bike in front of the burnout trough, a wet depression in the ground where she would spin the rear tire to generate friction. But first, Johnny connected an off-board starter mechanism to the bike's crankshaft. Doris flipped the ignition and the motor

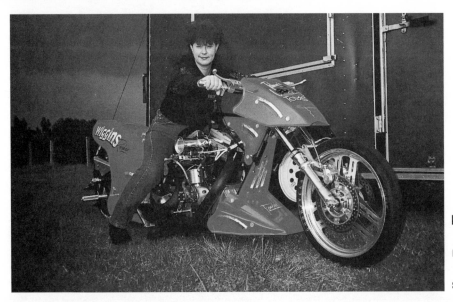

Doris Wiggins on her revamped nitro bike: same engine but shorter chassis.

kicked over with such fury that the torque (rotational force) flung the connector out.

Johnny pushed the bike back so the rear wheel was in the water. Doris grabbed the front brake and opened the throttle. The engine bellowed, and as it reached an ear-splitting crescendo, the back tire spun, melted, and blew up a cloud of black smoke. It appeared that Doris Wiggins was astride a mythical, fire-breathing dragon. The smoke, the noise, and the stinging smell of nitro and burnt rubber formed a booming cascade, like the aftermath of fireworks.

Wiggins eased off the front brake and let the beast lunge forward about ten feet for a "short hop." Satisfied that her tire had a good bite, she straddle-walked the monster to the starting line, where Johnny helped her line up straight.

Wiggins was lying down on the frame above the bike's twin combustion chambers. Her short arms were barely able to reach the handgrips. With her eyes dead-set over the handlebars, she concentrated fiercely while her rival delayed staging, hoping she'd lose her edge.

Fat chance. At the yellow light—four-tenths of a second before the green—Wiggins dropped the clutch, opened the throttle, and launched in spectacular fashion. With her front tire airborne a few inches, she roared down the strip on the rear wheel. In 7.9 seconds, she flew past the traps (timing lights) at 172 miles per hour. Through the adrenaline rush, she sensed what Johnny saw on the boards: She had made it into the "sevens." It was her personal best and she qualified number one for the next day's elimination rounds. Back in the pits, Wiggins chuckled, "It's a good thing I have a lot of hair 'cause my head does get big."

On the following day, Sunday, June 13, Pam Cummings strutted her stuff. This formerly overweight girl was now a platinum-blond woman with a spikey punk haircut, tall and svelte in a white leather suit. Astride a white, arrow-shaped drag bike with a carbureted, 99-cubic-inch nitro motor, she ran nose-to-nose with a rival, zooming past the traps at 154 miles per hour in 8.8 seconds. Cummings lost by one-*hundredth* of a second, but she'd made a perfect pass. It was nirvana, her fastest run ever. An awestruck woman came up to her and blurted, "Gosh, girl—when I watch you, it makes me proud to be a woman!"

Linda Jackson didn't fare as well in her Modified gas class. She experimented with new engine heads, which caused her motor to bog. Pro Stock champ Lori Francis moved up (temporarily) to Top Gas. Problems with her chassis and rear tire almost veered her into a guardrail, but she refused to pack it in. It took Bob Taft, peaking at 157 MPH on the world's fastest Top Gas Harley, to eliminate Francis. And then there was nothing left to do but see if Doris Wiggins would top her own personal best.

Wiggins did outgun herself. She soared through the traps at *175* miles per hour in 7.9 seconds, traveling more than eighty-five yards per second. Upon deceleration, her front wheel touched down and then—suddenly—her front tire skidded. Wiggins lost control. She flew up and over the handlebars, landed on the ground, and was knocked unconscious. The motorcycle was wrecked. Later she said, "Another pilot had raced in that lane just before me. His motor exploded and dumped oil at the finish line. My front wheel hit it."[1]

Wiggins sustained a serious concussion, lost her memory for five days, and couldn't get back on the bike for two months. She wasn't fazed: "I just love racing this bike. It's like riding a horse. Ya gotta get back on if you fall off."

Pam Cummings fell off her horse two weeks later. While cranked up to 125 miles per hour at the end of an eighth-mile strip, Cummings was blown off course by a 40-MPH crosswind. Hitting a rut, she and the bike were flung up in the air. The wheelie bar struck her leg and broke it. The following year, Cummings divorced her crew chief and had to sell the bike. She pit-crewed for a funny-car racing team while dreaming of piloting another nitro bike.

In the months to come, Doris Wiggins hit the pavement again, less harshly, but never quit. "I've done my body-slamming bit," she insisted. "I'm determined I'm gonna get the best of these motorcycles and not vice versa." In 1995, she had a shorter chassis built, one more within her reach and in a color more suited to a "gusto girl"—hot pink.

Meanwhile, the other women were still pushing the envelope in the AMRA. In a single season, Sharon Garrison set eight—count 'em, eight—national speed and ET records, and captured the Number One plate in Super Modified XL. Linda Jackson swept both national and regional championships in her class of '95. That same year, Lori Francis set a Pro Stock record of 158.4 MPH and placed second in the nation.

Like surfers waiting for the perfect wave, these denizens of the drag strip were forever searching for the perfect pass, that zone where concentration was so intense, where human reaction synergized with motion and the innards of the machine. The perfect pass. These women had found the thing that made them feel most alive, and they just did it.

A select group of women partake in the ultimate challenge: road-racing motorcycles on asphalt circuits, competing amongst men at breathtaking speeds.

Europeans began road racing after World War I, when motorcycles were slow enough to steer on public courses that webbed through countrysides and villages. But as machines became faster and faster, zooming through populated areas was too dangerous.

The sport then moved to closed outdoor circuits that mimicked the winding roads, and thus kept the name "road racing." In America, today's asphalt courses are designed for the brave, with banked corners, switchbacks, hills, and dips. In between, there are straightaways where

Road Warriors: Women Who Race Superbikes

the most high-tech machines can rocket from 150 to nearly 200 miles per hour. One lap is akin to a two- or three-mile roller-coaster ride. A sprint race may last a few laps, with a pack of jockeys vying to the finish. Endurance contests last from two to twenty-four hours; the longer races are relays, in which team members take turns on one bike.

Some racers describe the sport's feeling in the jargon of addicts.

"What a high!"

"It's such a rush!"

OPPOSITE: **Nancy Delgado on a Harley Sportster, hailed as a prototypical superbike.** (Brian J. Nelson/Euro Tech)

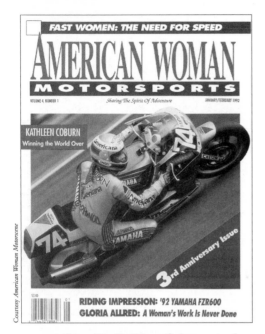

FAST WOMEN: THE NEED FOR SPEED

AMERICAN WOMAN
MOTORSPORTS

VOLUME 4, NUMBER 1   *Sharing The Spirit Of Adventure*   JANUARY/FEBRUARY 1992

KATHLEEN COBURN
Winning the World Over

3rd Anniversary Issue

RIDING IMPRESSION: '92 YAMAHA FZR600
GLORIA ALLRED: *A Woman's Work Is Never Done*

Courtesy American Woman Motorscene

**ABOVE: Canadian Kathleen Coburn raced internationally in the late 1980s. "I was different from other women," she said. "I didn't want to be a girl doing well for a girl. I wanted to win." She had major factory sponsorship until childbirth put her on the sidelines.
BELOW: Delgado spent her first two years as a pro (1991–92) aboard Sportsters.**

Like a hang glider, sky diver, or any other athlete who partakes in an "edge" sport, a road racer in the height of her passion is close to death yet most vibrantly alive. With pilots zooming toward hairpin curves at such high speeds, some argue that road racing is the riskiest motorcycle sport. Perhaps not coincidentally, women who advance to the pros tend to be single and childless.[1] But they aren't crazies with a death wish.

"They have a life wish, a desire to live life to its fullest." So says psychologist Frank Farley, a Ph.D. from the University of Wisconsin who has studied risk-taking behavior in a variety of people, from parachutists to entrepreneurs. He calls risk takers "Type Ts," for "thrill seekers."

Says Farley: "Type Ts feel their destiny is in their own hands, so they like to be in situations where they can act. They are usually self-confident, independent thinkers motivated by risk, intensity, and the unknown. The motorcycle offers a lot to this person."

A woman who road-races a motorcycle is a

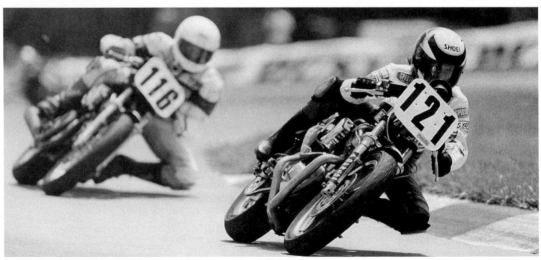

Brian J. Nelson/Euro Tech

technician with a specialty in speed. On a superbike, she straddles a primeval fault line: her need to survive versus her need to take risks. With such a whirlwind pace—at 120 miles per hour she covers 176 feet per *second*—there is no room for error. But if she hesitates and brakes a half-second too early in a curve, she's lost her edge and, perhaps, the race. In endurance contests, there's some leeway, since there's time to catch up.

Women who dare to enter this sport do so as underdogs. They are usually too old (in their twenties) by the time they qualify for a spot on the grid among men who have greater strength to muscle the machine, not to mention the advantage of social conditioning and phys-ed curricula that instill aggression and dominance into boys, but not girls. Further, very few parents will let girls compete on the rough-and-tumble dirt track, where most road-racing champions get their start. As adults, women may race with no family encouragement; some nail-biting parents can't bear to watch.

On the track, minor to moderate fractures, sprains, and contusions are common. The occasional high-speed crash into a barrier can be crippling, or fatal, despite the best helmet and padded leather suit. Tragedy does *not* strike often, but to brush it off as "rare" would be a lie. Every road racer knows of someone who's paid a price.

In the United States, most asphalt tracks are modern and well maintained, but in the early nineties, this wasn't exactly true of Ohio's Nelson Ledges Race Course, home of the grueling 24 Hours of Nelson Ledges, a quarter-of-a-century-old event. By Inde-

pendence Day Weekend 1993, endurance racers who braved the deteriorated circuit wore the experience like a badge. This was the story of a rare, all-woman team of privateers who competed in the 24 Hours that weekend. The women worked with a shoestring budget in the middleweight superbike class, where almost any performance modification to a factory bike was allowed.

TWENTY-FOUR HOURS OF GRIT

In the midst of the rural blackness near Garrettsville, Ohio, there was a primitive racetrack with no overhead lighting. The hot July night was pierced by the sound of thirty-four engines screaming at redline. Over and over the motors cranked up to 11, 12, 13,000 RPM, wound down a few grand, and shot back up to their limits. It was near midnight and the riders had been doing this—blasting away on the straights and braking hard into the corners—since three o'clock in the afternoon.

ABOVE: **Racers on the starting grid at Nelson Ledges Race Course in Ohio.** BELOW: **Endurance team members, FROM LEFT, Letha Jeffers, Nancy Delgado, and Cathy Creighton.**

The scene on Nelson Ledges Race Course was almost surreal. Thirty-four halogen head-lights flew around the course like bodiless spirits, because behind the lights you could barely see the bikes. The riders crouched behind their windscreens could barely see the track: Mist, dense fog, and smoke from spectators' campfires obscured their vision, making every lap a leap of faith.

The two-mile track was so badly broken up that the 24 Hours of Nelson Ledges was Darwinian—it was not so much a race that year as survival of the fittest. It was a test of which riders could keep the rubber down through incredible fatigue, which pit crew could keep the bike assembled through a day and night of bolt-rattling, tire-splitting ripples, bumps, and potholes.

Circling the course in the midst of this madness was a headlight attached to a black Yamaha FZR600 superbike. The pilot was

The race is suspended while workers clear the track of debris, one of many times that accidents or bike failures among the thirty-four teams stopped the action. As Cathy Creighton pulls into pit lane, crew chief Teri Sabin is ready to service the bike.

Letha Jeffers is about to race for another hour.

Letha Jeffers, captain of the nation's only all-woman endurance team. Jeffers was an ex–rugby player turned gardener and mechanic. A lanky six feet one, she had a weathered face, tired eyes, and a deep Virginia drawl. At thirty-eight, she was the oldest rider on the six-woman team. She was a motorhead who lived and breathed bikes.

Jeffers had barely slept since before the previous day's long drive to the track. While speeding, she scanned the course for oil and errant toads and critters from the surrounding swamp. Toad-kill, not to mention larger roadkill, could be awfully slippery stuff to a tire. The poor visibility forced her to concentrate so fiercely that she blew past riders who usually passed her in the daylight. Nothing existed beyond the bike and the next curve ahead. This was what she lived for, this

state of speeding, altered consciousness.

Jeffers thundered toward a corner at about 120 miles per hour. She clicked down a gear or two and hit the brakes firmly, slowing to perhaps 70 or 80. Centrifugal force and inertia tried to fling the bike straight off the track, but Jeffers fought the laws of physics by shifting her weight to the inside of the turn. Hanging off the speeding bike, she stuck out a padded knee and dragged it on the ground with a *chrrrrrrrrrrrr!* as the bike swooped into the corner.

She was leaned way over—her head was only a couple of feet from the ground—and in a flash she was at the apex of the curve. With eyes focused at the exit of the turn, she shifted her weight up, pivoted the bike, upshifted, and drove hard onto the straight. In the pitch-black night with the engine howling, she felt that *rush* as the speedo hit 130 miles per hour and then—*phfffftuh!*—the sudden splat of a flying insect on her helmet visor, right at eyeball level, tweaked her consciousness.

Back in the pits, Cathy Creighton, Jeffers's friend and cofounder of the women's team, was so wired she couldn't sit still. The top half of her one-piece leather racing suit was pulled down to reveal a tank top. Creighton strolled pit row with the arms of the suit dangling at her back. The humid air smelt of fuel, oil, solvents, sweaty leathers, and mud from the previous night's rain. People milled about beneath the line of colorful canopies. Some sat on lawn chairs or coolers filled with Gatorade and beer. Tools and spare parts

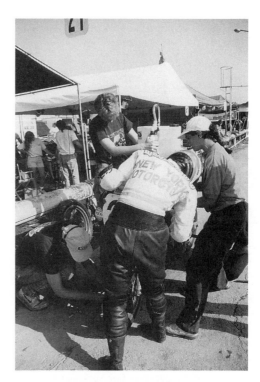

The crew descends upon the bike in a typical pit stop.

were everywhere. At least one crashed motorcycle was being pieced back together.

Creighton was itching for another hour on the FZR. At thirty-two, she was an admitted "adrenaline junkie" who cross-trained by running, lifting weights, swimming, and occasionally riding motocross bikes with her enduro champion boyfriend. Creighton was five feet eight, as wholesome looking as an Ivory girl, and made her living as a sous-chef. She learned to race a decade ago while studying culinary arts in England. She checked her watch as the clock ticked into July Fourth. Jeffers was scheduled to come in soon, so Creighton headed back to her team's pit and zipped up her racing suit.

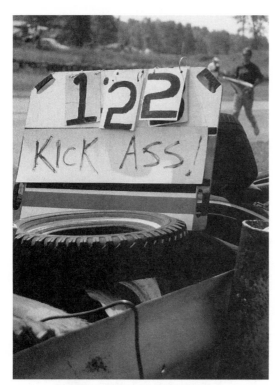

A rival team's booster message.

Having slept for about an hour, Delgado cools off while awaiting her turn to race.

Jeffers rolled in and was barely out of the saddle when the crew descended upon the bike. In about forty seconds, two men and two women dumped in four gallons of gas, topped off the motor oil, adjusted and lubed the chain, and scanned the bike for loose nuts and bolts. Then Creighton, wearing amber glasses behind her helmet visor, rode out into the blackness.

Past the front straight, she glided out from under the pedestrian bridge and was blinded by a billowing cloud of black smoke from the track's diesel generator. At about 110 miles per hour, Creighton couldn't see a thing, but she was prepared. The night before, she had walked the track and planted reflective tape on key braking and turning points. "There's

my dot!" she exclaimed with relief as she steered through the bog.

In a few seconds, she entered a tight, 180-degree horseshoe with ripples in the pavement. Creighton muscled the bike to hold her line as the FZR pogoed through the corner. Twelve hours around this obstacle course had squished the bike's shocks, but it had not put a dent in the team's determination.

They'd started with six riders. Newcomer Danielle Saxman, stricken with a stomach virus, withdrew early. Just before dawn, an eager Alanna Davis sped into a corner too hot, crashed, and went home with minor injuries. By sunrise, the team was left with four riders, two of whom had been up all night. The amateur pit crew spent well over an hour patching up the crashed bike.

In the morning, Nancy Delgado was the first to go out on the rolling wreck. At twenty-eight, the sloe-eyed Delgado looked more like a waif than the most tenacious woman ever to storm road-racing tracks in this country. She was small boned yet flicked the four-hundred-pound bike with fluid, almost balletic maneuvers as she weaved past slower competitors.

Delgado had raced many bikes since a boyfriend introduced her to the sport in 1987, but she learned to muscle a big machine in 1991. That year, she turned pro aboard a five-hundred-pound Harley Sportster 883 and was the only woman in the AMA Twin Sports Series. To qualify, Delgado lifted weights and built herself up from ninety-eight pounds to one hundred ten. To master the art of sliding, she cross-trained in winter by ice-racing a dirt bike with metal-studded tires.

Early on, she learned that competition would be fierce against a few men who resented her presence. "There were guys who said they wouldn't go home if they didn't beat me," she recalled. "Another guy introduced me to his sister as the token female. I said, 'Hi, I'm the token female who always beats your brother.'"

In one rookie race, Delgado taped a bikini-clad calendar pinup to the back of her bike. The guys ogled the photo and she crossed the finish line first. From then on, her in-your-face attitude enabled her to survive in the sport but made some rivals bristle. Delgado used her gender to get noticed by the press. Though her track record was respectable compared to most male privateers, at times even better, it wasn't always the stuff of champions. Some guys whined, "Why should *she* get the ink? If she was a man, they'd ignore her."

Delgado's response: "I benefited from my own PR efforts, got exposure for the sport, and opened doors for other women." In-your-face.

Her first year on the Harley ended when another rider crashed into her, hurling her against a concrete wall. Delgado sustained a fractured skull yet got back in the saddle the next season. When she wasn't networking for sponsorship, she cleaned houses to support her passion and relax her high-strung nerves.

On this day at Nelson Ledges Race Course, as Delgado circled the bumpy course in the seventeenth hour of the race, she held steady at one-minute, sixteen-second lap times. That was four seconds off the lead pace, but by then it didn't matter—her goal was to keep the sagging machine in one piece to the end. So she stayed out of trouble, finessing and forcing the FZR to do her bid-

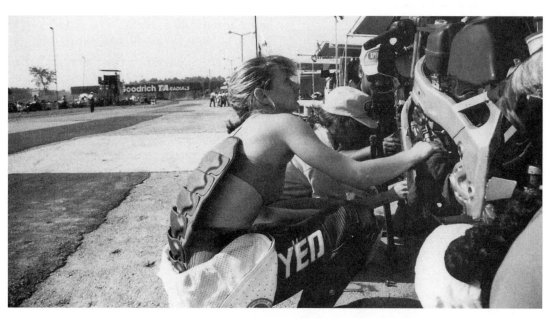

The FZR has been leaking oil; Delgado, still wearing her back protector, inspects the bike with Creighton.

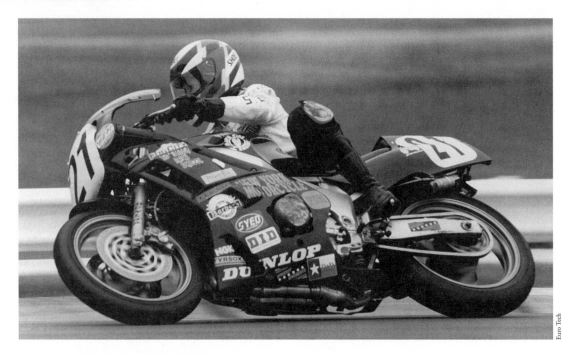

Euro Tech

ABOVE: Delgado on the FZR.
BELOW: Candace Gregoire.

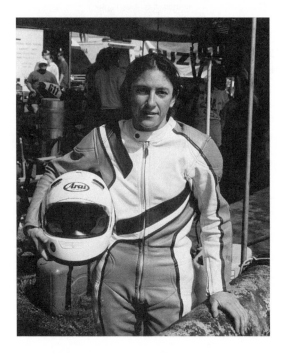

ding in this choreographed production that was part ballet, part bullfight.

The next rider up was Candace Gregoire, a New Hampshire novice who mustered 1:25s in her first endurance race. The FZR had been leaking oil since Alanna Davis's predawn crash and the fluid was dripping down Gregoire's leg. The rookie didn't know the source and hoped—no, prayed—that the slick stuff would stay off her tires.

At eleven A.M., the bike in the neighboring pit came back charred from a blowup. The crash left the rider with minor injuries and the race was suspended while cornerworkers cleared debris from the track. Jeffers and her pit crew changed the last of three sets of tires on the FZR.

Creighton rode out the twenty-fourth hour. The field had slowed down to a leisurely cruise—thirty-four riders dearly wished to see

The wearisome task of counting laps and recording lap times. Teri Sabin does it all.

the checkered flag from an upright position. Finally, at three P.M., they did.

A pasty-faced Creighton rolled into pit lane and dismounted. Quietly, her brother David handed her a beer. While some back-slapping and whoops could be heard down pit row, Delgado and Gregoire were expressionless. Andrea Brady, Jeffers's roommate, was shooting the scene on video. Jeffers mounted the bike, raised her arms in a V, and cried, "Thank you for not blowin' up!"

After a race that had seen countless bikes scraping, bouncing, and careening across the rough pavement, the women had completed 848 laps, or 1,696 miles. This put them twelfth in the middleweight superbike class and twenty-eighth in the whole field.

In privateer road racing—where the phrase "labor of love" was often stretched to dogged lengths—these women on their shoestring budget and ragtag schedule had just broken through an awesome gender barrier. They proved to the guys they were typical.

A track official strolled by and said, "Good job, ladies!"

"We suck and you know it," replied Creighton.

"We're not this bad," Delgado chimed in. "You should have seen us last year. Fourth place."

IN THE YEARS TO COME . . .

Each woman remained active in the sport as a racer or instructor. In 1995, Nancy Delgado became the first woman to win a championship in the new National American Superbike (NASB) series, aboard a 125cc grand prix bike. (She also posed for *Playboy*.) Candace Gregoire advanced to the expert ranks on a 125 at her home track in Louden, New Hampshire. Letha Jeffers opened her own repair shop. Cathy Creighton studied radiology and retired from competition, exclaiming, "I dedicated my last race to my mother, my boyfriend, and everyone who ever wanted to see me quit!"

I f rodeo cowgirls had wheels instead of horses, they'd race motocross. Because it takes one hell of a rider to wield a dirt bike weighing 150 to 230 pounds as it bucks and bounces through ruts, bumps, and dips. It takes a hell of a racer to slide the bike deep into a hairpin turn, whip the back

Cowgirls on Wheels: Women Who Race Motocross

end around while using one leg as an outrigger, power up a fifteen-foot hill . . . then launch the bike off the peak and land, as one coach has said, "as if you're jumping from a

two-story window." And it takes a fierce competitor to do this as fast as she can in a pack of like-minded loonies, most of whom are men.

Motocross is a wild, physically demanding sport. It is a mix of rodeo and steeplechase—except that the "jockeys" ride dirt bikes with springy suspensions and tall, knobby tires. Women and girls who race in the high-flying mud are fresh-faced jocks— the most athletic women you'll find astride motorcycles. For much of the race, they stand on the footpegs, leaning forward. With elbows up and out, they balance and vault their bikes over obstacles. They use muscles many of us don't know we have.

The word *motocross* (MX) combines "moto," short for motorcycle, and "cross," for cross-country. The sport originated in post–World War II Europe, where open country served as the track. It came to America in the 1960s and was popularized

OPPOSITE: **Women motocrossers let loose from the starting gate.**

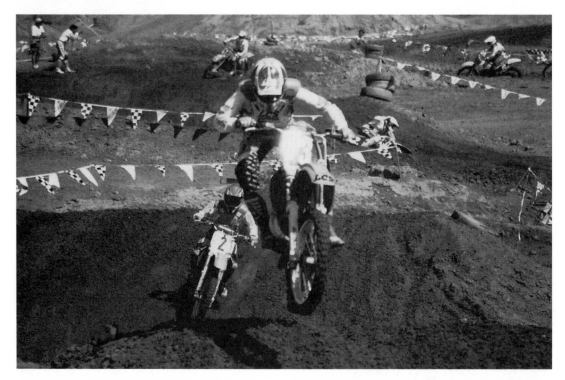

by Steve McQueen's 1971 documentary, *On Any Sunday.* The American Motorcyclist Association, the sport's premiere sanctioning organization, says motocross has been the fastest-growing form of motorcycle competition in two decades.

Today's outdoor motocross courses are closed circuits carved into natural terrain. They are generally a half-mile to a mile and a half in length. One race is comprised of two or three heats called motos. One moto can last anywhere from four to twelve laps and take ten to twenty minutes. Whoever finishes the best of two or three motos is the overall winner.

If the landscape is too tame, sadistic designers create obstacles for your riding terror. The wooliest sections have nicknames like Ten Commandments, Gravity Cavity, Animal Leap, King Kong, and Twin Peaks.

Respectively, these names denote a washboard section of whoops (large bumps), a crater-sized dip, two tabletop hills or launchpads, and a double jump. There are potholes, rocks, hairpin turns, wide sweepers, and berms (banked shoulders). Mercifully, there are also straightaways. On a long enough straight, a pro rider on a 250cc bike may top out in sixth gear at about 60 to 70 MPH, which is very fast in the dirt.

But in this sport, it's not how fast you can go, it's how far you can fly. The main attractions of motocross, and its indoor cousins, arenacross and supercross, are the spectacular double and triple jumps. Like acrobatic daredevils, the best riders fly their bikes over two or three hills. On average, the hills are ten to fifteen feet high; the total length of a double or triple jump can reach anywhere from twenty to sixty feet or more. Riders say jumping a bike is a "rush" or "natural high."

Retired national champion Mercedes Gonzalez of California, the dominant female motocrosser of the late 1980s and early '90s, excelled at indoor supercross. As an amateur in the United States, she was a consistent top-three to top-five finisher; internationally among pros, she placed top five to ten. Teenager Kristy Shealy of Houston, Texas, aspires to do even better.

Motocrossers and supercrossers fall down a lot, sometimes on top of one another in a pile-up of spokes and limbs. Even the AMA once quipped: "Motocross is the black-and-blue division of motorcycle racing." Although jockeys wear plastic armor, minor to moderate injuries are common. But they get so hooked, some still race with fractured fingers or broken ribs.

Motocross has drawn the widest age range of any motorcycle sport. Strikingly, children old enough to ride a bicycle without training wheels can start in the "peewee" classes on mild little tracks. The kids ride 50cc minibikes with automatic transmissions; without modifications, they can go up to about 25 miles per hour. Skilled adolescents graduate to 80cc machines, which are occasionally allowed in the same rugged field as larger bikes. There are veteran classes for riders over thirty, forty, and fifty, and events for owners of vintage bikes.

As in other types of motorcycle racing, women are a minority, yet there are probably more of them racing amateur motocross on a regular basis than any other type of motorcycle competition. Since the sport often runs in families, this is one likely reason.

Many women and teenage girls ride 125cc bikes, which are light enough to throw around yet powerful enough for hard competition. A handful of the most aggressive women also race heavier 250cc machines. There are no dilettantes in this class. These femme fatales have honed their skills by hammering with the men and boys every weekend. When these women vie against one another, their contests are as fierce as any men's race.

But as in other sports, venues for women are few and cash rewards are almost nil. This is controversial. A fledgling movement of female promoters want the industry to sanction separate women's classes. Some men are receptive, but most believe that there aren't enough "fast" women—or women, period—to make it cost-effective. Novices intimidated by the idea of racing with men may never enter the sport, so there will never be more than a few women—"fast" or otherwise.

The big question is: Who sets the standards for "fast"?

Every year in August, the lines are redrawn at Loretta Lynn's Dude Ranch in Hurricane Mills, Tennessee. This is the site of the prestigious, AMA-sanctioned Amateur and Youth National Motocross Championships. Out of twenty-eight classes, there is only one that pits women against women. The AMA has considered dividing the field, but for now, all are lumped in the same field. Novice girls, intermediates, and over-thirty veterans are at the gate with young pros. The pros lap the field; that is, they complete a lap so fast, they pass the stragglers. At other venues, the serious women go out against the men and admit it

At age eleven in 1993, Heather Matthews was the youngest rider to win a women's national event, on a Kawasaki KX60.

forces them to go faster. It's "kill or get killed." But, as in asphalt road racing, men—with greater strength, aggressive social conditioning, a serious phys-ed curricula, and generally an earlier start in the sport—have an edge. In a mixed field, the odds against women are great.

A recent article in *American Motorcyclist* magazine declared: "It's not written anywhere, but there is a pyramid to climb at the Amateur Nationals. . . . Why do these riders and their families devote so much time and money to racing? One powerful motivation is the invisible pyramid, the promise of a factory ride."[1]

It's not visible to the naked eye, but at the top of the pyramid is a sign that says, GIRLS NEED NOT APPLY. Beyond her pride and love for the sport, there is little motivation for a girl or her family to strive toward the male standard of "fast." The factory scouts are watching the boys.

Kristy Shealy, who may grow into the fastest woman motocrosser of all time, said, "It's unfair that there's only one women's class, but we can't say anything 'cause they'll get mad at us and not have a women's class at all."

Tami Rice, a longtime California motocrosser in her mid-thirties, never cared who got mad. While racing, she spent years banging at the dirt ceiling, insisting, "Women of all skill levels have the right to compete and be rated against their peers. Why should motocross be any different from tennis, golf, or the Olympics?"

In 1988, Rice formed a league, later called the Women's International Motorsport Association (WIMSA). With local promoters, she hosted several championship meets that drew forty to one hundred riders. But with tepid

Tami Rice, daughter of motocross pioneeer John Rice, started riding dirt bikes at age five.

industry support and some feathers ruffled by her outspokenness, WIMSA stood on shaky ground.

In *The Stronger Women Get, the More Men Love Football*, author Mariah Burton Nelson wrote:

We can read, on a daily basis, stories

told by men about men: male strength,

male bonding, male power and struggle

and sweat. Imagine if we could also

read stories told by women about

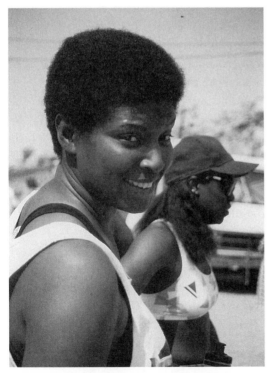

Racers Shirlyn Smith (foreground) and Brenda Yancey of California

women: female strength, female bonding,

female power and struggle and

sweat. What if, in the sports pages, we

could read how a friendship is chal-

lenged and strengthened when two

women compete for one position? . . .

What if we saw, on a daily basis, female

athletes in action, muscles taut, faces

intent on victory? [2]

This was the story of one woman's campaign to get the industry to recognize the heights that women in motor sports could reach, rather than to minimize their abilities by stacking them against the opposite sex. It was a day in the life of female strength, bonding, power and struggle and sweat—in a different venue: the hills, dips, bumps, and ruts of the motocross track.

A LEAGUE OF THEIR OWN

In the wee hours of the morning of May 29, 1994, the sky above Oklahoma City was astreak with lightning. Thunder shook Tami Rice awake from an overwound sleep. Then came the rain in torrents. Flash floods washed out roads and the red clay track of Motorcycle Raceway turned into a a quagmire of earth-sucking mud.

The first World Cup championship races of the Women's International Motorsport Association were to take place on this day. As wind gusts rattled the bedroom window, Rice—promoter, motocrosser, and president of WIMSA—had a tough time fighting back tears. This stormy Sunday was the culmination of Rice's seven-year struggle to wrest one day a year of track time from the men, so that women could go head-to-head in a series of heats separating novices from pros.

While working as a lab technician in the late 1980s, Rice had formed WIMSA. She had a meager budget, no business savvy, little industry backing, and, three years later, a newborn son. A single mother with boundless nervous energy, Rice tried to carve a niche in the old-boy motocross network while child rearing and commuting to work.

"I'm very competitive," said Rice. "Motorcycles are a power thing. All these years, I've heard women aren't supposed to do this, but I've proven they can."

Her WIMSA World Cup in Oklahoma was one of only two such events on American soil in 1994. Kat Spann, publisher of the monthly *Tex-MX News,* hosted the other one two weeks later in Texas. That was *it* for the whole year. Eight female racers—women *and* girls—from Russia, the Ukraine, France, Australia, and New Zealand journeyed with their trainers and families to compete against the Americans.

Rice hosted the foreigners at the track owner's Oklahoma City home. Starting at four A.M., as the rain kept pelting and the thunder kept booming, one by one the bedroom lights came on.

"This is good weather for my girls," said Leonid Majorov, the brawny coach of the Moscow team. The Aussies quipped, "This rain is nothing."

And so, by seven A.M., an international caravan of windshield-wiping, dirt bike–laden vans inched its way across flooded highways toward the track. And then, almost eerily, the rain stopped. The course at Motorcycle Raceway looked like a construction site after a landslide. Axle-deep in mud, a tractor heaved the earth until it loosely resembled a motocross course.

Meanwhile, Rice set up a registration booth for the racers who braved the squall. She hung banners and lined up the victory plaques to await the winners. Then it hit her: She had staged a field of dreams for women who love motocross and forty of them had come, despite the hazardous storm. They had come for love of the sport—certainly, not for the purse. A thousand dollars was all she could muster, to be divided among winners in several classes.

As the skies gradually cleared, pit row began to look like a cross between a vast aerobics studio and a parts swap meet for Japanese dirt bikes. Pitwear for these

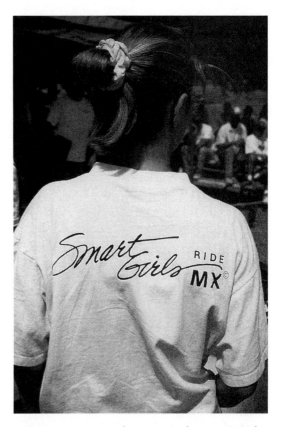

motocrossers was closer to jockwear: Besides T-shirts, the younger women sauntered around in gym tights and stretch halter tops that doubled as sports bras. There were lots of mud-caked sneakers.

These were the same women who, on the starting line, covered in protective gear, kickstarted their engines and thrashed at this gritty sport. These women were literally tough as nails—some had surgically implanted metal splints on various bones, the results of hard crashes. These motocrossers had pushed the envelope of athleticism, proven their ability in a "guy's sport," mastered—gasp!—*machines,* and gotten dirty doing it.

At noon, after a three-hour delay, the course was opened for practice in the mud. The women donned their armor, looking genderless beneath the padded plastic. Their helmets, jerseys, pants, and bikes were painted in startling fluorescent colors—the stuff was bright enough to land an airplane by.

After a brief practice, the races began. The woman to watch was the defending champion, twenty-five-year-old Dee Ann Wood of Dallas, Texas, who raced in the 125cc and 250cc pro classes. At five feet nine and 130 pounds, Wood was one of the fastest women motocrossers ever. Disarmingly, she was also one of the shyest. Mighty Mouse—the cartoon character on her helmet—summed up the contradiction that was Dee Ann Wood. A green-eyed brunette with long, wavy hair, she once prompted a male racer to shout, "That girl's faster 'n shit! She's faster 'n *me!*"

Wood had been raised on frequent doses of encouragement from her Harley-riding mother, who said, "Never be afraid to try anything. Who says girls aren't supposed to ride?" And so, at three, Wood got on a pint-sized Indian painted with stars and stripes like Evil Kneivel's stunt bike. At nine, she raced cross-country, then switched to moto-cross at fifteen.

At the time, Mercedes Gonzalez was the dominant female motocrosser. Wood couldn't catch her before quitting to shoot hoops on a basketball scholarship at Midwestern State University in Texas, where she earned a B.A. in business administration. "Basketball gave me the chance to be a leader," she said. "The game was intense and my teammates became like sisters. The bonding helped me cope with my greatest loss." Wood's mother died from breast cancer in 1990.

After college, Wood managed her father's Harley franchise near Dallas. "When basketball ended," she said, "I had to have something competitive and physical to focus my energy on, or I would've gone crazy." She returned to motocross and "got my chance at beating Mercedes." Gonzalez retired in 1991 at the age of twenty-eight, losing her last moto to Wood at Loretta Lynn's.

Wood's success was all the more phenomenal given her limited practice time. She rode dirt bikes mainly at night and cross-trained by weight lifting, mountain biking, and running. She earned a truckload of trophies and sustained numerous injuries. Her talent and perseverance earned her modest support from Kawasaki and some local business owners.

The deciding race in Oklahoma, and the one most telling of Wood's mettle, was the second moto of the 125 pro class, a come-from-behind affair at the end of the day. Her chief

Dee Wood of Dallas, Texas. Her plate number says it all.

Gale Webb: "Just Say MX!"

"Motocross is better than drugs" is the message purveyed by veteran racer and sports evangelist Gale Webb. Her jersey is emblazoned with the words MX MOM. With her bleached, cropped hair and ruddy complexion, Webb is over fifty but going on fifteen.

She is also the survivor of a near-fatal skydiving accident. At the age of twenty, when her main chute failed to open, Webb sustained massive head injuries, a broken neck and back, partial paralysis, memory loss, and learning disorders. She spent the next two years in a hospital but her rehabilitation has been a lifelong process.

She used sports—motocross, snowboarding, skiing, and mountain biking—as physical and emotional therapy. She fought doctors and inner demons who told her she'd never lead a normal life. "I was always wild," said Webb. "When they told me 'you can't,' I did."

Gale Webb

Corina Chinen

"America's Sports Mom" is a role she invented for herself in the late 1970s. After her best friend died from a drug overdose, Webb became an antidrug crusader. With help from her husband and grown son, she stages sports shows at fairs, parks, and malls. Her troupe of young bicyclists, in-line skaters, and skateboardists roll, flip, and leap to music while Webb cries, "Kids! You don't need drugs to have fun! Get high on sports!"

Corina Chinen, twenty-five, who began riding dirt bikes with her father in the pineapple fields of their native Hawaii, agrees with Webb. Said Chinen, "The sensation of flying a bike in the air is a natural high. Motocross keeps you focused. You have to stay healthy or you're going to get hurt." While working as a production assistant in her father's construction firm, Chinen saved money so she could come to the mainland and train for the pros.

Dee Wood soars off a tabletop jump.

opponent was Michaela Gonzalez, a thirty-three-year-old software engineer from Colorado Springs, who'd been racing since childhood.

Fourteen riders were called to the gate. By then, the rain-soaked ground had semi-coagulated but was slick as ice in spots. Speed alone couldn't win on this track. It would take skill, nerve, and endurance.

Wood's green eyes were piercing as she put on her steely "race face." The riders pulled on the last bit of protective gear, the bulbous goggles. Then they looked like superhero characters. At the first signal from the gatemaster, the women kickstarted their engines and the air reverberated with a loud, raucous sound. Were these motorcycles or kazoo-powered lawn mowers?

At the next signal, they shifted into gear and revved those little motors until they screamed. There wasn't a gut not aflutter, a vein not nearly bursting with adrenaline. These pumped-up jockeys on their neighing metal ponies were ready for the chase.

It was the holeshot they were after, these jockeys. The holeshot—the lead into the first turn—can make or break a race. Be first around that hallowed corner or close behind the leader, and you're in it to possibly win it. Get caught in the midst of the pack, and you may never break out. Except if you're Dee "Mighty Mouse" Wood.

The gate dropped and the jockeys blasted off in a cloud of red dust. Wood got caught in the middle. Michaela Gonzalez got the holeshot and hung on to the lead. "Mighty Mouse" turned into a lioness in pursuit.

Wood weaved through the pack, commanding the inside line through turn after turn. Like a boxer, she watched for weakness in her opponents, then darted through. She charged until she was at Gonzalez's tail, pushing her front wheel into the leader's peripheral vision. Wood's technique was visceral. She launched hard off the hills, landed hard on the flats, charged hard into the corners, and skimmed the ground with her pivoting leg as she whipped the back end of the bike around. It was a beautiful sight.

But Gonzalez was stubborn. For six rowdy laps, she blocked Wood and held her to the outside of the corners, then dusted her on the straights. The women battled until they came to a 180-degree turn. Gonzalez left an eyelet for Wood to bullet through. The two bikes shrieked as they raced down a straight and bucked over the whoops. Wood lunged her bike forward and then, in a sudden lash of momentum, she roosted Gonzalez. The checkered flag flew for Wood.

Tami Rice, watching from the observation tower, had goosebumps. "The level of competition was amazing," she said. "It was also a personal victory to realize how far WIMSA had come. But then I remembered the brick walls. Why hasn't the industry accepted that women can do this?"

By the end of the WIMSA World Cup in Oklahoma City, Dee Wood had swept both the 250cc and 125cc pro classes, defending her title as world champion.

The storm before dawn, the quagmire at the track, the ploughing through, the gradual clearing, and, finally, the success of the event, were a miniseries of Tami Rice's struggle to put women's motocross on the map. By the end of the year, flailing under a pile of debts, Rice was forced to fold WIMSA. Afterward, she taught women to race and helped promote local meets.

Yet on this day in Oklahoma City, as the legendary Mercedes Gonzalez handed out plaques to winners in eleven competitive classes, there was an unspoken sense that the World Cup had been a milestone.

Return of the Racers

In the 1970s, motocross was even more popular among young women than it is now. A California group called PURR (Powder Puffs Unlimited Riders and Racers) sanctioned its first "Powder Puff Nationals" in 1974. According to a newspaper account, there were more than 150 entrants and "the intensive training programs of the experts, including jogging and weights, produced top-notched athletes." But not for long—most women sat out the eighties. Male resistance, marriage, pregnancy, and the skyrocketing cost of bikes kept many on the sidelines.

Today, women are back on the motocross track and they've brought their daughters with them. Debbie Matthews, thirty-eight, from Mission Viejo, California, competed in the Powder Puff Nationals. Now she races in the over-thirty veteran class and is working to continue what Tami Rice started.

With Elaine Ruff of Acerbis, USA (a motocross equipment maker), and two other colleagues, Matthews manages the U.S. Women's Motocross League, a descendent of WIMSA formed in 1995. Ruff's industry experience and connections have helped her and Matthews make inroads where Rice had faced road-blocks. "Tami helped pave the way for what we are able to do," Matthews said. "She had the heart but not the tools. We saw the obstacles she faced and developed strategies to get around them."

Besides the new league, Matthews and Ruff manage the U.S. Women's Motocross Team, comprised of the top four racers, who may change every year. Team members receive corporate sponsorship and represent the United States in international competition.

The league may herald a boom in women's motocross. "We already have eight hundred members," said Matthews. "At our championships, we've had to turn girls away at the gate." In 1996, the league received an AMA charter and thus a guarantee of AMA sanctioning for league events. This victory is a first step toward gaining wider industry support for women's motocross.

It comes not a moment too soon for girls like Matthews's fourteen-year-old daughter, Heather, who began 50cc "peewee" racing when she was seven. Heather got knocked down five times in her first moto; undaunted, she finished the race. While growing up, Heather was easy to spot on the track. The antenna sticking up from her helmet was a giveaway. Using an intercom and hand signals, Debbie Matthews coached the child from the sidelines. Raising her fists, Matthews cheered, "C'mon, Heather, you can do it!" On a typical day, a boy rival's father would yell, "Johnny, don't let that girl beat you!" His wife might counter with, "Go, Heather!"

At age twelve, the resilient child began racing an 80cc bike, sometimes in the same field as her mother. Debbie Matthews said, "The sport gives the kids goals. It keeps 'em off the street and out of trouble."

Veteran racer Debbie Matthews (center) shows her trophies with daughter Heather (foreground) and peewee racer Jillian Bennett. When other mothers asked Matthews how she could let her daughter compete in such a rough sport, Matthews said, "I don't think she should be held back just because she's a girl."

"My worst nightmare came true! I was in a construction zone, and as far as the eye could see, it was ankle-deep in gooey mud. Well, 'Mush, baby, mush!' I got through the first eight hundred feet. Then my arms got tired of fighting the handlebars and my legs gave out from dragging the mud and trying to keep the Harley up. I didn't really drop her—I buried her! I had mud up to my knees with splatters all over me and a gob on my face. What a bath! I loved every minute of it."

—Amy Mullins, sixty-two, recalling her solo ride through the Canadian Yukon

Flying Solo: Adventurers and Explorers

"I was riding through sand trails in Costa Rica and came upon a river. I couldn't tell how deep it was and there was no other way to pass. I was nervous. I thought, I can't get the bike through, I'll have to turn back, which is against my religion. Then a local man came by and waded through. The water was knee-deep, so I plunged the bike in and made it across. I felt like that song, 'I am woman, hear me roar!' I can do anything! I can have grandchildren! I can cook! And I can ford rivers! It was a hoot!"

—Catharine Rambeau, sixty-one, recalling her solo ride through Central America

Some women use their motorcycles to go beyond the controlled environment of the racetrack ... beyond the local roads of a Sunday jaunt with friends ... away from the hangouts where bikers meet to kick tires.

These women want none of that. When they go out on their motorcycles, they go

OPPOSITE: **Amy Mullins geared up for a rough ride on the Alcan Highway** (Amy Mullins Collection)

Amy Mullins Collection

For Mullins, riding north on the Alcan from Haines Junction, Yukon, toward Alaska was like taking a giant mud bath.

into themselves. They ride alone and very far. As much as racers live on the edge, these women push their personal envelopes by embarking on long, solo flights to unknown places. Going in, they know that hardship and danger are likely to rear up as often as exhilaration and freedom. They get off on the mixture.

Amy Mullins, a retired power plant technician from St. Clair, Michigan, and Catharine Rambeau, a magazine editor and former film critic from Lantana, Florida, were two such women. Both divorced many years, both grandmothers, both stubborn. Far from retiring into the empty nest, Rambeau and Mullins were propelled by a relentless energy.

In the late 1980s, both women set aside the time and some modest resources to fulfill their dreams of adventure. They were never tourists. They were *travelers,* drinking in the highs and lows in a manner true to the original meaning of the word: *travail.*

NORTHERN EXPOSURE

What brought Amy Mullins to leave home in July 1988 and, for the duration of the month, to slosh and bounce her 650-pound Harley Low Rider up the infamous roads of the Canadian Yukon and the Alcan Highway to Fairbanks, Alaska? What goaded this five-foot-one, 110-pound woman to tackle what many

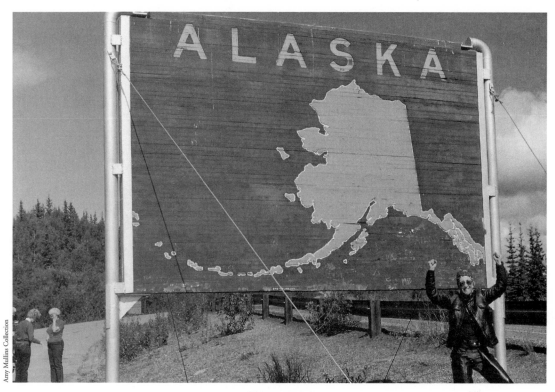

Amy Mullins Collection

She made it!

bikers say is one of the two last, great overland adventures on the continent? (Inuvik in the Arctic Circle, the northernmost point on the continent accessible by land, is the other.)

"I did it for the same reasons people climb mountains—for the sense of accomplishment," said Mullins. "I'd already ridden all over the country, so going to California on a motorcycle was no big deal anymore.

"I didn't just want to see Alaska," she continued. "I wanted to *ride* it. The north country is not like civilization as we know it. Up there, you are a real adventurer. The country reaches out and grabs you, especially on a bike."

Mullins was in her early fifties at the time

of the trek. She was (and still is) a walking powerhouse who lifts weights in competition and rock-climbs with her grown son. Mullins's inner and outer strength stood her well up north. Much of her journal read like this:

The rocks thrown up by passing trucks

could rearrange your front teeth.

The last stretch of road before the

Alaskan border was a terror. The frost

heaves (buckled road) were so bad, I hit

A peaceful moment at Kluane Lake, Yukon

Amy Mullins Collection

the frame of the bike a couple of times. I

really white-knuckled it through there.

She concluded: "It was *all* positive because I glory in that kind of challenge. It was worth it to see the crystal glaciers, the wildlife and landscapes so vivid, it looked like God had taken a paintbrush and dipped the land in color."

Years of self-sufficiency and resourcefulness had prepared Mullins for the rigors of the road. "I used to have a house where the toilet got clogged. A plumber wanted fifty bucks to clear it. I said, 'Forget it.' I took the toilet out of the floor and got the obstruction out. From

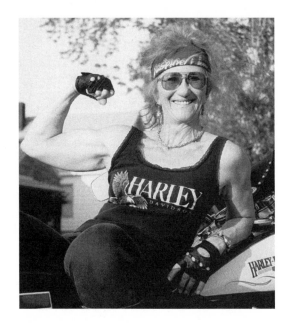

Readin', Ridin', and Rallyin'

At the end of every May for the past several years, Cindy Earle dismissed her fifth-grade students for summer recess, while Dan, her college professor husband, wrapped up his semester. Cindy packed her BMW K75S with camping gear while Dan loaded his van with canoe and kayak. They kissed good-bye and locked their house in Baton Rouge, Louisiana. Except for brief sojourns when their paths crossed, they didn't see each other for two months. She rode America's roads; he navigated its rivers.

Earle, in her fifties and the mother of a grown daughter, made a loop of the continent that typically traversed more than twenty-five states and a Canadian province or two. She saw old friends at a dozen BMW rallies and the Women on Wheels Ride-In. She won several long-distance mileage awards.

Her ongoing travels have been a study in extremes: The loneliness and monotony of the interstates have been relieved by the camaraderie of the rallygoers and explorations of scenic back roads. And yet, one of Earle's favorite encounters occurred in the midst of monotony.

"My itinerary forced me to ride I-70 through Kansas four times," she recalled. "I thought, Surely, there must be something that changes in Kansas. I needed to have a memorable encounter with someone other than having a meal and buying gas."

Cindy Earle

Nature provided the answer: an impending tornado. "I figured *now* would be the time to get my bike serviced." Earle pulled into a repair shop, where she exchanged laughter and road stories with another stranded rider. "It was a three-hour encounter while the storm passed. Now I love Kansas."

Many of her interstate miles have been meditative. She explained, "It's a good time to look at yourself and learn from your actions. Riding helps me keep my head on straight and it puts the stresses of school on hold. [She teaches underprivileged and some troubled youngsters.] The road shows me how to live *each day* and to view every moment as a gift. June and July on the road alone are my summer celebration."

Catharine S. Rambeau Collection

Catharine Rambeau rode "Mojo," her Honda XL250S, from the United States to the southernmost village in Latin America.

there, I started working on houses." Mullins designed her own home, did most of the plumbing and all of the wiring.

"The older I get, the more independent I get," she said. "I always travel alone because it's my time to do what I want. All your life you're confined; people set rules you have to obey. On my vacation, I want total freedom. Then I'm not gonna come home and cook dinner for any man."

Her next goal is Inuvik or bust. A true Harley lover, she may do it on a Sportster because "it's only five hundred pounds. If I drop it, it's light enough to lift by myself."

SOUTHERN ODYSSEY

Catharine Rambeau was fifty-three and the mother of a grown son when she embarked upon her South American odyssey in 1988. But she learned the most important thing she needed to know for that trip when she was twelve.

"One day my mother drove me and my brothers to the dentist," Rambeau said. "The roads were slick from a frozen rain. Suddenly, the car went out of control and spun around three times. My mother simply turned off the ignition and waited till the car calmed down. Then she smiled and asked, 'Is everybody all right?' She switched the car on, turned it the right way, and continued to drive. She never made a scene, never cried. Just took care of business. Thirty-five years later, I realized that what I'd seen had changed my life."

Like her mother, Rambeau became a woman who always took care of business. Whatever came up, she *dealt* with it. When faced with the choice of losing weight or

spending the rest of her life as a diabetic, she shed eighty-six pounds. In the summer of 1988, the magazine she worked for closed its doors. "I was out of work for the first time in decades. I'd saved some money and decided that now was the time to pursue a serious adventure, my reward for thirty years of hard work."

Rambeau combined her interest in Latin culture with her love of riding. She obtained her mother's blessing, drew up a will, and rented her house. That December, she left Florida on a used, 250cc Honda dual-sport (on/off road) bike with a kickstarter.

For Rambeau, there was no other choice but to go on a motorcycle. "In a car, you're a self-contained unit. You can even eat in a car. The bike meant I had to reach out to people. I had to ask how far to the next gas station? Where could I sleep? Is this road dangerous?"

She continued, "When you travel long distances on a motorcycle, it's you and the road, you and the machine, you and the weather. It's your decisions and your mistakes. When something unexpected happens, you make an adventure of it. A nut that's not properly tightened on the bike can be an introduction to a whole village. If you take that attitude home to family and work, everyone is enriched."

Rambeau's crash into a boulder in Ecuador and her failed attempts to ride the bike over the crest of a steep, sandy hill (with help, she pushed it over) were among her unplanned "adventures." She navigated roads that were thrilling and terrifying, like that mountain pass in Colombia—altitude: eleven thousand feet. "I was so high up, I was in the clouds,

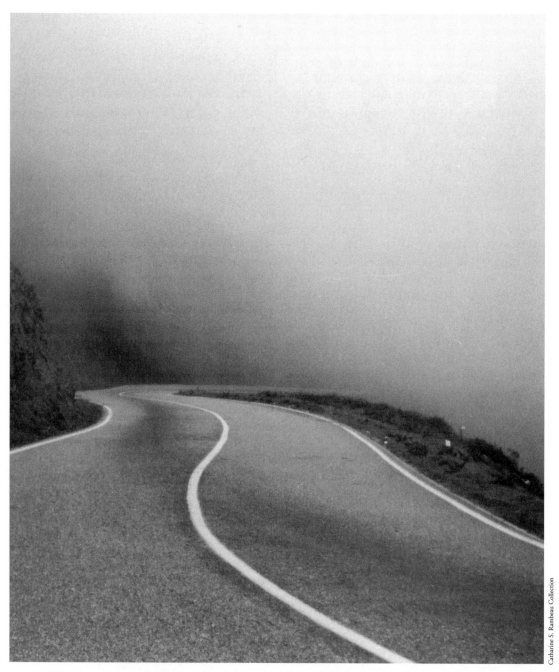

Catharine S. Rambeau Collection

In 1916, pioneer rider Adeline Van Buren said, "On a motorcycle, all roads lead to the end of the world if one has but the courage to follow them." On her 250cc Honda, Catharine Rambeau followed this road, literally, to the end of the world. This desolate portion of the Pan-American Highway is so high in the Colombian mountains, it is shrouded in clouds.

In 1993, FROM LEFT, Leenie Bachman, Doris Buksa, Gin Shear, and Sue Slate rode from the Atlantic coast to Inuvik in the Arctic Circle. Gravel, steep grades, and washouts caused a flat tire and "moving dismounts." Here, they relax at the Chuk campground, Northwest Territory, Yukon. Although they rode eighteen hours that day, Slate said, "When it's light at two in the morning, the child in you comes out."

Women's Motorcyclist Foundation

surrounded by their wetness," she recalled. Mist obscured her vision of the narrow road while cloud matter swirled through the spokes of her wheels. "It was a stiff haul and there were no guardrails, no margin for error. I was so scared, I sang "Amazing Grace" to myself because I thought I was going to die." But she *dealt* with it.

The Latin newspapers were intrigued by her moxie and a string of stories preceded her arrival in many villages. "I hated being defined as a motorcycling grandmother," Rambeau said, adding that her happiest times were the forty-four days she spent riding the high, cool Sechura and Atacama deserts, of Peru and Chile. "In the desert, there were no definitions. Everything was so stripped down, so lacking in falsity. There was a moment when I was able to disappear into the road. When I 'came to,' as it were, I'd forgotten the day, the month, even where I was. I'd forgotten my age, my sex, my color. I was just this creature.

It was a wonderful, freeing experience. The only expectations were mine."

A year after leaving home, when she'd ridden to the far, far underside of the globe, Rambeau fulfilled those expectations. She sat by herself, sipping wine and watching a late sunset over the Beagle Channel, where Charles Darwin had once sailed. Quietly, she celebrated the end of an arduous journey that had taken her through South American war zones, rain forests, and cobblestoned streets to where she was then: Argentina's most southern outpost—Ushuaia, a village on the island of Tierra del Fuego known as the end of the world. Local officials verified that Rambeau was the first woman to make the trek from the United States alone on a motorcycle.

Naturally, the first person she called was her mother.

Through tears of pride Rambeau exclaimed, "Hey, Ma! I made it! I bleeping made it!"

A Woman and Three Wheels

"People with disabilities can do an awful lot," said forty-six-year-old Marsha Wacker. Indeed, she should know.

Due to a birth defect, Wacker had both legs amputated above the knee when she was only one year old. With a wise mother who "never told me I wasn't supposed to do things," Wacker embarked on a life of exploring the possibilities. Today, this Cleveland, Ohio, resident is a vocational counselor to teenagers with disabilities—and a motorcycle sidecarist, downhill skier, and kayaker. She walks with artificial limbs and travels in a modified, 1000cc Moto Guzzi California II with a sidecar. Beaumont, her begoggled standard poodle, is her frequent passenger.

Wacker has driven the sidecar rig on roads that would challenge sport riders even on nimble two-wheelers—from the Rocky Mountains and the Oregon coastline to remote trails in Nova Scotia. She

Marsha Wacker and Beaumont

has never let her disability limit her horizons. "I'm adventurous," she said. "I really want to live life, and the motorcycle has given me a life I wouldn't have otherwise. I can't run or ride bicycles. But with the motorcycle, I'm on the same plane as a person who is able-bodied. I can enjoy the wind in my face."

She has come a long way from the nineteen-year-old girl who—against great odds—learned to ride a two-wheeled, 90cc Honda. "I have free-swinging knees, so when I stopped the bike, I lost my balance. I fell over so many times that my key was bent in the ignition. But I allowed myself to fall and then figured out another way."

That way was to add a third wheel. She is a certified sidecar safety instructor who says, "It's exhilarating to handle the sidecar rig in the twisties at speed." Deal's Gap at the Tennessee/North Carolina border—three hundred and eleven curves in eleven miles—"was just incredible. I know I'm good and I push the edge of what the bike can handle."

Echoing common sentiments among women who ride, Wacker added, "I've had so many great moments on the motorcycle. Plus I enjoy the independence."

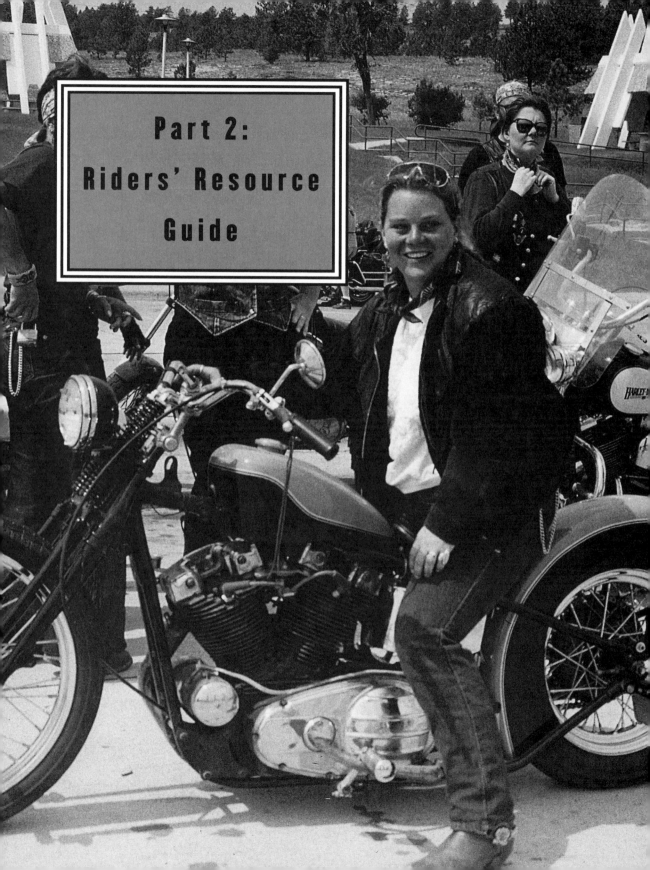

Part 2:
Riders' Resource
Guide

Motorcycle rallies are places where the sport's subcultures mingle. They are ad hoc cities—gatherings of tribes where motorcyclists from all rides of life are brought together by their passion for two-wheeled travel. The larger rallies are fun, fascinating panoramas of

A Biker's Social Calendar: Rallies, Runs, and Watering Holes

all the strata within the motorcycle community. They are places for tire kicking, camaraderie, and, of course, riding.

Sometimes, members of different motorcycle camps coexist but do not exactly mingle. In extreme cases, brand loyalty is so strong that some groups are snobbish toward outsiders. There are exceptions to every rule, but rallies are also laden with stereotypes, and it can be astounding to observe the lengths to which adults go to label one another.

Rallies range from fewer than five hundred people at a local one-day meet to two hundred thousand or more at a long-established national event spread over a week or so. The largest rallies offer amateur competitive riding events, parties, custom bike shows, scenic tours, informational seminars, shopping, demo rides of new bikes, professional races, and more. Smaller affairs have less of everything—including fewer hassles and fewer crowds.

Basically, the calendar consists of rallies geared to various groups: Harley riders, owners

OPPOSITE: **Main Street in Sturgis, South Dakota, during the Black Hills Motor Classic**

Vera Griffin Collection

Vera Griffin Collection

This motordrome or "Wall of Death" near Daytona dates back to the 1930s. Women have always been motordrome stunt riders. Here, Nita Nielsen rides the wall and Betty Fritz practices standing in the saddle, both circa late 1930s or '40s.

of other specific brands, owners of luxury touring bikes, women riders. There are events for other groups and lots of overlap. Rally addresses are in the Directory.

HARLEY-ORIENTED RALLIES

The Season Opener: Daytona Bike Week

The social and racing calendars begin in late February in Daytona Beach, Florida, with Bike Week, considered a rite of spring. Bike

Week has grown to about eleven days of festive and competitive events held within a twenty-five-mile radius of the town's Main Street. Although much of Bike Week is geared to Harley lovers, increasingly, riders of all brands have been coming to Daytona. They trek from all across the continent, even if it means trailer-towing their bikes through winter's chill. Typically, an estimated two hundred thousand people attend.

Main Street is a bikers' Mardi Gras, *the* place to see and be seen. The Harley-Davidson lifestyle is on parade. All day and into the wee hours, Harley riders cruise the crowded street. Many bikes are artwork-in-motion, with their gleaming chrome and custom paint jobs. During the evening party hours, the rumble and roar of thousands of Harleys, many with straight (unmuffled) pipes, can be deafening and so intense that the ground vibrates. Interspersed among the "hogs" are a few riders on plastic-covered Japanese and Italian sport bikes, BMWs, British bikes, and huge touring rigs.

While recovering from the blinding glare of all the chrome, occasionally the eye rests upon an archaeological dig-on-wheels. These are the beat-up rat bikes, dinosaurs that lumber along in proud defiance of Harley's Evolution motor, not to mention upscale Evolution bikers. A true rat bike is akin to a homeless person's shopping cart, replete with the trappings of a nomadic life. Cooking and camping utensils, arcane spare parts, and anything else from deer antlers to vintage memorabilia may adorn a rat bike.

The sidewalks and shops of Main Street are packed with bikers in denim jeans and leather vests. Most of the men appear to be auditioning for the same part in *Masters of Menace,* with their requisite beards, black T-shirts, potbellies, and tattoos. The majority of women in jeans and tank tops do not get photographed; the few in bikinis always do. There are also "profilers" and "rubbies" (rich urban bikers) in designer leathers. Depending on your point of view, the scene is awesome or a parody.

Away from Main Street, there are dozens of activities. At the Volusia County Fairgrounds, you can wander among the rust of an old-fashioned parts swap meet. At the Ocean Convention Center, you can sample the latest Harley-Davidson accessories and Motor-Clothes. You can wade through crowds at the Rat's Hole Custom Motorcycle Show. Here, practically every other machine is a radically chopped-out Harley with a skull or death gas tank mural. Voluptuous women, flames, demons, and Native American themes are also de rigueur. And if female coleslaw wrestling is your thing, Daytona has it.

The circus that has become today's Bike Week is a far cry from its humble beginnings, which lie in racing. In 1937, the original excuse for bikers to come here was the Daytona 200. Jocks raced their machines on the beach. In the early sixties, the race was moved to a closed-circuit asphalt track. Today, only a fraction of Bike Week attendees watch the races at Daytona International Speedway, which culminate with the 200. The attitude of some Harley lifestyle bikers is summed up on a T-shirt that says, "Fuck the races. I came to party."

In the speedway pits, the jocks downing

Bike Week in Florida: Motorcycles take over Daytona Beach.

Gatorade couldn't care less about Main Street. They do not consider themselves "bikers." They are "motorcyclists" who are here to see mostly foreign-made superbikes zoom around the high banks of Daytona. The visceral roar of these rockets blasting on a straightaway at 170 MPH can send chills up the spine.

Twenty miles north of Daytona at the Bulow Campground in Flagler Beach, another subculture of "motorcyclists" gathers. Every year, the local Space Coast BMW Riders Club reserves a chunk of the campground for "Beemer" owners and their guests. For two bucks, any rider (on any brand of bike) is welcome to a homey breakfast of pan-

cakes, coffee, and camaraderie. The camp is disarmingly quiet because BMWs don't roar.

It is often said that Daytona represents a clashing of cultures, but perhaps it is not so much a clashing as a juncture. Hoping to build on the popularity of Bike Week and create "a more family-oriented rally," a few years ago, organizers started Biketoberfest, a smaller event in the fall.

Sturgis Rally and Races: Thunder in the Hills

Tucked in a valley at the foot of South Dakota's Black Hills, there is a sleepy town called Sturgis, with a population of about

Sturgis draws bikers from all over the continent and a few from abroad. As one person put it, "On a motorcycle, you can go anywhere and find this common ground."

seven thousand. But for one week every August, that number may swell to two hundred thousand as bikers converge for the Black Hills Motor Classic, also known as the Sturgis Rally & Races. Like Daytona, Sturgis draws mostly Harley owners with a smattering of other riders.

Here, too, Main Street is a mecca, but the ambience at Sturgis is different. On the oil-soaked street, the undulating sea of leather, denim, and chrome has a rougher edge. Amongst the friendly lifestyle bikers, 1%er clubs are more visible. They keep mainly to themselves, but most years, a bar brawl or two makes the news.

For the duration of the Classic, local shopkeepers rent their stores to vendors selling leather, bike parts and accessories, silver jewelry, bandannas, greasy food, coonskin hats, and Nazi regalia favored by hardcore types. There are pins and patches that sneer "Die yuppie scum" and "If it has tits or wheels, it will give you trouble." The hardcore element frequents certain campgrounds. In some sections, the atmosphere can be so raunchy that unescorted women are ill-advised to enter. At every turn, drunken men blurt, "Show your tits." Some sit next to signs that say the same.

While these elements can be found in Daytona as well, they are more blatant at

Sturgis. Yet despite the sharp edges, the rally is what you make of it. If you love bikes, especially beautifully customized Harleys, and if you are fascinated by humanity in all its diversity, it's worth braving the gridlock to partake in what the local papers have dubbed "a Woodstock in leathers." Even the late billionaire biker Malcolm Forbes was a Sturgis fan. Several times in the 1980s, Forbes beat the traffic by floating over it—in his seventy-five-foot-high hot-air balloon, shaped like a Harley, of course.

At Sturgis, you'll meet two-wheeling crusaders for Christ and Brothers of the Third Wheel on trikes. For five bucks, you can have your picture taken with a six-foot snake on your shoulders. You can get a tattoo or sit on a curb and hear stories from old, grizzled bikers, nearly all of whom are named Pappy.

In fact, it was a local motorcycle dealer named Pappy Hoel who, with the Jackpine Gypsies Motorcycle Club, started this affair on a small scale in 1938. They held races on a dirt horse track and led bikers on scenic rides. Over the years, the event grew and changed for better and worse. Old-timers say that before the Vietnam era, the crowd was "cleaner cut." Today, only a fraction of rally-goers attend the dirt track races, though the all-Harley drags are quite popular.

Ladies of Harley member Jean Livermore shows her Heritage Softail at a HOG Ride-In Show. Custom touches include gold plating, a solo seat, snakeskin handgrips, and, of course, chrome.

Closeup of some radical paint at Daytona's Rat's Hole Custom Motorcycle Show

Activities around the area range from rock concerts to the *Harley Women* magazine Ladies Day Ride and Party. At bikers' amateur rodeos or field meets, riding skill and sense of humor are equally tested. Serious contenders race their machines around barrels and ride through cone weaves. For laughs, there is the infamous weenie bite for couples riding two-up. A hot dog slathered in mustard is hung from a rope suspended between two posts. As the driver passes beneath the dog, the passenger attempts to bite off a chunk. The biggest bite wins.

Many people come to Sturgis for what lies beyond the town. In the Black Hills, roads wind through spectacular landscapes. You may pass buffalo roaming a prairie. Nearby are Custer State Park, Mount Rushmore, the Crazy Horse Monument, and the Badlands, a geological wonderland of colored canyons and spires.

Laconia, the Granddaddy of Rallies

Every June in the days leading up to Father's Day, New Hampshire is the site of Laconia Rally & Race Week, a smaller version of Sturgis. Estimates on the typical number of attendees varies widely, from twenty thousand to an optimistic one hundred fifty thousand. The scene unfolds along a small boardwalk at

A biker wedding in front of 3700 West Juneau Avenue in Milwaukee.
If you don't recognize that address, you wouldn't understand.

Weirs Beach on the shore of Lake Winni-pesaukee. Problem is, since only a single, two-lane road leads to the area, it may take two hours of clutch-grinding and straddle-walking to inch your way in. The locals sit on lawn chairs to gawk at the stalled parade of bikes.

The Laconia rally originated in the 1920s, making it the oldest event of its kind. But Laconia, too, had a troubled past. Beginning in the mid-1960s outside the nearby town of Louden, outlaw bikers took over a hill behind the old Bryar Motor Sports Park. It became known as Animal Hill.

Today, New Hampshire International Speedway hosts the Louden Classic. This race is part of the U.S. Superbike Series, which means Daytona's Gatorade set migrates north.

A milder version of Animal Hill still exists, but most rallygoers in and around Laconia are peaceful, law-abiding lifestyle bikers. All riders can enjoy a modest array of rally activities and the tree-lined roads of New Hampshire's lake district.

In HOG We Trust:
A Kinder, Gentler Rally

Local chapters of the Harley Owners Group (HOG) and its affiliate, Ladies of Harley, host statewide and regional rallies and one giant national. HOG rallies are "cleaner," more family-oriented alternatives to hardcore events that are not sanctioned by the company. To enter, you must be a HOG member or an associate. "Hoggies" are easy to spot.

Besides the club colors (logo insignias), many members wear leather or denim vests laden with dozens of pins and patches commemorating every biker event they've attended.

The poker run is a highlight of many HOG (and other) rallies. In one type of poker run, riders pay an entrance fee to take a scenic ride. At checkpoints, they draw cards or chips. Prizes are based on the best poker hands, and proceeds from entrance fees are donated to charity. You can "Stud Your Duds" at a Ladies of Harley workshop or enter your bike in a ride-in show. All bikes, no matter how radically modified, must be ridden, not trailered, to the grounds. Most entries combine an elegant and costly mix of function and fantasy.

Now that Harley-Davidson has become an American institution, every five years, the company celebrates its anniversary by hosting a reunion or homecoming. June 1993 was Harley's ninetieth birthday. En route to the party in Milwaukee, about sixty-eight thousand motorcycles formed a thundering procession that stretched for thirty miles. The parade lasted over three hours—nothing but bikes as far as the eye could see. Thousands of spectators lined the route, giving the bikers high fives and waving American flags. Proceeds in excess of $1 million, collected from admissions to reunion events, were donated to the Muscular Dystrophy Association.

Hardcore Rallies: 1% of the Scene

At the opposite (low) end of the spectrum are the hardcore gatherings. These include the Easyriders Rodeos sponsored by the magazine of the same name. Similar events may have "American Motorcycle" or "Harley" in their titles, but they are *not* sanctioned by the Harley-Davidson Motor Company. You may be greeted at the gate by video cameramen urging you to "show your tits." The tattoo and wet T-shirt contests are the high culture here.

RALLIES FOR RIDERS OF ALL BIKES
Touring Rallies: Big-Bike Nations

There are many gatherings for riders of all brands. The touring rally is one such get-together. Americade, held each June in Lake George, New York, is the grandest of them all, drawing anywhere from twenty thousand to seventy-five thousand enthusiasts over the course of a week.

Touring riders who come to Americade include many older couples on behemoth, fully dressed touring rigs. "Full dressers" are powerful motorcycles equipped with so many amenities, they are akin to two-wheeled motor homes. The most popular of these is the Honda Gold Wing, seconded by similar rigs from the other Japanese manufacturers. BMW and Harley-Davidson have versions as well.

Touring couples are the Ozzie and Harriets of motorcycling. Typically, the husband steers the luxury vehicle while the wife sits back in a plush seat with armrests. Some couples wear matching outfits and helmets with intercoms and microphones. Many rear trunks are platforms for stuffed animals, while others are inscribed with the couples' names—Bob and Bitsy here, Hank and Hannah there.

Peeking out from among the rows of yachts-on-wheels are other types of bikes, especially those owned by sport riders who come to sample the curvy Adirondacks roads. The crowd is friendly but machines with

Courtesy Motor Maids

The Motor Maids at their 53d Annual Convention in 1993.

modified or unmuffled pipes are nearly booed out of town.

On the other hand, there is much applause for the full dresser light parade, where motorcycles are festooned with so many bulbs, they look like Disneyland floats. There are awards for the best-dressed couple, youngest and oldest riders, looniest license plate, and competitions for an Americade Queen and King. Anyone wearing too much leather—that is, anyone who looks too much like a "biker"—need not apply.

In short, Americade is a high-school prom for middle-aged "kids." Similar but smaller

are the Rider Rallies sponsored by *Rider* magazine at sites around the country. Other (brand-specific) touring rallies include the Honda Hoot, put on by the Honda Riders Club of America (HRCA), and the Wing Ding of the Gold Wing Road Riders Association (GWRRA).

Women's Rallies: Where "The Girls" Are

The three national women's clubs—Motor Maids, Women on Wheels, and Women in the Wind—hold annual rallies in different states. Women's rallies offer samplings of the usual social, competitive, and informational activities over three or four days, but the ambience at each gathering is as different as the clubs are from one another.

Of a Motor Maids convention, humorist Erma Bombeck once said, "It looked more like a midlife Tupperware party where 'the girls,' as they call themselves, sit around and spin stories."

Except that these are no ordinary "girls." These are members of the nation's oldest women's riding club, and the stories are about the many millions of miles that they, collectively, have ridden. The older members recall how motorcycling used to be, before the days of biker chic and outlaw bikers. Snippets of conversations overheard include:

"Did you ever think you'd be selling ladies' underwear in your Harley dealership?"

"Please don't call us meter maids or motorcycle mamas. You won't find any tattoos or halter tops here."

The Motor Maids hold their conventions in July. The first one in 1944 drew fourteen riders. Today, roughly two hundred of the club's five hundred members attend, but other than their numbers, not much has changed. A favorite contest is the decades-old

Vera Griffin Collection

Field games haven't changed much in half a century. Back in the 1940s, Helen Blansitt of St. Louis, Missouri, rode the plank, as rallygoers do today.

The Peterson family of Jacksonville, Illinois: three generations of motorcycle enthusiasts converge at a Women on Wheels Ride-In.

timed road run, in which riders navigate varying terrain and arrive at checkpoints within designated time slots. The traditional Motor Maids parade looks like a sea of blue, gray, and white. Behind their tall windshields are the blue shirts, gray slacks, white gloves, and white boots of their uniforms ... and the gray and white hair of the many lifetime members. If it sounds quaint, consider this: Club rules state that all Motor Maids must *ride* their bikes to the convention—trailering, even for octogenarians traveling a thousand miles or more, is unthinkable.

Believe the husbands when they say it isn't easy being married to a Motor Maid. One man complained: "You can't tell the guys you rode a million miles and sound macho, because your wife is right next to you doing the same thing!"

Stroll the parking lot at a Women on Wheels Ride-In, and you might wonder if WOW should change its name to WAF, for Warm and Fuzzy. Like the true touring riders that they are, many WOW members have stuffed animals bungeed to their bikes. Others have unicorns, owls, and Disney characters airbrushed on gas tanks. Inside the host hotel are two hundred to three hundred women, many in their forties and fifties.

WOW leaders, from left, Kathy Heller, Susan Konopka, and Sue Frish accept the AMA Brighter Image Award from AMA trustee Patty Mills.

Every July, they gather at what appears to be a giant coffee klatch.

But with WOW as with the Motor Maids, appearances are deceiving. The woman next to you in the cotton blouse and slacks has just ridden solo from Alaska. The young mother with her toddlers and their grandmother are veteran riders from a multigenerational motorcycling family where no one stays home to mind the kids—because the kids come everywhere in the sidecar. Husbands, boyfriends, even a few fathers are such strong supporters that nominations are taken for a "Mr. WOW."

When Women in the Wind get together in late June for their Summer Nationals, the host campground and nearby motel rock with the laughter of one hundred fifty boisterous women, many of whom are Harley lifestyle bikers in their thirties and forties. Local chapters have names like Wild Bunch, Smokey Mountain Thunder, Southern Maidinz, Free Spirits, and Empowered Sister-

hood. If you ride a foreign bike, you're welcome to join the club, but be prepared for some friendly ribbing.

The Women in the Wind "uniform" is ride-as-you-are: cowboy boots and jeans, bandannas over braids, and why bother with makeup when you know your face will be a mess from riding? Vests sport the club colors—a caricature of a woman riding, wearing shades, her hair blown wild by the wind.

Lin Litousky rode down from Canada for a Women in the Wind Ladies Run at Sturgis. That's a painting of a scantily clad *man* on the gas tank of her bike, "Lady's Night."

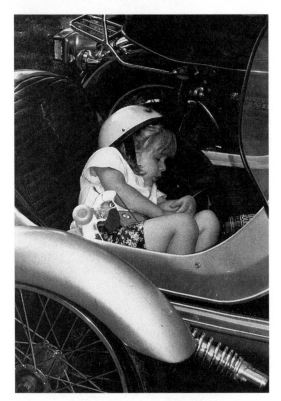

**A future biker catches a few
winks at a sidecar rally.**

Some husbands and boyfriends, who look as though they could hold their own in any brawl, have enough sense of humor to allow themselves to be whooped and hollered into donning T-shirts that say "Property of Women in the Wind." Don't miss the male "best buns" and beard contests.

There is something electric and liberating at the women-only Mid-Atlantic Women's Motorcycle Rally. This annual June gathering in Maryland was started in the early 1990s and has gotten good reviews for the diversity of the attendees, and the open, laid-back atmosphere where women of all ethnic backgrounds and persuasions mingle comfortably. Without male partners around, everyone can "let it all hang out." One attendee, sharing her experience in *Women on Wheels* magazine, wrote, "I loved my walk on the (sorta) wild side. I felt free to indulge my fantasies and be rid of conservatism and the restrictions I place on myself in real life.' " Rally proceeds go to the Susan G. Komen Breast Cancer Foundation.

Rallies Geared to
Specific Bike Brands

BMW Motorcycle Owners of America (MOA) and the BMW Riders Association (RA) each host a national rally drawing several thousand devotees, and local chapters of both clubs host smaller gatherings.

BMW riders are campers known for their wry humor and "secret society" clannishness. The local rallies have names like Beer Hunter, Udder Nonsense, It's Hard to Be Humble, and the Rolling Broccoli Camp Out and Nude Line Dancing Party. Within the ranks are many upscale professionals who get eccentric at the rallies. Aficionados of BMW's signature engine, the "boxer," with its horizontal-twin cylinders, may wear boxer shorts over their pants.

Beemers are built for autobahns, not boulevard cruising. Very few have custom paint jobs, and chrome sightings are rare. Rallygoers will inspect your odometer because hard miles, not paint, is the stuff of which war stories are made. The most superior, or insane, of BMW devotees are the Iron Butts, who rig auxiliary fuel cells to their bikes and ride thousand-mile days just to win mileage contests and bragging rights.

There are rallies for just about every type of bike and rider, including exotic Moto Guzzis, long-defunct Indians, and British bikes. In Ohio, the AMA hosts Vintage Motorcycle Days, featuring a bike auction, vintage road racing, motordrome stunt riders, and more. At sidecar rallies, you'll see lots of parents with children and dogs, as well as seniors and some disabled adults who enjoy motorcycling with a third wheel.

According to *Blackriders* magazine, there are an estimated two hundred thousand African-American motorcycle owners in the country. In recent years, more and more are attending all types of rallies. There are also gatherings organized by, and geared to, black riders. The week-long National Round-Up is considered one of the best.

Charity Rides

Charities have long been beneficiaries of bikers' generosity. Some charity rides have turned into enormous events, with parades of bikes that stretch for miles. The larger events conclude with a barbecue and recreation, including concerts, bike shows, and door prizes. At some events, you pay a flat entry fee; for others, you must raise pledges or bring checks from sponsors.

In Glendale, California, the Harley-dominated Love Ride to benefit the Muscular Dystrophy Association has become perhaps the largest single-day motorcycle fund-raiser in the world, with more than twenty thousand riders raising upward of a million dollars a year. It helps that the list of VIP participants is a who's who of Hollywood's celebrity biker set. Jay Leno, along with Peter Fonda and

Dennis Hopper, who starred in the cult film *Easy Rider,* are the grand marshals. Mary Hart of TV's *Entertainment Tonight* rides in the parade, as do actors Lorenzo Lamas, Larry Hagman, and others.

Honda's Ride for Kids, benefiting the Pediatric Brain Tumor Foundation of the United States, consists of a dozen rides in various states. Since their beginnings in 1984, the rides have raised more than $2.5 million. Bikers raise money for many other charities as well, ranging from the March of Dimes Birth Defects Foundation to the Make-a-Wish Foundation. Clubs hold bike washes and other events to benefit battered women's shelters and veterans' hospitals. For Christmas toy runs, riders turn out even in bone-chilling weather to deliver toys to children who are orphaned, troubled, or disabled.

In the week preceding each Memorial Day, tens of thousands of bikers from across the nation, including many Harley-riding Vietnam vets, join the Run to the Wall, a mass pilgrimage to Rolling Thunder in Washington, D.C. Rolling Thunder is a procession of bikes that begins at the Pentagon and ends with a subdued but emotionally charged visit to the Vietnam Memorial.

One-Day and Weekend Events

In most areas, there are plenty of one-day activities. The riding season may begin with a bike blessing, during which a priest sprinkles holy water on the bikes and riders.

Sunday is traditionally the day when local clubs host events like field meets, swap meets, poker runs, and observation runs (take a scenic ride, look for clues, win a door prize).

An annual rite of spring: the blessing of the bikes.

Gypsy tours, which date back to the mid-1920s, are longer group rides over one or two days; they usually end in an idyllic setting with a barbecue and recreation. Two-day, five-hundred-mile rides that cover challenging roads are popular. The most well known of these include the Ramapo 500 for street bikes in the New York tristate area, and the Ridgerunner 500 for dual-sport bikes in California. There are midnight runs and even polar bear runs in the winter.

Events are hosted by all types of specialty clubs. These include the Blue Knights, comprised of law enforcement personnel; the Red Knights, a group for firefighters; the Knights of Life, who are medical professionals; and the Retreads, who are over forty. There are meetings of the Christian Motorcyclist Association and of "clean and sober" groups for recovering alcoholics. There are clubs and events for just about everyone.

Cycle Watering Holes

Sometimes, rallies are where you make them. Unpretentious diners, dairy barns, and snack bars have a way of becoming biker landmarks if they're situated on or near great riding roads. These rest stops are Sunday-morning watering holes where bikers pause to exchange stories and show off a bit before roaring off in small groups to partake of their favorite pastime. Three of the most famous spots are Marcus Dairy in Danbury, Connecticut; Alice's Restaurant in Woodside, northern California; and the Rock Store, a deli nestled in the mountains near Malibu, just west of Hollywood. Here, celebrity bikers mingle with the nonfamous. And if you think cruise nights are only for cars, think again. On summer nights, hot-dog joints with big parking lots have a way of filling up with bikes.

With such a full social calendar of annual rallies, runs, and hangouts all across the continent, newcomers to motorcycling may wonder how they could have missed all this activity before. When bikers get together, motorcycles are social lubricants, demographic levelers, and, ultimately, adhesives for cherished friendships.

Choosing the right motorcycle to suit your needs, level of experience, and riding style is a highly personal decision and not often a simple one. As motorcycles have become safer (better brakes, better tires), faster, and more comfortable than those our parents and grandparents rode, they have become more specialized. The major considerations that should influence your choice of a motorcycle are:

- Type or classification of the bike, including its handling characteristics

- Type of riding you intend to do most. Do you plan to: Commute in urban traffic? Take leisurely long-distance tours? Challenge yourself with fast, sporting rides on twisty paved roads? Explore dirt trails? All of the above?

OPPOSITE: **BMW's R850 Roadster**
(BMW of North America)

About Bikes: A Primer on Choosing a First Motorcycle, with Tips on Lowering Ride Height

- Ergonomics, including seat height and seating posture

- Weight, including center of mass or gravity (CG)

- Configuration and power output of the engine

- Style or aesthetic appeal

- Initial purchase price
- Subsequent costs in money *and* time for repairs and maintenance

While some motorcycles are as different from one another as sports cars are from station wagons, most bikes have this in common: They are designed for that half of the population who tend to be taller, heavier, and have more upper-body strength than the average female. Women who are taller or stronger than average and those with more advanced riding skills may not be concerned with some of the issues addressed here.

Motorcycles in the cruiser class are popular among women because they have low seats and a low CG. But short riders may not wish to be limited to one type of bike. What can they do? There are ways to lower many bikes, but first, let's look at what is available straight from the factories.

Because it would take a separate volume to cover all there is to say about bikes, we'll make certain *generalizations to summarize the hallmarks* of each category. Only types and brands of bikes widely available in North America are included. Some discontinued models are mentioned because they are excellent examples of their class and can be found used. Prices aren't listed because the range is too great. Five hundred bucks could get you a used, running wreck; thirty thousand would bring you a custom showpiece. We'll focus on street bikes, meaning motorcycles that are legal to ride on paved roads.

Today's street motorcycles are shifted manually (unlike automatic scooters). Most new models have hydraulic disc brakes, though some have a mechanical drum brake in the rear. A drum is not as efficient as a disc, but on some models, a rear drum is adequate because the front brake has 70 to 80 percent of the bike's stopping power, anyway. BMWs were the first motorcycles to come with antilock disc brakes (ABS); only a few models from other manufacturers have them.

A motorcycle is driven by a chain, belt, or shaft. A chain is the cheapest method, and it is light, efficient, and provides smooth gear shifts, but a chain must be lubricated and adjusted frequently. This can be a messy, annoying task. Belts and shafts are practically maintenance-free.

Street motorcycles have four-stroke internal combustion engines with one to six cylinders. Each cylinder has a piston. To complete one revolution, or "rev," of the motor's crankshaft, each piston makes four strokes. RPM means revolutions per minute. Engines may be cooled by air, oil, or water. When stuck in a summer traffic jam, a liquid-cooled engine is less prone to overheating than one cooled only by airflow. Engine size is measured by the volume in cubic centimeters (cc's) or cubic inches (ci's) of fuel/air mixture that is displaced by the pistons. Small or "entry level" street bike engines may displace anything from 125 to 450cc's. Midsized bikes fall roughly in the 500 to 850cc range. Large bikes blow out 900 to 1500cc's.

You'd think that the larger the displacement, the more horsepower. That's not always true. A four-cylinder, state-of-the-art 600cc sport bike may outrun a two-cylinder cruiser with twice the engine displacement. What happens when rubber meets road is determined by many factors, including:

- The number of cylinders
- How quickly and efficiently engine power is transmitted to the crankshaft
- The weight of the bike
- How aerodynamic the bike's outer bodywork is

A motorcycle's weight varies widely according to bike type, size, accessories, and other factors. Dry (without gas), an entry-level 175cc bike may weigh a mere 250 pounds, while a large cruiser or tourer can weigh 600 to 800 pounds. A full tank of gas, saddlebags, and windshields add pounds.

In many cases, total poundage is not the issue, but center of gravity is. You want to know where the machine carries most of its weight or mass. A cruiser carries most of it low, so a small person may handle the machine comfortably in most situations. But a touring bike, top-heavy with accessories and a full fairing (a large windscreen that protects the head, hands, and legs), might be unwieldy for a small person.

Lawrence Grodsky, who runs a rider training school in Pennsylvania and writes a safety column for *Rider* magazine, points out that the average female has roughly half the upper-body strength of the average male, and her inseam is generally two inches shorter. If she cannot plant both feet squarely on the ground, she must support more of the bike's weight at rest. According to Grodsky, "on a tall machine, the difference may exceed a hundred pounds."[1]

Generally, the best advice for most beginners is to start on a small or "smallish" bike.

Too much power in the hands of a novice who is just learning to operate the machine can be counterproductive. A not-uncommon scenario is one that occurs when a novice has a well-intentioned male partner who encourages her to start on a bike that is too tall, too top-heavy, or too powerful for her skill level. The result may cause a real dip in confidence.

Learn to ride *before* purchasing a motorcycle! Believe it or not, many people buy motorcycles without a clue as to how to ride them out of the dealership. Start by taking the Motorcycle RiderCourse, taught by the Motorcycle Safety Foundation (see Chapter 11 and the appendix for more information).

Once you've learned the basics, buy a used, inexpensive motorcycle. Make your mistakes on that machine. Observe what you like about the bike and what you don't. Then listen to yourself. With experience, you now have a reference point for choosing a suitable motorcycle. Keep in mind that in many cases, men's motorcycling needs *are* different. To a 180-pound man who carries a passenger, a 650cc bike may seem puny and underpowered. But for a 115-pound woman riding solo, a 650 may be quite adequate. Bikes are affected by power-to-weight ratio—how heavy the bike and rider(s) are will affect how powerful the bike "feels."

Following are the different types or categories of motorcycles. Bikes pictured are 1996 models except where noted.

SPORT BIKES: TWO-WHEELED ROCKETS

Sport bikes are designed for performance, not long-distance comfort. They have aerody-

Discover Today's Motorcycling

The discontinued Honda Hawk GT 650. Fully loaded, this midsized standard had plenty of power in its performance V-twin to carry the author (BELOW) around the continent during her working travels.

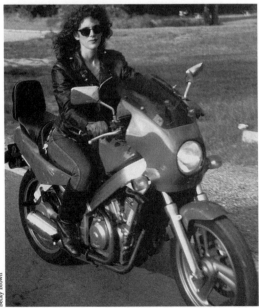

Becky Brown

namic plastic bodywork to help the bike punch a hole in the air with minimal wind drag. The handlebars are placed low and forward, while the footpegs are rearset. This forces you to crouch over the gas tank like a jockey. You support your weight primarily with your arms, wrists, and shoulders.

A sport bike has a short wheelbase (the distance between front and rear axles) and a steep rake. Basically, rake is the angle of the steering head (the front fork pivot, at the center of the handlebars) in relation to an imaginary vertical line. The shorter or steeper the rake angle, the closer the front axle is to the steering head, and the quicker the bike is to steer.

Sport bikes are generally chain-driven and they have powerful disc brakes and wide, sticky tires for maximum traction. They have high ground clearance to allow tremendous lean angles. This usually means two things: a seat height of thirty-one inches or more and a high center of gravity. In certain situations—like stopping on hills and pulling away from a stop on a sloped road—a large sport bike with a high seat and high mass may pose added challenges for a short rider. If both feet cannot reach the ground, you must slide to the left side of the seat and balance the bike using one leg as an outrigger. Since most women have good *lower*-body strength, this isn't a problem as long as the bike is straight up. If it starts to lean, you'll need a strong lower back, shoulders, pectorals, and arms to keep the bike up.

Many sport bikes have engines with an inline-four configuration, meaning four cylinders in line with the chassis. Inline-fours make their best power in the higher gears—when you're going fast. They can feel com-

paratively sluggish in stop-and-go traffic. Some modern sport bikes can rocket from zero to 150 and even up to 170 miles per hour right off the showroom floor. They are thrilling, but it is advisable to get some experience before you buy one. Street-legal sport bikes, when stripped of parts like lights and horns, become superbikes at the racetrack.

Midsized sport bikes include the Honda CBR 600, Kawasaki Ninja 600, Yamaha FZR 600, and Suzuki RF 600. Kawasaki's entry-level Ninjas, the 500 and 250R, have two cylinders instead of four.

CRUISERS: CHROME AND GLORY

Cruisers or "customs" are everything sport bikes are not. Cruisers have chromed parts and their owners tend to embellish them with accessories. Strip away the baubles and a cruiser is simplicity in motion. The engine is

American Honda Motor Company

Honda's CBR600F3, a quintessential sport bike with an inline four engine

1.

2.

An array of eye-catching cruisers:
1. Honda Rebel 250
2. Kawasaki Vulcan 500 LTD
3. Suzuki Savage 650
4. Yamaha Virago 750
5. Harley-Davidson Sportster 883 Hugger
6. Harley-Davidson Dyna Low Rider
7. Harley-Davidson Heritage Softail Classic

About half of all street bikes sold in 1995 were cruisers. Small cruisers are somewhat "forgiving" of a novice's clumsy techniques. It's advisable to have some experience before climbing aboard the larger bikes numbered 4 through 7.

3.

4.

5.

6.

7.

A luxury tourer, the Kawasaki Voyager XII

Kawasaki Motors Corp.

exposed and treated as part of the bike's over-all styling.

Cruisers have high, curved, or "buckhorn" handlebars sloped back toward the rider. The footpegs are set forward. This places you in a leisurely, laid-back position for boulevard cruising or long-haul interstate trips. Cruisers, especially small to midsized models, are favored by short riders because of their modest seat heights. Cruisers' low center of gravity, long rake, and long wheelbase provide rock-solid straight-line stability but make them slower to handle on twisty roads. Yet speed is so irrelevant that some cruisers don't have a tachometer to indicate RPM. The essence of the ride is the feel of the V-twin engine.

In the minds of most people, there are basi-cally two types of cruisers: Harleys and the Japanese look-alikes. Harley's V-shaped, dual-cylinder, air-cooled engine, essentially unchanged since before World War II, has a deep, loud rumble and vibration that is over-whelming and powerful. Most foreign cruisers have refined versions of the V-twin engine that are usually liquid cooled and shaft driven. They rumble but the ride is smoother and eas-ier on the bike. They require less maintenance.

Harleys are big-displacement machines. The "smallest" Harleys are the 883cc Sportster and the Hugger, a Sportster with a twenty-seven-inch seat height. Large Harley cruisers, or "Big Twins" (1340cc or 80ci), include the Heritage Softail Classic, Springer Softail, Fat Boy, and the Dyna Low Rider.

Cruisers have become so popular that three formerly discontinued, entry-level import models are back: Honda's Rebel 250; Yamaha's Virago 250 (formerly, the Route 66); and Suzuki's Savage 650. Kawasaki's Vulcan 500 LTD evokes the old 454 LTD. Midsized models include Suzuki's Intruder 800 and Honda's Shadow 600 and (four-cylinder) Magna 750. Discontinued entry-level cruisers that can be found used include Honda's Rebel 450, Shadow 500, and Magna 500. Not all of these models have a V-twin centerpiece, but all have that classic cruiser look.

TOURERS: ALL DRESSED UP

Tourers, a.k.a. full-dressers or rigs, are the Winnebagos of motorcycles, built for the long-distance comfort of driver and passenger. Touring bikes are huge, smooth, and powerful. Honda's new Gold Wing models have carlike, six-cylinder engines and a reverse gear. The dresser seating posture is upright, as in your favorite armchair.

There are so many options for full-luxury models that you can create your own rolling universe. Like cars, dressers have dashboards and sophisticated wiring systems to support amenities that may include anything from a CB radio, stereo, and tape deck to heated handgrips, blindingly bright headlights, and auxiliary lights. Fuel capacity is gargantuan, as is the luggage capacity of the built-in hard bags.

The downside is that dressers are top-heavy and their wide, plush saddles are beyond the reach of many short riders. These bikes glide on the interstate, but "flicking" one through twisty roads takes getting used to. Stopping all that mass requires careful attention to braking.

All of the manufacturers have dressers, which are great for experienced riders. The Kawasaki Voyager 1200 has a relatively low ride height of 29.7 inches. The adjustable seat on BMW's R1100RT goes down to 30.7 inches. Since both bikes are narrower than other tourers, they could work for some short riders.

SPORT-TOURERS: PERFORMANCE WITH SOME COMFORT

Sport-tourers are the "performance sedans" of motorcycles. These machines are hybrids for long-distance riders who want enough handling capabilities to make straying off the interstate fun, but don't confuse sport-touring with "dual-sport" or "adventure touring," as these bikes are not built for rough terrain. Sport-tourers are more passenger-friendly than true sport bikes, and many models come with integrated, removable hard luggage systems. Others carry soft luggage beautifully.

The innards and aerodynamic bodywork on the sportier models are descended from sport bikes. They have a relatively forward seating posture, relatively low, short handlebars, and a modest rake, all of which make them nimble enough for twisty roads, yet spare the rider from the cramped extremes of a true sport bike. Since most of these hybrids have a wholesome fuel capacity and high ground clearance, they tend to be tall and have a high center of gravity.

The designation itself—sport-tourer—is an oxymoron and a hint of compromise. If a sport-tourer has wind protection, it is usually an aerodynamic, frame-mounted fairing or

Yamaha Motor Corp.

Yamaha's Seca II 600 is a nimble, midsized sport-tourer that's fun to ride.

half-fairing that protects the torso and shoulders. Your helmet remains in the breeze and this can make or break the ride. If you're going slow enough or riding on narrow roads where trees block the wind, you'll be fine, but if you're droning on a windy interstate for hundreds of miles, you may experience heights of fatigue and discomfort that you never thought possible from a motorcycle.

The aerodynamic fairing/windshield is supposed to deflect the wind blast over your helmet to place your head in a pocket of "dead air." If you were tucked down as on a superbike, this would work. But you're touring, not racing. The slope, width, and height of the shield, the angle and height of the handlebars, the length of your arms and torso, may all conspire to place your head in a line

of turbulence. At interstate speeds, your head can bob like a dashboard doll. Your neck muscles may cramp as you attempt to hold your head level. The wind roar can be so loud, your ears may ring long after you're off the bike. Some full-face helmets and earplugs can lessen, but not prevent, the problem. Certain sport-touring windshields are adjustable, but often not enough to make a big difference. Aftermarket (nonfactory) designers have a variety of windshields and peripheral attachments to redirect the turbulence.

Despite the compromises, many riders love sport-tourers for their fine handling and versatility, but the pickings for entry-level and even midsized models are slim. There are Honda's Pacific Coast 800 and the Yamaha Seca II 600. The adjustable seat on BMW's

R1100RS makes it lower than other bikes of comparable engine displacement, but the bike is still massive.

STANDARD OR RETRO BIKES DO IT ALL

Standard motorcycles are all-around workhorses that harken back to what motorcycles were before they became specialized. Some models look like older bikes, hence the "retro" label. They are also known as "naked" bikes because typically they have minimal bodywork that leaves the engine exposed. They can be elegant or nondescript in their simplicity.

Standards don't accelerate or handle as quickly as sport bikes and they don't turn heads like cruisers. They don't offer the plush comfort of dressers and they're not overly happy on dirt roads. What they do is a little of everything, and they do it just fine. The seating posture is upright, sometimes slightly forward. There are many windshields for these bikes, so turbulence should not be a permanent problem. Standards tend to be tallish, with seats hovering at thirty inches or more.

A good standard is like a faithful dog—it's reliable and will come with you everywhere. Midsized models include the Honda Nighthawk 750 and Suzuki's Bandit 600 and GS500ET. BMW's R1100 and R850 Roadsters have adjustable seats and a lower CG than many standards in this displacement range. Entry-level standards include the Honda Nighthawk 250 and Suzuki GN125ET. Good

American Suzuki Motor Corp.

Suzuki's standard Bandit 600 is another nimble handler that's fun in the short haul. The Bandit, like the Seca II and Hawk GT, has a relatively forward seating posture that can feel cramped after a while.

American Suzuki Motor Corp.

Suzuki's DR125SET, an entry-level dual-sport

discontinued models are Kawasaki's 750 and 550 Zephyrs, the Suzuki Bandit 400, and the Honda Hawk GT 650 (different from the Nighthawk).

DUAL-SPORT OR ON/OFF-ROAD BIKES

Dual-sport, a.k.a. dual-purpose, motorcycles double as rugged street commuters and "adventure touring" bikes that can take you over hill, dale, and dirt. Most are light and narrow but very tall—seat heights tend to start around thirty-three inches. A high center of mass, long-travel suspension, and lots of ground clearance get these bikes over ruts and rocks. If you can manage the height, they are a hoot. Their resilient suspension may feel a bit wobbly on asphalt, but once you get used

to it, you'll find them very maneuverable for skitting around urban traffic.

Most Japanese dual-sport bikes are small to midsized "thumpers" (single-cylindered). They are chain-driven and kick- or electric-started. Entry-level models include the Yamaha Serow 225 and Suzuki's DR 350, 200, and 125 SETs. The 125 is a relative midget with a narrow, 31.5-inch seat. If you're heavy enough, sometimes merely sitting on the smaller bikes lowers the suspension by a couple of inches.

OFF-ROAD OR DIRT-ONLY BIKES

Dirt bikes are built for off-road use only. They are lighter than dual-sports, and have high seats and lots of ground clearance for trail riding, motocross, and enduro competition. Dirt bikes for children come as small as 50cc so that kids old enough to ride bicycles can compete in "peewee" motocross races. Kawasaki's KX models in 125 and 80cc are popular among female motocrossers.

LOWERING A STREET BIKE TO FIT YOU

Sometimes, especially for short riders, the ideal street bike doesn't exist from the factory. Enter the aftermarket and the world of customization. Many bikes can be lowered by installing a lower seat, lower profile tires, a shorter rear shock absorber, and by adjusting the front suspension. With a combination of steps, ride height may be lowered by a couple of inches. These are fairly routine modifica-

tions that many repair shops do—but be aware that as soon as a bike is modified from its factory specifications, you may void your warranty. Some dealers will not modify bikes due to liability concerns. This section is *not* intended as a do-it-yourself guide, nor as a substitute for consultation with a trained mechanic.

Lowering modifications must be done carefully. If the motorcycle's rear end is lowered more than a tad, the bike's steering geometry is altered and its handling may be compromised. Your mechanic must adjust the front suspension proportionally. On some bikes, this is done by raising the fork tubes in the triple-clamps (for simplicity's sake, this is a minor adjustment that lowers the front

Kawasaki Motors Corp.

The Kawasaki KX 80, a favorite among young motocrossers

end). Sometimes, different fork springs are also needed. Not all bikes are built with leeway for such alterations.

Research tires carefully. A lower-profile tire means a wider tire. Will it fit the rim and clear the wheel supports? Call the tire manufacturers. Their customer service reps will tell you if they make a tire to fit your bike, though at the same time, they will not go on record as *recommending* anything other than the OEM (original equipment manufactured) tire that came with the bike.

Lowering a motorcycle may cost some ground clearance. It will be harder to lift the bike onto its centerstand. The angle of the sidestand will be steeper, which means the bike will lean less when parked. You may need to have the sidestand shortened and welded by a professional. As for the seat, sometimes shaving off a bit of foam from the top and sides can make the difference. If this proves uncomfortable, turn to the aftermarket seat companies.

If you have your heart set on a certain bike, the compromises may be worth the initial outlay of cash and time, but before you have any modifications done, talk to several dealers

and mechanics. Hang around the shop and talk to other riders, especially riders of the same model. Find out if there is a club or owners network devoted to your particular bike or marque—newsletters are great for word-of-mouth information.

The motorcycle magazines are excellent sources from which to learn about bike anatomy, parts, accessories, and all kinds of customizations. Most topics are perennials—pick up several magazines in any month, and you may find an article (and surely plenty of ads) about the subject you're researching, whether it's the right seat, the right motor oil—or the right new or used bike. A highly informative, easily readable textbook is *Motorcycles: Fundamentals, Service, Repair* by Bruce Johns and David Edmundson (Goodheart-Willcox, 1987). For details on specific new and out-of-production models, check out Ian Smith's Motorcycle Reports and bound volumes of *Cycle World* road tests. See the Riders' Resource Directory (page 178) for addresses of manufacturers and distributors of motorcycles, parts, and accessories, as well as sources for more information.

Triumph USA

Triumph motorcycles made a comeback in recent years. This 885cc Thunderbird recalls British "cafe racers" of the fifties and sixties. The Rockers (rivals of the Mods—remember them?) hung out at London's Ace Cafe and held impromptu drag races. Comic-book biker Barb Wire rides a T-bird on film.

BMW of North America

And They Said It Couldn't Be Done . . .

The BMW K75RT is a discontinued midsized touring bike with a loyal ridership. BMW's low-seat kit brings the saddle down to 29.9 inches, but since the bike is as wide as a hippopotamus, it is still quite a reach. A Progressive Suspension short shock and low-profile Metzeler street radial tires brought the ride height down dramatically on the author's K75RT. The front fork tubes were raised in the triple clamps; this shortened the steering rake, making the bike slightly more responsive, or quicker to steer, in corners. The Metzeler radials improved traction. Although the shorter shock didn't always absorb bumps as well, and the side-stand and centerstand had to be shortened, in some ways the lowered bike was a better bike.

Shop work: Lindner Cycle

Before lowering . . .   **. . . and after**

It's midnight when a sudden downpour takes you by surprise...

Do you know what to do? Take the *Motorcycle RiderCourse*®.

Motorcycle Safety Foundation

Motorcycling is often described as a healthy risk-taking activity. And it is—as long as you have a healthy awareness of the fact that the risks are real and that they apply to you, too.

Basic Motorcycle Safety and Risk Management, with Tips on Choosing Protective Gear

The Motorcycle Safety Foundation (MSF) runs a nationwide program of excellent rider training courses. According to the MSF, mile for mile, riding a motorcycle is sixteen times more likely to result in a fatality than driving a car. But that is a "blanket" statistic that doesn't reveal age, gender, or cause. The MSF says the two major factors that determine who gets in accidents are age and experience. The older you are and the more riding experience you have, the less likely you are to have an accident. Traffic safety expert James McNight was once quoted as saying, "Males crash because of testosterone, females from inexperience." The first six months of riding are when mishaps are most likely.

In 1981, a comprehensive study of nine hundred motorcycle accidents in the Los Angeles area was published by the University of Southern California Traffic Safety Center. Commonly called the Hurt Study (after head researcher Dr. Harry Hurt), the report is still considered a landmark.[1]

The findings revealed that three-fourths of motorcycle accidents involved collision with a car, and two-thirds of these accidents were caused when the car violated the motorcycle's right-of-way, mostly by turning left in front of the oncoming bike at an intersection. The most common excuse car drivers gave was, basically, "Officer, I didn't see the motorcycle."

Hurt noted that typically, the rider had less than two seconds to take evasive action, adding, "The ability to countersteer and swerve was essentially absent." Many riders overbraked and skidded the rear wheel and underbraked the front. (The front brake has 70 to 80 percent of a bike's stopping power.)

Almost half of the fatalities in the study involved alcohol. Operating a motorcycle requires three to five times more coordination skills than driving a car. The MSF points out that, theoretically, the same amount of alcohol that might not be a problem for a person driving a car could make a lethal difference to the same person when riding a motorcycle. (This does *not* mean it is okay to drink alcohol and operate a car!)

HOW TO MANAGE THE RISKS

Covering every principle of motorcycle safety is beyond the scope of this book, but there are several important areas that the MSF and other safety groups emphasize. Here are some guidelines. *Guidelines are not intended as a substitute for a safety course.* Phone numbers and addresses for all the resources and products mentioned are in the appendix.

Take a Rider Training Course

The Hurt Study found that rider training reduced accident involvement and was related to reduced injuries. Since the time the study was conducted, motorcycle fatalities have declined by nearly half.[2] Rider training is often cited as a major reason.

MSF courses are taught at more than seven hundred sites around the country. To find a site near you, call 800-446-9227. Novices use demo bikes provided by the MSF. If you have at least three months of experience, you are ready for the MSF's Experienced RiderCourse (ERC), for which you use your own bike.

Those with more advanced skills might consider California's Leading Advanced Safety School (CLASS), which travels to racetracks around the country. It is geared toward improving your riding *performance,* with emphasis on smoothness. As you get smoother, you get faster. You will come away with valuable skills that are applicable to the street.

Practice Evasive Maneuvers and Emergency Braking, and Be Alert to Predict Hazards

Riding a motorcycle as safely as possible requires a combination of defensiveness and "aggression" (for lack of a better word). Hurt noted that "lack of attention to the riding task is a common factor for the motorcyclist in an accident." You must always be alert and constantly predict potential traffic hazards. When riding, you make hundreds of decisions per mile. Be wary of those ubiquitous left-turning cars and slow down at intersections. It's common sense, but some riders, figuring they have the right-of-way, do not slow down enough. There's a saying: "You can be right or dead right."

As for "aggression," your bike is much more maneuverable than a car, and therefore you are better able to speed up, if appropriate, or swerve quickly to get out of the way of a hazard. A motorcycle does not steer according to the same principles as a four-wheeled vehicle. When swerving or turning, a bike leans, and so you must understand and use the technique of "countersteering."

Your motorcycle can stop quicker than the car or truck behind you—watch those rearview mirrors. Motorcycle brakes are powerful and must be applied properly. Chomping abruptly on the front brake, for instance, can cause your front wheel to lock, which would put you on the pavement immediately. In an emergency, though, you need all the stopping power you can get. Learn the art of what some call "threshold braking"—braking smoothly, firmly, but progressively.

Too much rear brake can cause a rear-wheel skid, which could also put you down if the motorcycle isn't moving in a straight line. Braking on wet pavement or gravel, in a curve, or when riding downhill require caution. The MSF has practice drills for these situations and others. As with martial arts, tennis, or anything else that requires mental and manual dexterity, these skills must be practiced to be perfected. You want to be so good at them that in an emergency, you'd do them automatically.

Every time you start the bike, psyche yourself up to concentrate on what you're about to do. Hurt found that most accidents happen close to home. Expect the unexpected. Think of every ride as a practice session and an opportunity to improve. This is part of the fun and challenge of riding. Exercise your mind by playing "what if" games. Having escape routes in mind could save your life.

Ride Within Your Limits

One-fourth of motorcycle accidents in the Hurt Study were single-vehicle mishaps. Of these, rider error was the major cause two-thirds of the time. The typical error was a slide-out and fall due to overbraking or running wide on a curve due to excess speed or undercornering. Ride with a margin for error. Knowing your limits also means getting off the bike if you're fatigued.

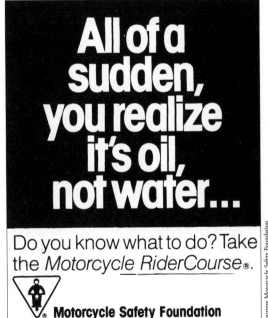

All of a sudden, you realize it's oil, not water...

Do you know what to do? Take the *Motorcycle RiderCourse*®.

Motorcycle Safety Foundation

Courtesy Motorcycle Safety Foundation

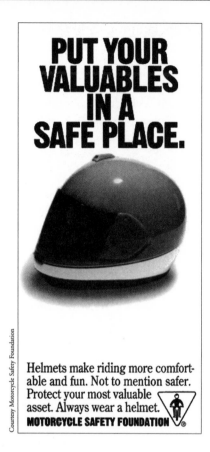

PUT YOUR VALUABLES IN A SAFE PLACE.

Helmets make riding more comfortable and fun. Not to mention safer. Protect your most valuable asset. Always wear a helmet.
MOTORCYCLE SAFETY FOUNDATION

Courtesy Motorcycle Safety Foundation

Increase Your Visibility to Other Motorists

Hurt found that riders who made themselves conspicuous by wearing high-visibility yellow, orange, or bright red jackets were less likely to get hit. If you don't want to give up your black leather jacket, consider a removable, over-the-jacket vest made by a company that calls itself Conspicuity. The vests are made of a sheer, netted material that is available in black; brightly colored stripes are sewn on the netted material. The stripes are either fluorescent (for daytime visibility) or reflective (for nighttime). A light-colored helmet is preferable to a dark one. At the very least, put reflective stickers on your helmet. There is a removable band called a Halo that fits around the bottom of a full-face helmet. The Halo bands are either fluorescent or reflective.

Proper lane positioning is necessary to promote visibility. Ride in that portion of the lane that puts you in the best spot to scan the road and predict hazards, and also to be seen by others. Don't tailgate and don't ride in people's blind spots.

Wear Protective Gear

According to Hurt, the most deadly injuries were to the chest and head. A helmet was the single critical factor in the prevention of head injuries. At the least, Hurt recommended a helmet that was DOT approved; better still was a helmet approved by the Snell Foundation. Full-facial coverage helmets offered the most protection.

Not every injury is to the head, of course, and that is why it is advisable to wear a full set of protective gear. Besides a helmet, that would include a leather jacket, leather pants or chaps, boots or shoes above the ankle, leather gloves, and eye protection. If this sounds awfully stuffy for hot weather, it is, but there's another saying: "Better rawhide than your hide." Heavy-grade leather can withstand about a hundred feet of sliding on pavement before it will wear through. Cotton denim will be in tatters in just five or ten feet. Nylon can actually melt from the friction of a slide. All-season garments made of Kevlar, a highly abrasion-resistant fabric, are an alternative to leather.

There are also vented leather and Kevlar jackets with zippered areas that open to reveal a lining with airholes. These vented jackets do work, even in summer, except if you're stopped in traffic. In hot weather, you can sometimes stay *cooler* wearing a vented jacket over a wet shirt. Motorcyclists who live in desert climes sometimes wear several water-soaked layers and peel them off as they dry.

Women's motorcycle apparel has become all the rage, but designer leather duds are for disco dancing, not riding. Designer jackets and pants are made of softer, thinner leather, they are sewn with less sturdy stitching, and they lack certain features you'd want on the road. A real motorcycle jacket should have a wind flap behind the main zipper, zippered pockets, and zippered wrists to keep the wind from blowing up the sleeves. To accommodate the riding position, the jacket should also have longer sleeves, a longer waist in the back, and room at the shoulders. Roomy shouldn't mean loose or "blousy," as many women's jackets are. If the jacket is blousy, the wind will get in and cause the jacket to balloon. A loose jacket could also ride up in the event of a slide, exposing you to the pavement.

A few manufacturers of genuine motorcycle gear offer jackets in women's sizes, but be aware that some women's jackets aren't as functional as men's. The sleeves and waists are too short, they don't have as many (sometimes, not any) zippered compartments, and they may be sorely lacking in other basics. If you're willing to spend the bucks, some companies will custom-tailor garments for you.

In cool weather, look for gauntlet gloves, which have long, wide cuffs that extend over

Courtesy Harley-Davidson MotorClothes

Sturdy boots, such as these from Harley-Davidson MotorClothes, protect the ankles and shins. Boots can also shield the legs from excessive engine and exhaust heat.

your jacket wrists to keep the wind out. Designer gloves are better than nothing, but real motorcycle gloves are thicker; some have an extra layer of leather or padding on the palms.

Be Ready to Battle the Elements
One of the great joys—and potential health hazards—of riding a motorcycle is being exposed to the elements. On long trips especially, prepare for changes in the weather. Carry rain gear and extra layers.

Copyright © Femmegear

Dee Modglin, ABOVE, president of Femmegear in San Francisco, custom-tailors leather garments for women and is attentive to the needs of full-figured riders. According to Modglin, leathers for street riding should be at least 1.1 millimeters thick; sturdy, drum-dyed cowhide or buffalo hide are best. Femmegear selections are shown at LEFT. Seated on the bike, RIGHT, is motojournalist Jamie Elvidge, who road tests gear for *Motorcyclist* magazine.

In the warm months, take steps to prevent dehydration, heat fatigue, and heat stroke. As mentioned in the section on protective gear, sometimes covering up can be more comfortable than leaving your skin exposed to the hot sun. In any case, carry sunblock and water. You might also want to try a neckerchief called a Kool Tie. The Kool Tie is filled with absorbent granules, which, when soaked in water, expand and retain moisture. Unlike a conventional bandanna that dries in minutes from a warm wind, the Kool Tie may stay moist for days.

Dehydration can also occur in the cool months, as can hypothermia and frostbite. At rest stops, get inside, move around, stretch your limbs, and stay away from caffeine and nicotine. Caffeine is a diuretic that can rob your body of liquids. Caffeine and nicotine constrict capillaries and can leave your extremities more vulnerable to frostbite. Keep in mind that when you're riding, especially on an unfaired or minimally shielded bike, the windchill factor is much colder than what you hear on the weather report.

Your leather jacket is a windbreaker, but it is not warm in itself. You need to layer up beneath it. Start with underwear made of silk or a synthetic sweat-wicking fabric such as polypropylene. Real wool, which traps air and thus body heat, is best for subsequent layers. "Heated" vests, gloves, and even jackets and chaps are also available. These garments use your bike's battery power to heat up and stay toasty. Your rain jacket can double as a windbreaker. Worn *under* your leather jacket, it will really hold your body heat.

Prepare for the Unexpected

Carry these items:

- A first-aid kit. There are many compact kits available. Two geared toward motorcyclists are Adventure Medical Kits' Day Tripper and Pro-Light Cyclist. If you are allergic to any medications or have any conditions that medics should know about, carry the appropriate identification.

- Earplugs. On a long trip, you'll be glad you have them.

- Your bike's owner's manual and a tool kit for emergency repairs. New motorcycles come with tool kits. If your bike doesn't have one, the owner manual will tell you which tools to get. Supplement the kit with a small vise grip (handy for a broken clutch cable), electrical tape (handy for a hundred potential things), spare fuses, spark plugs, spare bulbs for headlight and brake light, a flashlight, a chain master-link if your bike has a chain, and a tire patch kit or spray can of compressed air and tire sealant. If your bike drinks a lot of oil, carry at least enough to "top off" until you get to a repair shop.

Maintain Your Bike and Inspect It Before Riding

Today's motorcycles are generally so reliable, many riders neglect the obvious. Keep your

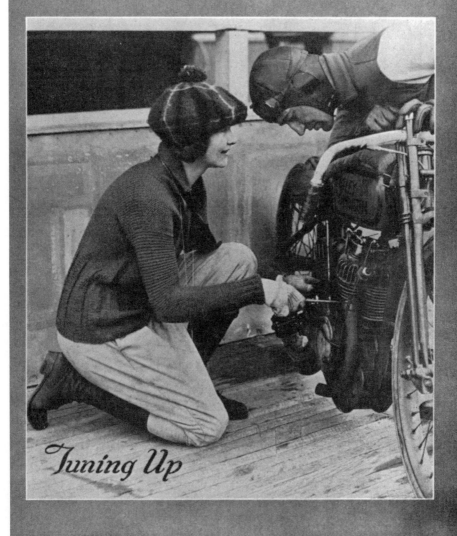

The Harley-Davidson Enthusiast

Tuning Up

July, 1921

bike well maintained by following the service schedule in the owner's manual. Something as simple as a clogged fuel filter can put you on the side of the road. Change the oil, and if your bike doesn't have a "maintenance-free" battery, be sure to check the electrolyte level. Learn how your bike works. An unfamiliar rattling or "ratchety" noise can stem from something as basic as a loose chain.

If your bike feels wobbly, especially in a curve, pull over and check your tires. Underinflated tires are the most common cause of handling problems. The Motopump is a very compact pump and CO_2 cartridge kit that is handy to top off an underinflated tire. A flat tire, needless to say, would cause a *major* handling problem. A blowout can cause you to fall, so inspect your tires for nails and cracks before you set out. Also check the adjustment on your shock absorber; if your suspension isn't properly adjusted, the bike may feel unstable in corners.

T-CLOCK is an MSF acronym to remind you of what to check in your pre-ride inspection.

T: Tires and wheels
C: Controls (cables, hoses, throttle)
L: Lights (battery, lenses, reflectors, wiring, headlamp)
O: Oil (levels, leaks)
C: Chassis (frame, suspension, chain or belt, fasteners)
K: Kickstand (centerstand, sidestand)

The MSF has compiled a handbook called *Motorcycling Excellence: Skills, Knowledge and Strategies for Riding Right* (Boston: Whitehouse Press, 1995), which details the T-CLOCK routine, along with many other areas indicated in the book's title. It even has tips on lifting a fallen bike.

A Twist of the Wrist, a book and video set by road racing guru Keith Code, is geared to improving performance on the track, but Code has some excellent advice on concentration and the art of using visual reference points to get you safely (and quickly) through a curve. *Street Smarts* is a useful, multipart video and book for street riders. The motorcycle magazines have lots of articles on riding skills. Two of the best monthly columns are David Hough's nuts-and-bolts "Proficient Motorcycling" in *Motorcycle Consumer News* and Lawrence Grodsky's thought-provoking "Stayin' Safe" in *Rider.*

Trail, dirt, or off-road riding requires a different set of skills, a different type of bike and protective gear. The MSF book has a good section on off-road riding. Incidentally, learning to ride in the dirt can help your street skills.

A WORD ON GROUP RIDING

It is tempting for new riders, eager to be accepted in their local motorcycle community, to want to ride with a group. If you are unfamiliar with a particular group's riding style, don't "ride someone else's ride." If you are not comfortable with the group's pace, slow down. Ask the leader or road captain to establish a plan. Many groups allow for different skill levels. Faster riders go at their pace and wait at crossroads for slower ones. In this manner, everyone can enjoy the ride safely.

WHO YA GONNA CALL?

If traveling alone for any distance, consider carrying a cellular phone. Subscribe to an emergency roadside towing service geared to motorcyclists. One of the best is Motorcycle Towing Service (MTS), which offers a variety of benefits, including cellular phone rental, an emergency cash loan, and a guarantee that the proper equipment will be used to tow your bike. The American Motorcyclist Association and some of the large, nation-wide motorcycle clubs have emergency "help" networks. BMW Motorcycle Owners of America (BMWMOA), BMW Riders Association (BMWRA), Gold Wing Road Riders Association (GWRRA), and Harley Owners Group (HOG) are among such clubs.

As in any sport or endeavor that involves risks, the risks of motorcycling can be, and are, managed and minimized by responsible riders. With proper training, practice, and common sense, you can master the challenge and experience the joy of safe cycling.

Give Your Bike a "Brake"

This beautiful shovelhead Sportster, so nicknamed for the shape of its cylinder heads, is nearly twenty years old but wears its age well. Preventive maintenance is especially important on older bikes and those with high mileage. Brakes are among the most often neglected vital systems. Most bikes from the early seventies have a hydraulic disc brake in the front and a mechanical drum brake in the rear. To get the most power out of the front brake (or brakes, if there is a double disc), inspect and top off the fluid in the

master cylinder on a regular basis. Change the fluid at the service intervals in your owner's manual. Check brake pads for wear and change pads accordingly, and inspect calipers and hoses for leaks. Drum brakes must be adjusted periodically and worn linings must be replaced. Dirt and rust inside the drum can also hinder the mechanism. Overall, keeping a bike clean is the first step in maintaining it. When lubricating or cleaning, keep slippery substances off brake parts and tires.

T-CLOCK INSPECTION

T-CLOCK ITEM	WHAT TO CHECK	WHAT TO LOOK FOR	CHECK-OFF	
T—TIRES & WHEELS				
Tires	Condition	Tread depth, wear, weathering, evenly seated, bulges, imbedded objects.	Front	Rear
	Air Pressure	Check when cold, adjust to load/speed.	Front	Rear
Wheels	Spokes	Bent, broken, missing, tension, check at top of wheel "ring" okay—"thud," loose spoke.	Front	Rear
	Cast	Cracks, dents.	Front	Rear
	Rims	Out of round/true = 5mm. Spin wheel, index against stationary pointer.	Front	Rear
	Bearings	Grab top and bottom of tire and flex: No freeplay (click) between hub and axle, no growl when spinning.	Front	Rear
	Seals	Cracked, cut or torn, excessive grease on outside, reddish brown around outside.	Front	Rear
C—CONTROLS				
Levers	Condition	Broken, bent, cracked, mounts, tight, ball ends on handlebar lever.	Front	Rear
	Pivots	Lubricated.		
Cables	Condition	Fraying, kinks, lubrication: ends and length.		
	Routing	No interference or pulling at steering head, suspension, no sharp angles, wire looms in place.		
Hoses	Condition	Cuts, cracks, leaks, bulges, chafing, deterioration.		
	Routing	No interference or pulling at steering head, suspension, no sharp angles, wire looms in place.		
Throttle	Operation	Moves freely, snaps closed, no revving.		
L—LIGHTS				
Battery	Condition	Terminals, clean and tight, electrolyte level, held down securely.		
	Vent Tube	Not kinked, routed properly, not plugged.		
Lenses	Condition	Cracked, broken, securely mounted, excessive condensation.		
Reflectors	Condition	Cracked, broken, securely mounted.		
Wiring	Condition	Fraying, chafing, insulation.		
	Routing	Pinched, no interference or pulling at steering head or suspension, wire looms and ties in place, connectors tight, clean.		
Headlamp	Condition	Cracks, reflector, mounting and adjustment system.		
	Aim	Height and right/left.		

O—OIL

Levels				
	Engine Oil	Check warm or centerstand, dipstick, sight glass.		
	Hypoid Gear Oil	Transmission, rear driver, shaft.		
	Hydraulic Fluid	Brakes, clutch, reservoir or sight glass.		
	Coolant	Reservoir and/or coolant recovery tank—cool only.		
	Fuel	Tank or gauge.		
Leaks	Engine Oil	Gaskets, housings, seals.		
	Hypoid Gear	Gaskets, seals, breathers.		
	Hydraulic Fluid	Hoses, master cylinders, calipers.		
	Coolant	Radiator, hoses, tanks, fittings, pipes.		
	Fuel	Lines, fuel taps, carbs.		

C—CHASSIS

Frame				
	Condition	Cracks at gussets, accessory mounts, look for paint lifting.		
	Steering-Head Bearings	No detent or tight spots through full travel, raise front wheel, check for play by pulling/pushing forks.		
	Swingarm Bushings/ Bearings	Raise rear wheel, check for play by pushing/pulling swingarm.		
Suspension	Forks	Smooth travel, equal air pressure/damping antidive settings.	Left	Right
	Shock(s)	Smooth travel, equal preload/air pressure/damping settings, linkage moves freely and is lubricated.	Left	Right
Chain or	Tension	Check at tightest point.		
Belt	Lubrication	Side plates when hot. *Note:* Do not lubricate belts.		
	Sprockets	Teeth not hooked, securely mounted.		
Fasteners	Threaded	Tight, missing bolts, nuts.		
	Clips	Broken, missing.		
	Cotter Pins	Broken, missing.		

K—KICKSTAND

Centerstand	Condition	Cracks, bent.
	Retention	Springs in place, tension to hold position.
Sidestand	Condition	Cracks, bent (safety cut-out switch or pad if equipped).
	Retention	Springs in place, tension to hold position.

RIDERS' RESOURCE DIRECTORY

CONTENTS

Listings appear under these headings and subheads.*

*A listing does not necessarily indicate a recommendation.

ACCESSORIES AND PARTS FOR MOTORCYCLES; RIDER GEAR

General Mail-Order Catalogs

Chaparral Cycle Supply
555 H Street
San Bernardino, CA 92410
800-841-2960

Competition Accessories
345 W. Leffel Lane
Springfield, OH 45506
800-543-4710
513-323-0513

Dennis Kirk
955 South Field Ave.
Rush City, MN 55069
800-328-9280

Lockhart-Phillips USA
151 Calle Iglesia
San Clemente, CA 92673
800-221-7291
714-498-9090

Motorcycle Accessory
  Warehouse
925 E. Fillmore St.
Colorado Springs, CO
  80907
800-241-2222
719-520-9000

Targa Accessories
21 Journey
Aliso Viejo, CA 92656
800-521-7945
714-362-2505

J.C. Whitney
1917-19 Archer Ave.
P.O. Box 8410
Chicago, IL 60680
312-431-6102

Brand-Specific Mail-Order Distributors

For BMWs
Capital Eurosport
21580 Beaumeade Circle
#170
Ashburn, VA 22011
800-642-5100 (USA)
800-445-4175 (Canada)
703-729-7900

Bob's BMW
10630 Riggs Hill Rd.
Jessup, MD 20794
800-BMW-BOBS
301-924-5155

For British Bikes
British Cycle Supply Ltd.
P.O. Box 119
Wolfville
Nova Scotia B0P 1X0
Canada
902-542-7478

For Ducatis
Motofixx
505 N. Main St.
Port Chester, NY 10573
800-8-DUCATI

For Harleys
Custom Chrome (CCI)
16100 Jacqueline Ct.
Morgan Hill, CA 95037
800-729-3332

Drag Specialties
P.O. Box 9336
Minneapolis, MN 55440
800-222-3400
612-942-7890

Harley-Davidson
Genuine Parts & Accessories
3700 W. Juneau Ave.
P.O. Box 653
Milwaukee, WI 53201
800-443-2153

J & P Cycles
P.O. Box 138
Anamosa, IA 52205-0138
800-397-4844 (USA)
800-944-2201 (Canada)

Arlen Ness
16520 E. 14 St.
San Leandro, CA 94578
510-276-3395

For Moto Guzzis
Harper's Moto Guzzi
32401 Stringtown Rd.
Greenwood, MO 64034
800-752-9735
816-697-4311

For Motocross & Off-Road Bikes
Acerbis Plastica USA
9402 Wheatlands Court
Ste. A
Santee, CA 92071
800-659-1440
619-562-1440

APPAREL FOR RIDING

Leathers, Miscellaneous

Aerostitch Riderwear
8 South 18th Ave. West
Duluth, MN 55806
800-222-1994
218-722-1927
Leather alternatives:
abrasion-resistant fabrics.

Bates
3700 N. Industry Ave.
#102
Lakewood, CA 90712
310-426-8668

Brooks Leather Sportswear
14511 W. 11-Mile Rd.
Oak Park, MI 48237
800-727-6657
810-548-8633

Femmegear
5214-F Diamond Heights
  Blvd.
Ste. 623
San Francisco, CA 94131
415-826-3598

Femmegear Outlet: Riders
  Motorcycle
1115 California Dr.
Burlingame, CA 94010
415-348-5706

Fieldsheer
485 E. 17 St.
Ste. 400
Costa Mesa, CA 92627
714-642-6877

Firstgear, Hein Gericke,
  Vetter
Intersport Fashions West
333 S. Anita Dr.
Ste. 1025
Orange, CA 92668
714-978-7718

Gypsy Leather
71 Saint John St.
Lancaster, NY 14086
716-681-7535

Harley-Davidson
  MotorClothes
3700 W. Juneau Ave.
P.O. Box 653
Milwaukee, WI 53201
800-443-2153

Iron Horse Clothing
#3 Vaquero Rd.
Santa Fe, NM 87505
800-784-8401

Langlitz Leathers
2440 S.E. Division
Portland, OR 97202
503-235-0959

LMO Leather Outlet
258 Broadhollow Road
Farmingdale, NY 11735
516-694-0200

Motoport USA
6110 Yarrow Drive
Carlsbad, CA 92009
800-777-6499
619-929-4880

Orchard Leathers
36-06 43rd Ave.
Long Island City, NY 11101
718-361-2072

Protech Leather
40 Christa McAuliffe Blvd.
Plymouth, MA 02360
508-747-4494

Pure Leather Gold
317 St. Pauls Ave.
Bldg 1 – 5th Floor
Jersey City, NJ 07306
800-783-1225

S&S Highway
S&S Cycle & Supply
304 Rolling Trail
Amarillo, TX 79108
800-321-2735
806-355-8541

Schott Brothers
358 Lehigh Ave.
Perth Amboy, NJ 08862
800-25-SCHOTT

Thurlow Leatherworld
4807 Mercury St.
Ste. E
San Diego, CA 92111
619-279-9004

Tour Master Riding Gear
Outlet: Helmet House
2360 Townsgate Rd.
Westlake Village, CA 91361
800-421-7247
805-373-6868

Tucker-Rocky
1775 Hurd Dr.
Irving, TX 75038
800-347-1010
714-488-3930
Wholesale; ask for retail
outlets.

Unik International
P.O. Box 9
Hasbrouck Heights, NJ
    07604
201-779-0222

Vanguard Leather
258 Broadhollow Rd.
P.O. Box 3208
Farmingdale, NY 11735
516-420-1010

Vanson
213 Turnpike St.
Stoughton, MA 02072
617-344-5444

Vent-Tech Leathers
1106 Oceannaire Dr.
Ste. J
Glendale, CA 91208
800-331-8408

Heated Apparel

Gerbings Heated Clothing
E750 Dalby Rd.
Union, WA 98592
360-898-4225

Eclipse
3771 E. Ellsworth Rd.
Ann Arbor, MI 48108
800-666-1500
313-971-5552

Widder Enterprises
410 Bryant Circle
Unit D
Ojai, CA 93023
800-WYBCOLD
805-640-1295

Rain Gear

Dry Rider
Neese Industries
P.O. Box 1059
Gonzales, LA 70707
800-535-8042
504-647-6553

Nelson Rigg
1048 Irvine Ave.
Ste. 384
Newport Beach, CA 92660
714-645-5161

Thunderwear
1060-C Calle Negocio
San Clemente, CA 92672
800-422-6565
714-492-1141

Boots

Bates
See Apparel.

Dayton Shoe Co.
2250 E. Hastings St.
Vancouver, B.C. V5L 1V4
Canada
604-253-6671

Femmegear
See Apparel.

Harley-Davidson
    MotorClothes
See Apparel.

West Coast Shoe Co.
P.O. Box 607
Scappoose, OR 97056-0607
800-326-2711
503-543-7114
Custom fitting.

ASSOCIATIONS AND CLUBS

Associations, Foundations: Women's

Women Motorcyclists of
    Southern California
Vivian Escalante, President
P.O. Box 292135
Los Angeles, CA 90027
213-664-3964
310-438-9354
"An umbrella organization
for women motorcycle
enthusiasts of all ages, colors
and occupations. Our goals
are to change the negative
views that have been cast
upon us [as motorcyclists]."

WMSC runs group rides for
beginners and advanced riders, and organizes women to
participate in other events,
including charity benefits.

Women's Motorcyclist
    Foundation (WMF)
Sue Slate & Gin Shear,
    Directors
7 Lent Ave.
LeRoy, NY 14482
716-768-6054

A not-for-profit networking
organization. Their philoso-
phy: "Diversity based on
race, religion, national origin,
age, physical challenge, mari-
tal status and/or sexual orientation is welcomed as a way
to enrich each of our lives."
WMF organized the Pony
Express Tour '96 National
Ride for Breast Cancer
Research.

Associations, Foundations: General

ABATE
American Bikers Aimed
    Toward Education
To find your nearest state office,
inquire at your AMA district
office, local bike shops, or
regional publications. ABATE
works for bikers' rights.

American Motorcyclist
    Association (AMA)
33 Collegeview Rd.
P.O. Box 6114
Westerville, OH 43081-6114
800-AMA-JOIN
614-891-2425
A not-for-profit umbrella
organization that convenes
road riding tours, sanctions
competitive events, lobbies
for bikers' rights, publishes a
magazine, runs a museum,
and offers a variety of perks
to its 200,000 members.

Canadian Motorcycle
    Association
Box 448
Hamilton, Ontario L8L 8C4
905-522-5705
Canada's version of the
AMA.

Five-Borough Motorcycle
    Association
Gloria Green, President
1653 Straight Path
Wheatley Heights, NY
    11798
A coalition of African-
American and Latino clubs
in New York City and Long
Island.

Motorcycle Industry Council
2 Jenner St.
Ste. 150
Irvine, CA 92718
714-727-4211
Trade organization.

Motorcycle Industry
    Council,
Government Relations
    Officer
1235 Jefferson Davis Hwy.
Ste. 600
Arlington, VA 22202
703-416-0444

Motorcycle Safety
    Foundation (MSF)
2 Jenner St.
Ste. 150
Irvine, CA 92718
714-727-3227 (executive
    offices)
800-446-9227 (for safety
    course locations)

Motorcycle Riders
    Foundation (MRF)
Wayne Curtin, National
    Director
P.O. Box 1808
Washington, DC 20013-
    1808
202-546-0983
Bikers' rights.

NCOM
National Coalition of
    Motorcyclists
Pepper Massey
15910 Ventura Blvd.
Encino, CA 91436
800-235-2424 (in Calif.)
800-525-5355 (National)
800-521-2425 (Canada)
Bikers' rights.

National Handicap
    Motorcyclist Assn.
    (NHMA)
Bob Nevola
315 W. 21 St., #6F
New York, NY 10011
212-242-3376
A network for riders with
physical disabilities.

Specialty Vehicle Institute of
    America
2 Jenner St.
Ste. 150
Irvine, CA 92718
714-727-3727 (executive
    offices)

Women's Clubs: Nationwide

The beauty of women's motorcycle clubs is that most welcome diversity. Listings that mention clubs primarily comprised of one group or another are provided as a service to those seeking the camaraderie of women of like ethnicity, persuasion, or brand of bike. Clubs with memberships that are mainly "this" or "that" usually welcome all women, including passenger riders.

Ladies of Harley (LOH)
Harley-Davidson Motor Co.
3700 W. Juneau Ave.
P.O. Box 453
Milwaukee, WI 53201
800-CLUB-HOG
800-242-2464
Part of Harley Owners
Group (HOG). Of HOG's
280,000 worldwide mem-
bers, roughly 30,000 are
women (riders and passen-
gers). Membership is automatic with purchase of a new
Harley.

Motor Maids
Jan Barrett, President
601 N. McCall Rd.
Englewood, FL 34223
813-474-3970
About 500 members on all
brands of bikes. Est. 1940.

Women in the Wind
    (WITW)
Mother Chapter
P.O. Box 8392
Toledo, OH 43605
About 600 members in 20
states, four Canadian
provinces, England, and New
Zealand. Lots of Harleys but
all brands welcome. Est.
1979.

Women on Wheels (WOW)
P.O. Box 081454
Racine, WI 53408-1454
800-322-1969
414-681-9325
About 1,800 members in
48 states, five Canadian
provinces, England,
Germany, Italy, and Finland.
All brands. Est. 1982.

Associations and Clubs (*cont'd*)

Women's Clubs: Regional, Local

Local women's clubs run the gamut from upscale professionals who have time to ride together only once a month, to Harley lifestyle bikers who live and breathe bikes. Clubs that carry no description didn't provide one. Inclusion here is not an endorsement; use your own judgment.

Desert Hearts
Deb Lotardo
Phoenix, AZ
602-279-9228

Hardly Angels
Lynell Corbett
13492 County Rd. 250
Durango, CO 81301
All-women motorcycle drill team.

Iron Angels
412 East Oak Lane
Front Royal, VA 22630

J.U.G.G.S.
(Just Us Girls Gettin' Scooters)
Plaza 94, Ste. 109
St. Peters, MO 63376
All brands; male support members.

Lady Rider Club
Lillian "Wills" Shores
1015 Madison Lane
Falls Church, VA 22046
703-237-2824
All brands, all levels of experience welcome; gentlemen associates.

Leather & Lace
Lady Harley/Motorcycle
    Riders Assn.
Empire State Chapter
P.O. Box 2
Clintondale, NY 12515-0002
800-526-LACE
Harleys only. Eight chapters in California, Florida, Missouri, New Hampshire, New Mexico, New York, Pennsylvania, and Texas.

Medusa's Maidens
P.O. Box 66009
Chateauguay, P.Q. J6J 3X0
Canada

Metric Maidens
Lynda Thais, Chapter
    President
670 Lottie St.
Monterey, CA 93940

Professional Motorcycling
    Sisters (PMS)
Nancy Powers
275 Battery St.
San Francisco, CA 94111
415-392-7000
Business and riding network for upscale professionals; men's auxiliary.

Silken Steel Women's Riding
    Assn.
P.O. Box 16014
Wichita, KS 67216

Sisters of Silk N'Steel
403 W. Grangeville Ave.
Hanford, CA 93202
209-584-2809
and
1300 Ottawa Ave.
Corcoran, CA 93202
209-992-4402

Spokes-Women
Janet Britland
6 Sarah Lane
Jamesburg, NJ 08831
908-446-3866
Professional women, all brands, male associates.

Steel Magnolias
P.O. Box 7732
Houston, TX 77270
713-661-0987
An AMA-chartered club.

Untamed Spirits
610 5th Ave. NW
Mandan, ND 58554

Vixen Riders Ladies M/C
Box 128-1338 Eastern Blvd.
Essex, MD 21221

Zodiac Angels
Jesse Grooms, President
1699 Bahama St.
Aurora, CO 80011
Five chapters in Colorado, Nebraska, New York, and Rhode Island. Their slogan is "You've packed the rest, now ride with the best!"

Women's Clubs: Ethnic

Ebony Queens
P.O. Box 311021
Flint, MI 48504
"Pie," President: 616-452-
    7306
http://cstore-
    zserver.cl.msu.edu/eqmc/
    eqmc.htm
"We are the Ebony Queens,
all shades of fine." All races
welcome.

Lady Hawks
Paula Kelly, President
15475 Homeland Drive
Hughesville, MD 20637-
    2523
301-507-5270 (weekdays)
301-870-0572 (eves)
FAX: 301-507-5199
African-American members;
all races welcome.

Na Wahine O Mana
P.O. Box 22685
Honolulu, HI 96823-2685
808-528-2819
"We are like family and welcome diversity of race, sexual orientation, and religion.
Our name means women of
strength, power, and spiritu-
al enlightment."

Women's Clubs: Lesbian

Athena
1223 Wilshire Blvd.
Ste. 638
Santa Monica, CA 94013

Artemis
Ellen Wickersham
P.O. Box 934
Kingsburg, CA 93631
"Predominantly a lesbian
clean & sober club."

Hell's Belles
San Franscisco, CA
415-585-5707
All Harleys; mixed: gay and
straight.

Moving Violations
P.O. Box 382356
Cambridge, MA 02238
Mixed: gay and straight.

Sirens
c/o Gay and Lesbian
    Community Center
208 W. 13 St.
New York, NY 10011
212-749-6177
E-mail: SirenNYC@aol.com
Predominantly lesbian;
straight women welcome.

Sirens San Francisco Chapter
P.O. Box 423702
San Francisco, CA 94102

Vamps
2201 The Alameda
Ste. 13
Santa Clara, CA 95050
"We're into Goth, the
undead, horror flicks and the
more theatrical side of life as
well as riding."

ASSOCIATIONS AND CLUBS (*cont'd*)

Co-Ed Clubs: National, Regional

There are thousands of clubs, many of which host rallies and one-day meets. AMA members can get information on clubs in their AMA district. *Motorcycle Consumer News* updates a list of national clubs every year. *Rider* publishes a monthly list of local clubs on its "Rider Club Connection" page. *Old Bike Journal* lists clubs catering to vintage bikes, obscure marques and networks for owners of specific models. Clubs often leave flyers at dealerships and biker watering holes when they are hosting events. Attend an event to get a feel for the club.

All American Indian
  Motorcycle Club
25801 Clark Rd.
Wellington, OH 44090

American Voyager Assn.
P.O. Box 188
Redgranite, WI 54970-0188
414-566-2149

Antique Motorcycle Club of
  America
P.O. Box 333
Sweetster, IN 46987

American Sport-Touring
  Riders Assn. (ASTRA)
P.O. Box 672051
Marietta, GA 30067-0035
404-443-2614

Association of Recovering
  Motorcyclists (ARM)
1503 Market St.
La Crosse, WI 54601
608-784-8462

BMW Motorcycle Owners
  of America (BMWMOA)
P.O. Box 489
Chesterfield, MO 63006-
  0489
314-537-5511

BMW Riders Association
  (BMWRA)
P.O. Box 510309
Melbourne, FL 32951-0309
407-984-7800

Blue Knights Law
  Enforcement M/C
38 Alden St.
Bangor, ME 04401
207-947-4600

British International
  Motorcycle Assn.
P.O. Box 28713
Atlanta, GA 30358

Christian Motorcyclists
  Assn. (CMA)
P.O. Box 9
Hatfield, AR 71945
501-389-6196

Classic Japanese Motorcycle
  Club
358 St. Julie Dr.
San Jose, CA 95119
408-225-3274

Concours Owners Group
P.O. Box 0505
Acme, MI 49610

Ducati International
  Owners Club
P.O. Box 65-0857
Miami, FL 33265-0857

Gold Wing Road Riders
  Assn. (GWRRA)
21423 N. 11th Ave.
Phoenix, AZ 85027
800-843-9460
602-581-2500

Gold Wing Touring Assoc.
6010 Cadillac Dr.
Speedway, IN 46224
317-486-9982

GSX Katana Club
P.O. Box 7528
Torrance, CA 90504
310-538-3625

Harley Owners Group
  (HOG)
See Ladies of Harley.

Honda Hawk GT Owners
  Network
121 Hawkins Pl.
Boonton, NJ 07005

Honda Pacific Coast
  Owners Club
4316 Marina City Dr.
#321
Marina Del Ray, CA 90202
310-822-6317

Honda Riders Club of
   America (HRCA)
American Honda Motor
   Company
1919 Torrance Blvd.
Torrance, CA 90501-2746
800-847-HRCA

Honda Sport Touring Assn.
   (HSTA)
9310 167th Ave. NE
Redmond, WA 98052-3739

Indian Motorcycle Club of
   America
P.O. Box 1743
Perris, CA 92370-1743

International Brotherhood of
   Motorcycle Campers
P.O. Box 2395
Chandler, AZ 85244-2395
602-963-6992

International Suzuki Owners
   Club
P.O. Box 262613
Houston, TX 77207

Italian Motorcycle Owners
   Club
P.O. Box 332
Brooklyn, CT 06234
203-774-8365

Knights of Life
P.O. Box 168
Iselin, NJ 08830-0168
Health care professionals.

Life Riders International
34 Hillview Ave.
Franklin Park, NJ 08823
908-297-4050
Health care professionals.

Midwest Antique & Classic
   Motorcycle Club
2023 Sycamore Rd.
DeKalb, IL 60115

Moto Guzzi National
   Owners Club
P.O. Box 98
Olmitz, KS 67564
316-586-3275

Nassau Wings
Ron Mare, President
38 Hommel St.
Valley Stream, NY 11580
516-285-9713
All brands.

Red Knights International
   Firefighters Motorcycle
   Club
P.O. Box 710
Boylston, MA 01505

Retreads
528 N. Main St.
Albany, IN 47320
317-789-4070
Riders age 40 and up.

Scoot-Tours
Sally and Bob Reinhardt
10528 Canter Way
St. Louis, MO 63114-1902
Automatic step-through
scooters; family members on
motorcycles welcome.

Shadow Riders Club (SRC)
Bob Maynard
P.O. Box 867511
Plano, TX 75086-7511
214-684-7063
214-422-1461
Honda Shadows and other
cruisers.

Spanish Motorcycle Owners
   Group (SMOG)
1320 Cathy Lane
Minden, NV 89423
702-267-2103

Sport Touring Motorcycle
   Club (STMC)
393 W. Hudson Ave.
Englewood, NJ 07631
201-871-8425

Sportys
Assn. of Sportster Enthusiasts
P.O. Box 593
E. Bridgewater, MA 02333-
   0593
508-378-2233

Triumph International
   Owners Club
P.O. Box 6676
Holliston, MA 01746-6676
508-429-4221

United Sidecar Assn.
130 S. Michigan Ave.
Villa Park, IL 60181

Venture Touring Society
1615 S. Eastern Ave.
Las Vegas, NV 89104
702-457-6657
800-833-3687

Vintage Japanese Motorcycle
   Club (VJMC)
24 Cathy St.
Merrimack, NH 03054
603-429-2436

Virago Owners Club
6785 S. Threshold Pt.
Homosassa, FL 34446
800-315-3209

Yamaha 650 Society
P.O. Box 234
O'Fallon, MO 63366-0234

BOOKS AND VIDEOS

Autobooks Etc.
3524 W. Magnolia
Burbank, CA 91505

Classic Motorbooks
P.O. Box 1
Osceola, WI 54020
800-826-6600

Garage Company
13211 Washington Blvd.
Los Angeles, CA 90066
310-821-1793

Hosking Bookworks
136 Hosking Lane
Accord, NY 12404
800-626-4231

Infosport Publications
30011 Ivy Glenn Dr.
Ste. 122
Laguna Niguel, CA 92677
714-249-2270

Main Attractions
P.O. Box 4923
Chatsworth, CA 91313-4923
818-883-3408
"B" biker videos.

Motovideo
P.O. Box 6342
Laguna Niguel, CA 92607
800-688-6686

Pacific Motorbooks
1880 E. Main St.
Ventura, CA 93001
805-641-9545
and
11 W. Anapamu
Santa Barbara, CA 93101
805-965-5797

Roundabout Publications
2767 S. Parker Rd.
Ste. 240
Aurora, CO 80014-2701
800-455-2207
Travel and road guides.

Whitehorse Press
3424 N. Main St.
P.O. Box 60
North Conway, NH 03860-0060
800-531-1133
603-356-6590

T. E. Warth Automotive
Books
No. 5 Lumberyard Shops
Marine on St. Croix, MN 55047
612-433-5744
Out-of-print books.

Memorabilia

Motorcycle Memories
Robbie "Dale" Jackson
6784 Camp John Rd.
Millington, TN 38053
901-876-6883
Buy-sell-trade: computer searches: advertising brochures, posters, old magazines, manuals.

Recommended

On the Perimeter by Hazel Kolb with Bill Stermer (New London, MO: Maverick, 1983). Kolb's autobiography, chronicling her motorcycle ride around the U.S. perimeter.

She Lives To Ride
Filkela Films
539 Tremont St.
Ste. 409
Boston, MA 02116
617-542-7699
Video documentary about five women motorcyclists.

CYCLE INTERCOMS

Cycle Comm
3300 Castle Rd.
Woodstock, IL 60098
800-527-6798
815-337-0790

Maxon America
10828 Air World Dr.
Kansas City, MO 64153
816-891-1093

Nady Systems
6701 Bay St.
Emeryville, CA 94608
510-652-2411

EMERGENCY ROADSIDE ASSISTANCE

BMW Motorcycle Owners of
   America
See BMWMOA in Clubs; all
brands welcome.

BMW Riders Assn.
See BMWRA in Clubs.

Cross Country Motor Club
4040 Mystic Valley Pkwy.
Boston, MA 02155-6918

Gold Wing Road Riders
   Assn.
See GWRRA in Clubs.

Harley Owners Group
See HOG in Clubs.

Honda Riders Club of
   America
See HRCA in Clubs.

International Help'n'Hands
Through the AMA; see
Associations.

Motorcycle Towing Service
   (MTS)
1500 E. Tropicana
Ste. 221
Las Vegas, NV 89119
800-999-7064

Shell Motorist Club
P.O. Box 60199
Chicago, IL 60660
800-852-0555

HELMETS

AGV
5711 Industry Ln.
Frederick, MD 21701
800-777-7066
301-663-4550

Arai
P.O. Box 9485
Daytona, FL 32120
800-766-ARAI
904-253-5100

Bell
1565 McGaw Ave.
Irvine, CA 92714
800-848-3879

Bieffe USA
6630 Patterson Pass Road
Livermore, CA 94550
510-606-1505

FM/Kiwi
Triton International
1111 Lake Cook Rd.
Buffalo Grove, IL 60089
708-215-9914

Arthur Fulmer
122 Gayoso
Memphis, TN 38103
901-525-5711

HJC
See Tour Master Riding Gear
in Apparel.

Lazer
P.O. Box 279
Bellvue, CO 80512
800-321-6621
303-482-6623

Nolan
CIMA International
284 N. Main
Glen Ellyn, IL 60137

Shoei
22605 E. La Palma Ave.
Ste. 507
Yorba Linda, CA 92687
714-692-8776

Simpson Race Products
2415 Amsler St.
Torrance, CA 90505
800-621-6507

Helmet Liners

Silkys
P.O. Box 34294
Indianapolis, IN 46234
800-770-2689

Sliks Helmet Liners
0036 N. Meadowview Ct.
Glenwood Springs, CO
   81601
800-242-5339

LOWERING A BIKE

The major components needed to lower a bike are shorter shocks (and sometimes other suspension components), lower profile tires, and lower seats. See separate listings for Shock Absorbers/Lowering Kits, Tires, and Seats. Useful magazine articles are:

"How Low to Go" by Ron Lindquist, *Hot Rod Harleys* (Sept. 1994).

"Shock Therapy: Finding an Aftermarket Shock Absorber that Works" by Bill Stermer, *Rider* (March 1994).

"Suspension Mods: How Low Should You Go?" by John Frank, *American Iron* (Dec. 1994).

MECHANICS' SCHOOLS

American Motorcycle
Institute (AMI)
3042 International Speedway
Blvd.
Daytona Beach, FL 32124
800-874-0645
800-881-2AMI
904-255-0295

Motorcycle Mechanics
Institute (MMI)
2844 W. Deer Valley Rd.
Phoenix, AZ 85027
800-528-7995
602-869-9644

MOTORCYCLE MANUFACTURERS AND DISTRIBUTORS

American Dirt Bike
5430 Union Pacific Ave.
City of Commerce, CA
90022
800-426-6869
213-722-8880

Aprilla, Montesa, Scorpa
The Tryals Shop
6106 Land O'Lakes Blvd.
Land O'Lakes, FL 34639
813-996-3754

ATK
ATK America
P.O. Box 100
Bountiful, UT 84010
800-285-8724
801-298-8288

BMW
BMW of North America
300 Chestnut Ridge Rd.
Woodcliff Lake, NJ 07675
800-345-4BMW (dealer info)
201-307-4000
201-307-0783

Beta, Italjet
Cosmopolitan Motors
301 Jacksonville Rd.
Hatboro, PA 19040
800-523-2522
215-672-9100

Bimota
Moto Cycle
401 Jones Mills Rd.
Stahlstown, PA 15687
412-593-6208

Buell
Buell Motor Co.
214 Jefferson St.
Wukwonago, WI 53149
800-490-9635 (dealer info)

Bultaco
Hugh's Bultaco
Rd. 1 Box 205
Craryville, NY 12521
518-851-7184

Cagiva, Ducati, Husqvarna
Cagiva of North America
237 West Parkway
Pompton Plains, NJ 07444
201-839-2600

Cobra
Cobra Motorcycle Mfg.
10593 Main St.
New Middletown, OH
44442
216-542-2000

Harley-Davidson
Harley-Davidson Motor Co.
3700 W. Juneau Ave.
P.O. Box 653
Milwaukee, WI 53201
800-443-2153 (dealer info)
414-342-4680
414-935-4056

Hodaka
E & K Cycles
205 E. Jefferson
Sweet Springs, MO 65351
816-335-4481

Honda
American Honda Motor
    Company
1919 Torrance Blvd.
Torrance, CA 90501-2746
310-783-2000

Jawa/MZ
American Jawa Ltd.
185 Express St.
Plainview, NY 11803
516-938-3210

Kawasaki
Kawasaki Motors Corp.,
    USA
9950 Jeronimo Rd.
Irvine, CA 92718
714-770-0400

KTM, Husaberg
KTM America
1906 Broadway
Lorain, OH 44052
216-244-4939

Laverda
Slater Brothers
P.O. Box 1
Mica, WA 99023
509-924-5131

LEM Motor
Motomarina Ltd.
P.O. Box 327
21 Forest Rd.
Dumont, NJ 07628
201-848-0400

Moto Guzzi
Moto America
1004 Main St.
Lillington, NC 27546
800-USA-MOTO
910-893-3914

Moto Morini
Herdan Corp.
Rt. 61 Box 65
Port Clinton, PA 19549
610-562-3155

Rokon
Rokon International
140 West Road
Portsmouth, NH 03801
603-431-5100

Suzuki
American Suzuki Motor
    Corp.
3251 E. Imperial Hwy.
Brea, CA 92621
714-996-7040

Triumph
Triumph USA
403 Dividend Dr.
Peachtree City, GA 30269
770-631-9500
800-RIDE-TRI

Ural
Ural America
1-90 Preston Industrial Pk.
8146 304th Ave. SE
Preston, WA 98050
800-832-2845

Yamaha
Yamaha Motor Corp. USA
6555 Katella Ave.
Cypress, CA 90630
714-761-7300 (main office)
800-88-YAMAHA (for
    dealer info)

ON-LINE SERVICES: BULLETIN BOARDS, CHAT LINES

There are thousands. Here is a selective list to get you started.

Annie Fetter's "Chez Annie"
http://olmo.swarthmore.edu/
annie/

AT&T's 800 Directory
(Includes motorcycles)
http://att.net/

Harley Mom's Home Page
http://www.wp.com/
HarleyMom

MotoCentral, on the
    Microsoft Network
Motorcycling RoundTable,
    on GEnie
For info on both:

Joanna Strohn, President
Electronic Motorcyclists
3938 E. Grant Rd.
Tucson, AZ 85712
520-326-0792
520-326-7864
joanna_msn@msn.com
MotoCentral@msn.com

Motorcycle Links
    Compendium
Motorcycle Online Magazine
http://www.motorcycle.com/
motorcycle.html
"The world's first all-digital
motorcycle magazine."

Motorcycle Safety Mailing
    List
http://www.imat.com/
safety.html

Northeast Motorcycle
    Resources
http://hea-www.harvard.edu/
motorcyclist/HomePage.html

Wheelbase
http://www.wheelbase.com

PERIODICALS

National

American Iron
TAM Communications
1010 Summer St.
Stamford, CT 06905
203-855-0008

American Motorcyclist
Comes with AMA member-
ship; see AMA in
Associations.

American Rider
TL Enterprises
2575 Vista Del Mar Drive
Ventura, CA 93001
805-667-4100

American Roadracing
P.O. Box 3320
Carefree, AZ 85377-3320
602-488-4500

American Woman Motorscene
1510 11th St.
Ste. 201B
Santa Monica, CA 90401
800-LADY-RDR
310-260-0192

Big Twin
1499 Monrovia Ave.
Newport Beach, CA 92663
714-720-5300

BlackRiders Magazine
P.O. Box 58
4320 Hamilton St.
Hyattsville, MD 20781

BMW ON (Owners News)
Available with BMWMOA
membership; see Clubs.

Classic Cycle Review
641-645 Seneca St.
Harrisburg, PA 17110
800-232-9369
717-233-5569

Classic Motorcycle Journal
P.O. Box 36110
San Jose, CA 95158-6110
408-436-1400

Cruiser
c/o Art Friedman
213-782-2230
See *Dirt Rider.*

Cycle News
2201 Cherry Ave.
Long Beach, CA 90806
800-831-2220
310-427-7433

Cycle World
See *Big Twin.*

Dirt Rider
6420 Wilshire Blvd.
Los Angeles, CA 90048-
    5515
213-782-2390

Drag Times
P.O. Box 17
West Berlin, NJ 08091
609-770-0985
Harley drag racing.

Dual Sporter
8535 Amestoy Ave.
Northridge, CA 91325-3403
818-701-1913

Easyriders
Paisano Publications
28210 Dorothy Dr.
Agoura Hills, CA 91301-
2693
818-889-8740
Adult; has several spinoff
magazines.

Enthusiast
Harley-Davidson Motor Co.
3700 W. Juneau Ave.
P.O. Box 653
Milwaukee, WI 53201
414-342-4680

Feet-Up
L-Squared Publishing
P.O. Box 3685
Whittier, CA 90605-0685
310-944-0453
Observed trials.

Hack'd
P.O. Box 813
Buckhannon, WV 26201
304-472-6146
Sidecars.

Harley Women
Asphalt Angels, Inc.
P.O. Box 374
Streamwood, IL 60107
708-888-2645

Indian Motorcycle Illustrated
See *American Iron.*

IronWorks
Editor
P.O. Box 1096
Morganton, NC 28680-
1096
334-834-1170

Motocross Action
See *Dual Sporter.*

Motocross Journal
See *Dual Sporter.*

Motorcycle Collector
30011 Ivy Glenn Dr. #114
Laguna Niguel, CA 92677
714-249-2270

Motorcycle Consumer News
P.O. Box 6050
Mission Viejo, CA 92690
714-855-8822

Motorcycle Shopper
1353 Herndon Ave.
Deltona, FL 32725-9046
407-860-1989

Motorcycle Sport
550 Honey Locust Rd.
Jonesburg, MO 63351-9600
314-488-3113

Motorcycle Tour & Travel
See *American Iron.*

Motorcyclist
213-782-2230
See *Dirt Rider.*

MX Action/Dirt Bike
P.O. Box 958
Valencia, CA 91380
800-767-0345

NADA Appraisal Guides
P.O. Box 7800
Costa Mesa, CA 92628
800-966-6232
714-556-8511
Used motorcycles.

Old Bike Journal
See *American Iron.*

Rider
See *American Rider.*

Roadracing World &
  Motorcycle Technology
581-C Birch St.
Lake Elsinore, CA 92530
909-245-6411

The Sidecarist
See United Sidecar
Association in Clubs.

Shootin' the Breeze
Comes with WITW mem-
bership; see Women's Clubs.

Sportbike
See *Big Twin.*

Sport Rider
213-782-2584
See *Dirt Rider.*

Sport Tour Reader
W. G. Norman
P.O. Box 840566
Houston, TX 77284-0566
713-463-3794

Street Bike
RPM Publishing
6514 Glade Ave.
Canoga Park, CA 91303
818-888-4921

Thunder Alley
See *American Iron.*

Walneck's Classic Cycle Trader
7923 Janes Ave.
Woodridge, IL 60517
708-985-4995

Women on Wheels
Contact WOW; see Women's
Clubs.

PERIODICALS (*cont'd*)

Regional

Backroads
P.O. Box 3062
Teaneck, NJ 07666
201-569-1973
(New Jersey tri-state area)

Carolina Motorcycle News
P.O. Box 566
Campobello, SC 29322
803-457-2293

Citybike
323 10th St.
San Francisco, CA 94103
415-982-7242
(Northern California)

County Wheels
16499 NE 19th Ave.
North Miami Beach, FL
   33162
305-940-6185
(Southeast U.S.)

Free 2 Wheel
P.O. Box 1390
Simi Valley, CA 93062
805-581-0248
(Southern California)

*Independent Biker and Street
   Bike*
1339 Mission St.
San Francisco, CA 94103
415-252-6669
(Northern California;
Harley-oriented)

Iron Biker News
P.O. Box 201
Landisville, NJ 08326
609-697-1335
(Harleys, Northeast U.S.)

Keystone Motorcycle Press
P.O. Box 296
Ambridge, PA 15003
412-774-6542
(Pennsylvania)

Motomag
P.O. Box 1046
Nyack, NY 10960
800-MOTOMAG
(NY tri-state area)

Motorcycle Dispatch
P.O. Box 227
Anamosa, IA 52205
319-462-4855
(Harleys, North Central U.S.)

Motorcyclist's Post
P.O. Box 154
Rochdale, MA 01542
508-885-5221
(New England)

Southeastern Bike News
1125 Oak Creek Trail
Birmingham, AL 35215
205-681-0303

Tex-MX News
200 Madeline Lane
Burleson, TX 76028
817-295-NEWS
(Amateur motocross, Texas)

Thunder Press
12 Camp Evers Lane
Scotts Valley, CA 95066
408-438-7882
(Harleys, Calif. and Nevada)

Winding Roads
2550 Albert Rill Rd.
Westminster, MD 21157
410-374-6282
(Mid-Atlantic states)

Trade

Motorcycle Industry Magazine
P.O. Box 160
1267 Hwy 395 N.
Gardnerville, NV 89410
702-782-0222

Dealernews
201 E. Sandpointe Ave.
Ste. 600
Santa Ana, CA 92707

Foreign

Canadian Biker
735 Market St.
Box 4122
Victoria, B.C.
   V8X 3X4
Canada
604-384-0333

Cycle Canada
Turbopress
86 Parliament St.
Studio 3B
Toronto, Ontario
   M5A 2Y6
Canada

*Motorcycle
   International*
P.O. Box 10
Whitchurch
Shropshire
   SY13 1ZZ
United Kingdom

RACE SANCTIONING ORGANIZATIONS

The AMA sanctions many forms of amateur and pro competition, including drag racing, motocross, road racing, enduro (cross-country), hillclimbing, and more. See AMA in Associations. Below are other groups.

Drag Racing

All-Harley Drag Racing Assn.
Dane Miller, President
P.O. Box 1429
Elon College, NC 27244
910-229-4877

AMA-ProStar
Keith Kizer
P.O. Box 18039
Huntsville, AL 35804
205-852-1101
(All brands)

American Motorcycle Racing
    Assn.
Richard Wegner, President
Box 50
Itasca, IL 60143
708-250-0838
(Harleys)

East Coast Racing Assn.
Ben Petrovic, President
219 E. White Horse Pike
Galloway Twp., NJ 08201
609-652-1159
(Harleys)

International Drag Bike Assn.
3936 Raceway Park Road
Mt. Olive, AL 35117
205-849-7886

National Hot Rod Assn.
P.O. Box 5555
Glendora, CA 91740
818-914-4761
(Pro Stock bikes)

Motocross

U.S. Women's Motocross
    Team
Elaine Ruff, Executive
    Director
c/o Acerbis Plastica USA
9402 Wheatlands Court
Ste. A
Santee, CA 92071
800-659-1440
619-562-1440

Road Racing

National American
    Superbike Series (NASB)
Pat Murphy, 916-442-7985

Western Eastern Racing
    Assn. (WERA)
P.O. Box 440549
Kennesaw, GA 30144
770-924-8404
916-582-0451

American Federation of
    Motorcyclists (AFM)
P.O. Box 5018-333
Newark, CA 94560
510-796-7005

Vintage Racing

American Historic Racing
    Motorcycle Assn.
    (AHRMA)
P.O. Box 882
Wausau, WI 54402-0882
715-842-9699

RALLIES, RIDES, ATTRACTIONS

There are scores of rallies. At the start of each riding season (often in a March/April issue), the touring magazines such as *Rider, Motorcycle Tour & Travel,* and *Motorcycle Consumer News* publish calendars of national and regional rallies, and those devoted to single marques (many welcome all brands). The AMA hosts District Tours, Gypsy Tours, Road Riding Conventions, and other events throughout the season in various states. See AMA in Associations.

Rallies

Americade
P.O. Box 2205
Glens Falls, NY 12801
518-656-3696
(June, Lake George, N.Y.)

Bike Week
Daytona Convention
   & Visitors Bureau
800-854-1234
(March, Daytona Beach,
Fla.)

Biketoberfest
Daytona Convention
   & Visitors Bureau
800-854-1234
(October, Daytona Beach,
Fla.)

BMW Motorcycle Owners
   of America International
   Rally
(July, see BMWMOA in
Clubs)

BMW Riders Assn.
   International Rally
(August, see BMWRA in
Clubs)

Harley Owners Group
   Rallies
(several, various dates and
states, see HOG in Clubs)

Honda Hoot
(June, see HRCA in Clubs)

Indian Day
(July, see Indian Motocycle
Museum in Museums)

Laconia Rally & Race Week
603-366-2000
(June, Laconia, N.H.)

Mid-Atlantic Women's
   Motorcycle Rally
5707 Kenwood Ave.
Baltimore, MD 21206
(June)

Motor Maids Convention
(July, see Motor Maids in
Women's Clubs)

National Round-Up
(Summer; see *BlackRiders*
in Periodicals)

Rider Rallies
800-507-4337
805-667-4100
(Several, various dates and
states, see *Rider* in
Periodicals)

Sturgis Rally & Races
(Black Hills Motor Classic)
P.O. Box 189
Sturgis, SD 57785
605-347-6570
(August)

Vintage Motorcycle Days
(July, see AMA in
Associations)

Virago Owners Club Family
   Reunion
(See Virago Owners Club
in Clubs)

Women in the Wind
   Nationals
(June, see WITW in
Women's Clubs)

Women on Wheels Ride-In
(July, see WOW in Women's
Clubs)

Charity Rides

BMW's Miracle Ride
Crohn's & Colitis
   Foundation of America
34 W. Putnam Ave.
Greenwich, CT 06830-5341
203-629-5353
(October)

Love Ride
Harley-Davidson of Glendale
3717 San Fernando Rd.
Glendale, CA 91204
818-246-5618
MDA: 818-986-1793
(November, benefits the
Muscular Dystrophy Assn.
For a registration packet,
you can also contact your
local Harley dealer.)

Ride for Kids
Pediatric Brain Tumor
   Foundation of the U.S.
6350-B McDonough Dr.
Norcross, GA 30093
404-449-0789
(Several rides throughout
the season in various states)

Rolling Thunder
c/o Artie Muller
P.O. Box 216
Neshanic Sta., NJ 08853-
   0216
(Memorial Day Weekend,
Washington, DC;
commemorates those
who died in Vietnam,
POW/MIAs)

Museums & Attractions

Barbour Vintage
   Motorsports Museum
2721 5th Ave. South
Birmingham, AL 35210

Harley-Davidson Cafe
1370 Ave. of the Americas
New York, N.Y. 10019
Harley memorabilia,
souvenirs.

Harley-Davidson Museum
Harley-Davidson Motor Co.
1425 Eden Rd.
York, PA 17402
717-848-1177

Indian Motocycle Museum
33 Hendee St.
Springfield, MA 01109
413-737-2624

Motorcycle Heritage
   Museum
See AMA in Associations.

National Motorcycle
   Museum and Hall
   of Fame
2438 Junction Ave.
Sturgis, SD 57785
605-347-4875

Petersen Automotive
   Museum
6060 Wilshire Blvd.
Los Angeles, CA 90036
213-930-2277

Southeast Harley-Davidson
23105 Aurora Rd.
Cleveland, OH 44146
216-439-5300
Harley franchise with Elvis
memorabilia, vintage gas
station, diner, mall.

Trev Deeley Motorcycle
   Museum
13500 Verdun Pl.
Richmond, Vancouver
British Columbia,
   Canada V51X6
604-876-3326

Wheels Through Time
   Museum
Harley-Davidson of Mt.
   Vernon
12th St. & Waltonville Rd.
Mt. Vernon, IL 62864
618-244-4118

Sunday-Morning Gathering Spots

Alice's Restaurant
17288 Skyline Blvd.
Woodside, CA 94062
415-851-0303

Marcus Dairy
Sugar Hollow Rd.
Exit 3 off I-80
Danbury, CT 06810
203-748-9427
203-355-9771

Rock Store
30354 W. Mulholland Hwy.
Cornell, CA 91301
818-889-1311

Trade Shows

International Motorcycle
  Shows
Advanstar Expositions
800-331-5706
Off-season consumer expos
in various cities.

REFERENCES AND INFORMATION SERVICES

Biker Broadcasting
216-881-8969
Syndicated talk-radio shows
in various cities; headquar-
tered in Cleveland, Ohio.

Centerstand
KPFK-FM
3727 Cahuenga Blvd.
N. Hollywood, CA 91604
818-985-2711
One-hour talk-radio show
for Southern California
motorcyclists, hosted by
Margaret Fowler, Saturdays,
7 A.M.

Discover Today's
  Motorcycling (DTM)
Motorcycle Industry Council
2 Jenner St.
Ste. 150
Irvine, CA 92718
714-727-4211
800-833-3995
24-hour info line, basic
brochures on bikes, financ-
ing, insurance.

Motorcycle Reports
Ian Smith Information
P.O. Box 9440
Denver, CO 80209-0440
303-777-2385
Reprints of magazine articles
about most bikes from
1960–present.

*Motorcycles: Fundamentals,
  Service, Repair*
Textbook by Bruce Johns
and David Edmundson
(South Holland, Ill.:
Goodheart-Willcox, 1987)

*Trelland's Motorcycle Reference
  Guide*
MRGI
Box 8110
Ste. 903
Blaine, WA 98231
General directory.

*American Motorcyclist Yellow
  Pages*
General directory
supplement to *American
Motorcyclist* magazine,
updated yearly.

RIDING AND RACING INSTRUCTION

Rider Training (Street Skills)

California's Leading
  Advanced Safety School
  (CLASS)
15500 W. Telegraph Rd.
Ste. C24
Santa Paula, CA 93060
805-933-9936
Taught at the racetrack but
applicable to the street.

Lawrence Grodsky's
Stayin' Safe Motorcycle
  Training
P.O. Box 81810
Pittsburgh, PA 15217
412-421-5711

Motorcycle Safety
  Foundation (MSF)
See Associations.

Sidecar Safety Program
Northern Illinois University
College of Continuing Ed.
DeKalb, IL 60115-2860
815-753-1683

Trama's Auto School
87-15 Jamaica Ave.
Woodhaven, NY 11421
718-847-2015

Racing Schools

Ed Bargy Racing Services
P.O. Box 250222
Atlanta, GA 30325
404-352-5750

Keith Code's California
  Superbike School
255 Harlow Drive
Glendale, CA 91206
800-530-3350
818-246-0717

DP Safety School
805-772-8301
(Morro Bay, CA)

Fastrack Riders
805-256-7320
(Rosamond, CA)

Hallett Roadracing School
918-446-6657
(Tulsa, OK)

Penguin Racing School
207-548-2100
(Mansfield, MA)

Team Suzuki Endurance
Advanced Riding School
P.O. Box 964
Guasti, CA 91743
909-245-6414

Safe-Riding References

Motorcycling Excellence:
  Skills, Knowledge and
  Strategies for Riding Right
Compilation of MSF materi-
al, available from Whitehorse
Press and Classic Motor-
books; see Books, Videos.

Street Smarts
CFK Inc.
8033 Sunset Blvd.
Ste. 369
Los Angeles, CA 90046
213-876-3541
Book and video; urban
street riding strategies.

A Twist of the Wrist
Two books and a video from
Keith Code's California
Superbike School; see
Racing Schools.

SADDLEBAGS AND TANKBAGS

Black Hills Leather Co.
1324 Shephard St.
Sturgis, SD 57785-1820

Chase Harper
427 Olive St.
Santa Barbara, CA 93103
805-965-7977

Eclipse
3771 E. Ellsworth Rd.
Ann Arbor, MI 48108
800-666-1500
313-971-5552

Givi Luggage Systems
c/o Capital Cycle
21580 Beaumeade Circle
#170
Ashburn, VA 22011
800-642-5100 (USA)
800-445-4175 (Canada)
703-729-7900

Saddlebags and Tankbags (cont'd)

RKA
2175 Bluebell Dr.
Santa Rosa, CA 95403
707-579-5045

S&S Cycle & Supply
304 Rolling Trail
Amarillo, TX 79108
800-321-2735
806-355-8541

SAFETY AND COMFORT PRODUCTS

Adventure Medical First-Aid
 Kits
Available from Whitehorse
Press; see Books, Videos.

BMW Tubeless Tire Flat
 Repair Kit
BMW of North America
P.O. Box 1227
Westwood, NJ 07675-1227
800-345-4BMW
201-307-3785

Conspicuity
P.O. Box 608
Elgin, IL
708-697-4550
Reflective and fluorescent
vests and appliques.

Fog City Fog Shield
Modern World Ventures
P.O. Box 16010
Oakland, CA 94610
800-436-4248
See-through shield, sticks
to inside of full-face helmet
visor, prevents fogging if
used properly.

Halo Helmet Bands
MDC
3145 Geary Blvd.
Ste. 108
San Francisco, CA 94118
415-752-3200
Removable reflective and
fluorescent bands.

Kafka's Kool Tie
10443 N. Cave Creek Rd.
Phoenix, AZ 85020
602-943-8119
Stay-moist neckerchief.

Motopump
Moto-Vated Products
P.O. Box 5472
Pleasanton, CA 94566-5472
510-462-7544
Small CO_2 air pump to
regulate tire pressure.
Not a repair device.

SEATS

Corbin
11445 Commercial Pkwy.
Castroville, CA 95012
800-538-7035 (California)
800-223-4332 (Florida)

Diamond Custom Seats
902 Ave. R
Carter Lake, IA 51510
712-347-5316

Hartco
716 Parkway
Sevierville, TN 37862
800-446-7772
615-428-5262

LeMans
c/o Drag Specialties
P.O. Box 9336
Minneapolis, MN 55440
800-222-3400
612-942-7890

Le Pera Enterprises
8207 Lankershim Blvd.
N. Hollywood, CA 91605
818-767-5110

Mustang
P.O. Box 29
Terryville, CT 06786
800-243-1392

Russell Day Long Saddles
P.O. Box 609
Fall River Mills, CA 96028
800-4-DAY-LONG
916-336-5323

Sargent Cycle Upholstery
44 E. 1st St.
Jacksonville, FL 32206
800-749-SEAT
904-354-4531

Second Look
P.O. Box 661721
Sacramento, CA 95866-1721
916-920-8113

Travelcade
6325 Alondra
Paramount, CA 90723
800-397-7709
310-630-4522

Utopia Products
3867 W. Market St.
Akron, OH 44333
216-666-2602

SHOCK ABSORBERS AND LOWERING KITS

EMC Dynamics
c/o Capital Eurosport
21580 Beaumeade Circle
#170
Ashburn, VA 22011
800-642-5100 (USA)
800-445-4175 (Canada)
703-729-7900

Fox Racing Shox
3610 Snell Ave.
San Jose, CA 95136
408-365-9700

Hagon
c/o Quinn Motorcycles
335 Litchfield Turnpike
Bethany, CT 06524
203-393-2651
For vintage bikes.

Koni America
8085 Production Ave.
Florence, KY 41042
606-727-5000

Lindemann Engineering
520 McGlincey
Lane #3
Campbell, CA 95008
408-371-6151

Marzocchi
c/o Cosmopolitan Motors
301 Jacksonville Rd.
Hatboro, PA 19040
800-523-2522
215-672-9100
Mostly dual-shocks.

Ohlins
c/o Noleen Racing
16276 Koala Rd.
Adelanto, CA 92301
619-246-5000

Pettersson Pro Suspension
817 Lakeview
Unit B
Placentia, CA 92670
714-970-2423

Progressive Suspension
11129 G Ave.
Hesperia, CA 92345
619-948-4012

George Quay's
3201 6th Ave.
Beaver Falls, PA 15010
412-846-9055
Dirt bike specialists.

Race Tech Suspension
3227 Producer Way
#127
Pomona, CA 91768
909-594-7755

Ride One
11301 Olympic Blvd.
Ste. 534
Los Angeles, CA 90064
800-292-3960
213-299-3960
For Evolution Harleys.

Shoc Connection
1559 Sequia Ave.
Simi Valley, CA 93063
805-584-2805

Too-Tech Racing
19333 Sturgess Dr.
Torrance, CA 90503
310-371-3887

White Brothers
24845 Corbit Pl.
Yorba Linda, CA 92687
714-692-3404

Works Performance
8730 Shirley Ave.
Northridge, CA 91324
818-701-1010

SIDECARS AND TRAILERS

American Jawa Ltd.
See Jawa/MZ in Motorcycle
Manufacturers.

Bushtec
Rt #1 Mt. Paron Rd.
Jacksboro, TN 37757
615-562-9900

California Sidecar/Escapade
  Trailer
15641 Computer Lane
Huntington Beach, CA
  92649
800-824-1523
714-891-1033

Chariot
209 Pickney St.
Oldsmar, FL 34677
813-855-5801

Hitchhiker Sidecars
Trailers II Inc.
1675 Cumberland Rd. SE
  (Rt. 40)
London, OH 43140
614-852-5373

Motorvation
941 Fourth Ave.
Sibley, IA 51249
712-754-3664

See also United Sidecar Assn.
in Clubs; *Hack'd* in
Periodicals

TIRES

Avon
P.O. Box 336
Edmonds, WA 98020
800-624-7470
206-771-2115

Bridgestone
One Bridgestone Park
P.O. Box 140991
Nashville, TN 37214-0991
615-391-0088

Cheng Shin
545 Old Peachtree Rd.
Suwanee, GA 30174
404-962-5932

Continental
41 Strong St.
Wallington, NJ 07057
201-471-8890

Dunlop
P.O. Box 1109
Buffalo, NY 14240-1109
716-879-8200

Firestone
One Bridgestone Park
P.O. Box 140991
Nashville, TN 37214-0991
615-391-0088

IRC
2851 B Whipple Rd.
Union City, CA 94587
510-441-0126

Kenda USA
7095 Americana Pkwy.
Reynoldsburg, OH 43068
614-866-9803

Kings Tire USA
(Nichols Motorcycle Supply)
135 W. 126 St.
Alsip, IL 60658
708-597-3340

Metzeler
410 Eagleview Blvd.
Ste. 106
Exton, PA 19341
800-722-3336
610-458-9662

Michelin
P.O. Box 19001
Greenville, SC 29602-9001
803-458-5000
803-458-6053

Pirelli
410 Eagleview Blvd.
Ste. 106
Exton, PA 19341
800-722-3336
610-458-9662

TOURING AND CAMPING RESOURCES

AMA Travel Desk
800-AMA-DESK
Touring & travel agency for
AMA members.

International Motorcycle
Touring Council
1823 W. Selden Lane
Phoenix, AZ 85021
602-943-9030
Tour info worldwide.

Skip Mascorro's Pancho Villa
Moto-Tours
685 Persimmon Hill
Bulverde, TX 78163
800-233-0564
Women-only group tours
through Mexico.

Handbooks and Gadgets

*Motorcycle Touring: An
International Directory, with
1993/94 Supplement.* Lists
tours, tour operators, motorcycle rental and transport
companies in the U.S. and
abroad. Available from
Whitehorse Press; see Books,
Videos.

*Motorcycle Touring and
Travel: A Handbook of Travel
by Motorcycle* by Bill Stermer.
A nuts'n'bolts guide to plan-
ning and packing for the
road. From Whitehorse
Press; see Books, Videos.

MTS Dealer Handbook. Lists
U.S. motorcycle dealers.
From MTS, 800-999-7064.

Touring Gadgets, P.O. Box
340, Vinemont, AL 35179,
800-874-8276 and 813-921-
2939. Compact gear and
gadgets.

WINDSHIELDS AND FAIRINGS

Aeroflow
P.O. Box 11990
Costa Mesa, CA 92627
714-557-3119
For BMWs.

Clearview Shields
59113 Hwy. 285
P.O. Box 747
Bailey, CO 80421
800-798-6089
Custom-built shields.

National Cycle
P.O. Box 158
Maywood, IL 60153-0158
708-343-0400

Parabellum
Rt. 1 Box 412
Dahlonega, GA 30533
706-864-8051
For BMWs.

Rifle
3140 El Camino Real
Atascadero, CA 93422
800-262-1237 (USA)
800-663-1016 (Canada)

Slipstreamer
10820 Mankato St. NE
Blaine, MN 55449
612-780-9757

Swanee/Pacifico
1550 S. Main
Milton, Freewater, OR
97862
800-547-8273
503-938-6174

Tracey Design
158 Mills St.
Collierville, TN 38017
901-853-0293

Attachments

Saeng TA
P.O. Box 1246
Columbus, NE 68602
800-TOURING
402-563-3444
Winglets and adhesive edging
to redirect turbulence.

ACKNOWLEDGMENTS

I'd like to thank my inspirations—all the great women motorcyclists who gave their time and energy to participate in this book. Most especially I'd like to thank my "Charter Girls"—the women who, starting in the spring of 1990, were with me and behind me 100 percent as I began this long journey of writing and riding: Becky Brown and Sandy Couture of Women in the Wind, Patty Mills of Women on Wheels, Dot Robinson of the Motor Maids, Jo Giovannoni of *Harley Women,* Courtney Caldwell of *American Woman Motorscene,* Fran Crane, Pam Cummings, Nancy Delgado, Amy Mullins, Catharine Rambeau, and the inimitable Bessie B. Stringfield, who I regret is no longer among us to see the results. Each of these women—and others too many to name!—shared their lives through words, photographs, and hospitality during repeated interviews over the years. A project of this scope relies also on networking. Many women recommended other great riders.

How do I adequately thank the love of my life, Frank Dusek? The moment we first laid eyes on each other in 1993 at a vintage bike show, when I parked my motorcycle on soft grass, immediately he knelt down to wedge a support under my kickstand to prevent my bike from sinking. After that day, he became my greatest support and has—in ways too numerous to count—prevented me from sinking. I could not have finished the book without his unwavering love, friendship, and encouragement.

And how do I adequately thank my mother, Marie Ferrar, for everything she has done? Mom has been a tremendous help in every way that a mother could be, and more. Among other tasks, my mother called her top-notch secretarial skills out of retirement to transcribe endless hours of interview tapes.

My dear friend Nelly Edmondson-Gupta was the first person to lay eyes on the draft, way back in its proposal stage, and several times thereafter. Nelly's insight and feedback helped me see with clarity what I needed to submit to Crown, and what I didn't. Like me, Nelly had once been a full-time freelance writer who toughed it in the toughest city on earth, New York, and she *understood everything* I went through. I thank her for her empathy whenever I needed an ear to bend. My other dear friends, Joanne Flaster, Barbara "The Source" Giannoccaro, Kathleen Kiss, and Ron "El Presidente" Mare, lent their ears and much encouragement, as did Inez Boyce, my wonderful, creative aunt.

My gratitude goes to Sharon Squibb, my editor at Crown, and Patricia Haskell, my literary agent, for their efforts on behalf of me and the book, for embracing my subject matter, having faith in me, and "hanging in" while I finished the project. And thank you to designer Kay Schuckhart and to Lara Webb, Crown's editorial assistant extraordinaire.

Several key people and companies supported me in a variety of ways at each stage of my journey. They include Steve Piehl and Dr. Martin Jack Rosenblum of the Harley-Davidson Motor Company, who graciously arranged for me to reprint some wonderful photos from H-D's Juneau Avenue Archives, among other favors. Thanks also to Kal Demitros of H-D, without whom I could never have made it to Sturgis in 1990.

I am grateful to BMW of North America, which has been supportive through the efforts of Scott Arigot, Rob Mitchell, and, years ago, Carla Harmon. My gratitude goes to Beverly St. Clair-Baird of the Motorcycle Industry Council and Discover Today's Motorcycling, Ed Youngblood of the American Motorcyclist Association, Diane Carter of Suzuki, Mel Moore of Kawasaki, Jim Bates of Honda,

Scott Heath of Yamaha, Sammy Yoo of Shoei Helmets, and to the folks at Progressive Suspension, Metzeler Tires, LMO Leather Outlet, Chase-Harper, and Eclipse luggage companies.

Special thanks to rider Denney Colt of the all-women rock band She-Wolff for gracing the cover of this book, and to her friend Brian Elder. Thanks also to Kathy Heller of Women on Wheels, Debbie Matthews and Elaine Ruff of the U.S. Women's Motocross League, Sue Slate and Gin Shear of the Women's Motorcyclist Foundation, Patti Carpenter of *Motorcycle Consumer News,* Joanna Strohn of the Motorcycling RoundTable, Rudy and Anne Tully Ruderman, and Gasper ("It's All Your Fault") Trama. And thank you to God, especially for the bit about "all things must pass."

To this great motorcycle community of ours, I have to say "thanks for the memories." Through our common passion, I met so many diverse people whom I would never have otherwise encountered. People who at first were complete strangers opened their homes to me when I needed places to stay during my journeys. I made some friendships that will last a lifetime, and I retain some priceless, and humorous, memories of encounters on the road.

One such was the summer afternoon in 1993 when I met Rusty Dennis, the woman portrayed by Cher in the film *Mask.* Rusty said, "C'mon. I'll take ya to the clubhouse and introduce ya to some folks that the movie characters were based on." I didn't know what to expect of a 1%er clubhouse in Southern California, which was probably a good thing. Inside, all I saw were a couple of folks chatting and a sign that warned, THROWING BUTTS ON THE FLOOR COULD BE CAUSE FOR YOU TO LEAVE.

Rusty blurted, "Where's the depravity?"

Best of all was the weekend in July of '93, which I spent with eighty-year-old Vera

Griffin. Her legacy lives in the stories and vintage photographs of herself and other Motor Maids, which she shared for this book. If you recall Chapter Two, to ride through a construction zone filled with rattlesnakes, Vera rode a hardtail with her feet up on the handlebars. Some tough cookie, this lady was.

In my working travels, I wanted to meet as many women as possible and spend as much time as possible with each one. To cover miles quickly, I rode the superslabs. As I was packing my bike to leave Vera's, I confessed that at interstate speeds, my bubble-shaped windshield directed turbulence at my head and caused an awful wind roar inside my helmet. Earplugs were no match for this misfire of progress.

For a second-and-a-half, Vera contemplated the difficulty I must be having riding a high-tech machine on paved roads. Then she said, "Powder puffs. Stuff 'em inside your helmet liner. Perhaps they will muffle the noise."

She rode with me to the border of her home state, Indiana, where we stopped at a mini-mall and bought the puffs. To the wide-eyed locals, we must have been as weird a sight in 1993 as the Van Buren sisters had been in 1916. Here was Vera, a senior citizen astride a Harley-Davidson Sportster. And here was me, a road-weary, thirty-something woman who could barely wedge her butt onto the Hawk GT's saddle, because the bike was piled so thoroughly with junk. And here was Vera and me, sitting in McDonald's, stuffing powder puffs in a motorcycle helmet.

Soon we said good-bye and rode our separate ways. Vera handled her machine with agility as she banked toward a curve and disappeared from my sight.

The puffs didn't work as hoped. Fed up, I pulled off the interstate, pulled out my tool kit, and removed the evil windshield. Then I pulled out a map, followed it to the nearest squiggly line, and remembered why I loved riding in the first place.

Notes

Introduction—Unsung Heroines: Turning a New Page in Herstory

1. "My Mother the Motorcyclist" copyright © 1978 Anne Tully Ruderman (unpublished).

One—"Everywoman" As a Rebel: The Voices of Women Who Ride

1. From a letter to *Harley Women* magazine, November/December 1993.
2. Kolb wrote *On the Perimeter* with Bill Stermer (New London, Mo.: Maverick, 1983).
3. From a letter to *Women on Wheels* magazine, September/October 1994.

Two—Incredible Women and Their Freedom Machines: A Chronicle, from the Turn of the Century to the Fifties

1. Frances E. Willard, *A Wheel Within a Wheel* (1895). Republished as *How I Learned to Ride the Bicycle: Reflections of an Influential 19th Century Woman* (Sunnyvale, Calif.: Fair Oaks Publishing, 1991).
2. Frederick A. Talbot, "Across America by Motor-Cycle: A Four-Thousand Mile Race Against Time," *Wide World,* American Edition (1906). The story reappeared as "Pioneer Tourist" in Ruth Calif's *The World on Wheels: An Illustrated History of the Bicycle and Its Relatives* (New York: Cornwall, 1983). W. C. Chadeayne was said to be the second man to cross the continent by motorcycle.
3. Bob Carpenter et al., "The History of Women in Motorcycling," *Road Rider* magazine, July 1985 and July 1990. These articles formed the basis of "Women in Motorcycling," the 1990 inaugural exhibit at the American Motorcyclist Association's Heritage Museum.

4. *Second to None: A Documentary History of American Women,* edited by Ruth Barnes Moynihan, Cynthia Russert, and Laurie Crumpacker (University of Nebraska Press, 1993).
5. Betty Friedan wrote about her suburban, prefeminist lifestyle in *It Changed My Life* (New York: W. W. Norton, 1976), which was excerpted in *Second to None: A Documentary History of American Women.*
6. Bob Carpenter et al., op. cit.
7. Bob and Patti Carpenter, "Theresa Wallach: A Brief Biography and Interview with One of Motorcycling's Most Remarkable Women," *Road Rider,* Vol. 8, No. 4, April 1977.
8. Ibid. Copyright © *Road Rider.* Reprinted with permission.
9. Gill's story ran in *The Enthusiast* in January 1994 with the title "Motorcycling to the Bowling Tournaments."

Three—We've Ridden a Long Way: A Chronicle, from the Sixties to the Present

1. Susan J. Douglas, *Where the Girls Are: Growing Up Female with the Mass Media* (New York: Times Books, 1994).
2. "The Female Factor: Mr. Cheap Tour Has a Problem with Girls," *Cycle,* April 1988.
3. From the AMA Heritage Museum's "Women in Motorcycling" exhibit.
4. Tommy Sandham, *The Castrol Book of the Scottish Six Days Trial* (Somerset, U.K.: Haynes, 1982).
5. Gail Sheehy, *Passages: Predictable Crises of Adult Life* (New York: Bantam, 1977).
6. *Harley Women,* November/December 1990.
7. Billye Nipper, "Maybe Rodney Dangerfield Should Ride a Motorcycle—I Get a Lot of Respect," *Women on Wheels,* July/August 1991.

FOUR—FROM BIKER CHIC TO B MOVIES: THE MOTORCYCLE WOMAN AS AN ICON TO GLAMORIZE—AND TO TRASH

1. Ann-Margret with Todd Gold, *Ann-Margret: My Story* (New York: G. P. Putnam's Sons, 1994).
2. Caressa French, *Hog Heaven* (Freedom, Calif.: Crossing Press, 1994).
3. Woody Hockswender, "Born to Be Wild, but Feminine," *The New York Times,* July 16, 1991.
4. John Marchese, "Forever Harley," *The New York Times,* October 17, 1993.
5. Ann-Margret, *Ann-Margret.*
6. According to a long-term participant-observation study, "Women in Outlaw Motorcycle Gangs," by Columbus B. Hopper and Johnny Moore, published in the *Journal of Contemporary Ethnography,* January 4, 1990.

FIVE—ZOOM AND THE ART OF MOTORCYCLE MADNESS: WOMEN WHO DRAG-RACE HARLEYS

1. Race officials disagreed with the cause of the accident, claiming there was no oil.

SIX—ROAD WARRIORS: WOMEN WHO RACE SUPERBIKES

1. Male road racers are often husbands and fathers. Over the decades, a few men have suffered disabling injuries and a few have died. At this writing, there were no reported incidents of permanent disability or death among female road racers in this country. Some would argue that women race more conservatively than men, thus lowering their risks.

SEVEN—COWGIRLS ON WHEELS: WOMEN WHO RACE MOTOCROSS

1. Chris Kallfelz, "Class of '94—Loretta Lynn's: The Past, Present and Future of Motocross," *American Motorcyclist,* November 1994.
2. Mariah Burton Nelson, *The Stronger Women Get, the More Men Love Football—Sexism and the American Culture of Sports* (New York: Harcourt Brace, 1994).

TEN—ABOUT BIKES: A PRIMER ON CHOOSING A FIRST MOTORCYCLE, WITH TIPS ON LOWERING RIDE HEIGHT

1. Lawrence Grodsky, "Stayin' Safe: Gender Bender," *Rider,* October 1992.

ELEVEN—BASIC MOTORCYCLE SAFETY AND RISK MANAGEMENT, WITH TIPS ON CHOOSING PROTECTIVE GEAR

1. The full title of the study is *Motorcycle Accident Cause Factors and Identification of Countermeasures,* by Dr. Harry Hurt et al.
2. In 1993, there were twenty-four hundred fatalities. Nearly half of all fatalities are among riders under age twenty-five. Friday-night crashes are three times more likely to be lethal.
3. From the *Experienced RiderCourse Participant's Handbook* (Irvine, Calif.: Motorcycle Safety Foundation, 1992). Reprinted with permission.

INDEX

Science in Ancient Egypt

Geraldine Woods

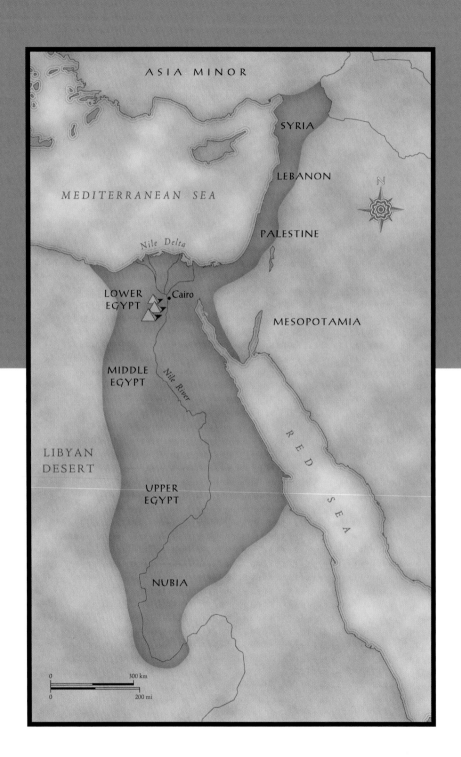

ASIA MINOR

SYRIA

LEBANON

MEDITERRANEAN SEA

PALESTINE

Nile Delta

LOWER
EGYPT   • Cairo

MESOPOTAMIA

MIDDLE
EGYPT   *Nile River*

LIBYAN
DESERT

UPPER
EGYPT

R E D

S E A

NUBIA

0   300 km

0   200 mi

Science in Ancient Egypt

Geraldine Woods

Science of the Past

FRANKLIN WATTS

A Division of Grolier Publishing
New York • London • Hong Kong • Sydney
Danbury, Connecticut

Photographs ©: Ancient Art & Architecture Collection Ltd.: 10 (Mary Jelliffe), 49 (Mary Jelliffe), 6, 30, 44, 45, 46 (Ronald Sheridan), 24 (John P. Stevens); Archive Photos: 17; Art Resource: 52, 55 (Werner Forman Archive, Schimmel Collection, New York); Bendick Association: 58; Boltin Picture Library: 27, 28, 56; Corbis-Bettmann: 9, 26, 31, 47; Erich Lessing/Art Resource: 42, 48 top; Folio, Inc.: 13 (Ira Wexler); Giraudon/Art Resource: 48 bottom; The Metropolitan Museum of Art, Rogers Fund, 1948: 41; Peter Arnold Inc.: 12 (Malcom S. Kirk); Photo Researchers: 11, 25 (Carolyn Brown), 53 (Roemer-Pelizaeus Museum, Hildesheim); Photri: 32; Reuters/Mohamed el-Dakhakhny/Archive Photos: 54; Scala/Art Resource: 15, 51; Superstock, Inc.: cover (Egyptian National Museum, Cairo, Egypt/ET Archive) 7, 40; Tony Stone Images: 50 (Rex A. Butcher), 38 (Charles Thatcher); Visuals Unlimited: 8 (Les Christman).

Map created by XNR Productions Inc.

Illustrations by Drew-Brook-Cormack Associates

Library of Congress Cataloging-in-Publication Data

Woods, Geraldine
    Science in ancient Egypt / Geraldine Woods
    p. cm. (Science of the past)
    Includes bibliographical references and index.
    Summary: Discusses the achievements of the ancient Egyptians in science, mathematics, astronomy, agriculture, and technology.
    ISBN 0-531-20341-7 (lib. bdg.)   0-531-15915-9 (pbk.)
    1. Science—Egypt—History—Juvenile literature. 2. Engineering—Egypt—History—Juvenile literature. 3. Science, Ancient—Juvenile literature. [1. Science—Egypt—History. 2. Technology—Egypt—History. 3. Science, Ancient.] I. Title.
II. Series.
Q127.E3W66   1998
509'.32—dc21   97-649
                                                 CIP
                                                 AC

CONTENTS

Ancient Egypt developed along the
shores of the Nile River.

The Nile River winds through more than 4,000 miles (6,400 km) of Africa before emptying into the Mediterranean Sea. About 10,000 years ago, the Egyptian civilization began developing along a narrow strip of land on either side of the Nile. Beyond this strip lay vast desert. The Nile made it possible for a great civilization to grow in an area with a dry, harsh climate.

For most of the year, the Nile flows peacefully to the sea. But each summer, when heavy rains fall, the river rises and rises until it floods. Before modern dams were built, the Nile overflowed its banks every year.

The rich soil along the banks of the Nile was ideal for growing grains such as wheat and barley.

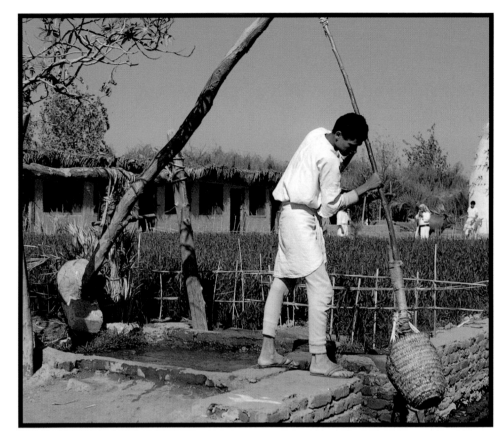

The early Egyptians used a *shaduf,* a long pole balanced on a wooden beam with a weight at one end and a bucket at the other. to move water from the canals to the fields.

The floods watered Egyptian farmers' crops and enriched the soil with *silt* from the river.

The earliest farmers had no choice but to wait patiently for the Nile to flood. But then, about 7,000 years ago, the Egyptians invented the world's first irrigation system. They dug canals to direct water from the river to distant fields. Later, the Egyptians began to build reservoirs to hold the water, so that they would have water to use during the dry season.

Besides being among the first societies to grow crops, the Egyptians were also one of the first groups of people to tame animals and breed them for work or food. They raised oxen, cattle, sheep, goats, pigs, and

This mural from a 3,500-year-old tomb shows Egyptans plowing their fields, sowing seeds, and harvesting crops.

donkeys. They kept antelopes, geese, and ducks for meat and collected honey and wax from beehives.

The ancient Egyptians knew how to preserve animal meat by drying it in the sun or salting it. They were the first people to make leather from animal hides. They even brewed beer and wine from the plants they grew. All of this was possible because the Nile supplied the Egyptians with a source of water and fertile land.

The Nile also inspired early Egyptian science. To predict the flooding of the Nile, the Egyptians made a calendar. To measure the flood, they created mathematical formulas. To record their findings, they learned to write on *papyrus.* To sail on the Nile, they designed boats.

Ancient Egypt's success as a civilization can also be attributed to the deserts that surrounded it. Because crossing these deserts was difficult, Egypt was relatively free from attack by other groups of people. Long periods of peace gave the Egyptians time to concentrate on building their society and their pyramids.

The Egyptians may have been the first people to make wine and brew beer.

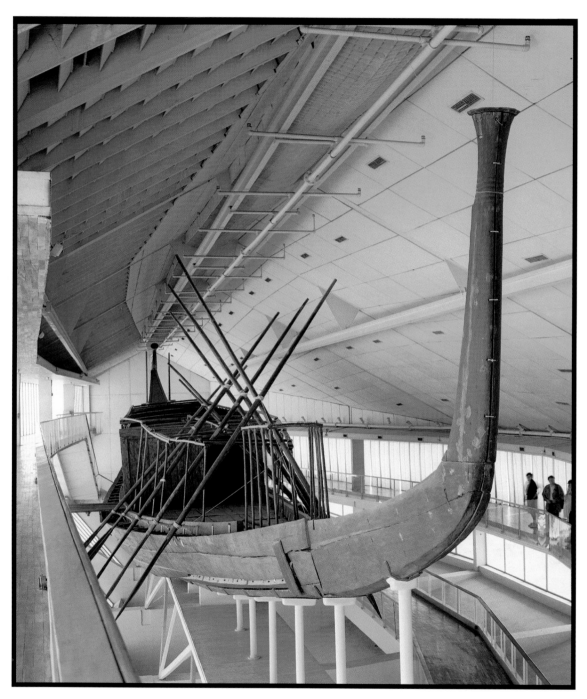

This ancient Egyptian boat was
intended to provide transportation
for the pharaoh after death.

chapter 2

Building the Pyramids

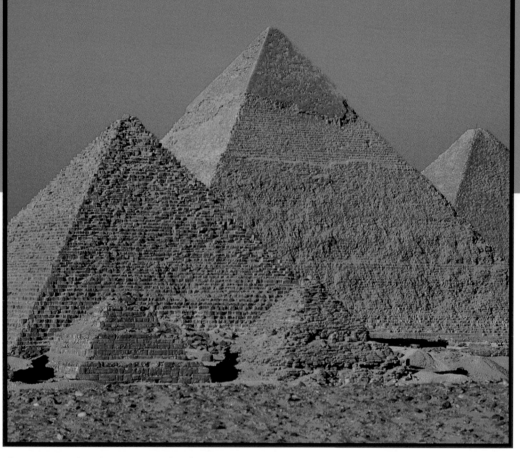

The pyramids of Giza were built
about 4,500 years ago.

The Egyptian pyramids were built as tombs for *pharaohs*—Egypt's rulers—and other nobles. King Zoser's step pyramid, was built about 4,500 years ago. It was the first large building ever constructed entirely of stone. The Great Pyramid of Khufu is the largest pyramid ever built. Its base is as large as ten football fields. Each of the 2,250,000 stone blocks used to build the pyramid weighs close to 5,000 pounds (2,300 kg).

Zoser's pyramid, which is also called the Step Pyramid, was the first pyramid ever built.

It's hard to imagine how anyone could construct something as large as a pyramid, even in modern times. And yet the Egyptians did it with just four simple tools-the lever, the inclined plane, the wedge, and the pulley.

Preparing the Building Site

Before construction could begin, workers cleared sand and gravel away from the chosen site until they reached the desert's solid-rock floor. The ground had to be perfectly level—even a slight difference in height between one side of the pyramid and another could cause the entire structure to come crashing down.

Workers used A-shaped tools to make sure the ground was level.

To make sure the ground was level, the Egyptians may have used a wooden frame shaped like an A. By marking the center of the crossbar and hanging a weighted cord from the top of the A, the builders could determine whether a surface was perfectly level.

The builders may have also dug ditches crisscrossing the base area and then filled them with water. Since free-flowing water always forms a flat surface, the workers knew that the waterline was perfectly level.

Crisscross channels were built across the pyramid site and filled with water. The waterline was used to determine whether the ground was level.

After draining the ditches, laborers cut the ground down to the water-lines and filled the ditches with rubble.

Meanwhile, architects were drawing plans on clay tablets. A pyramid appears to be a solid mass of stone, but it actually contains a number of tunnels and rooms as well as a passage from the outside. One room will house the pharaoh's *sarcophagus*, or coffin. Some pyramids also have rooms for the pharaoh's relatives and possessions. To confuse robbers, many pyramids have false tunnels and empty rooms.

All mummies were placed inside a sarcophagus.

Capstone

Airshafts

Pharaoh's chamber

Grand gallery

Ascending corridor

Entrance

Shaft

Chamber

Descending Corridor

Inside the Great Pyramid, which still stands today, are three burial chambers, a gallery, and a series of passages and shafts.

The ramp between the steps inside this pyramid corridor was used to slide the pharaoh's sarcophagus to its final resting place.

To make the pyramid's underground rooms and tunnels, the workers probably worked with *caissons*—large hollow tubes made of brick and stone. Each caisson was placed at the entrance of a tunnel and pushed forward while the workers inside removed dirt and rock from the caisson's path. The caisson's strong walls kept the tunnel from caving in. Laborers following behind the caisson reinforced the sides of the tunnel with stone. Caissons are still used to construct tunnels today.

The rock used to build pyramids came from quarries. After each stone was marked and cut, workers raised it onto a wooden sled and pulled it to the Nile. The blocks were loaded onto flat-bottomed boats and transported to the building site.

At the Quarry

The outer surfaces of the pyramids were covered with pure white lime-stone. The inner rooms were usually made of granite, a harder stone. Both types of rock came from quarries on the east side of the Nile. Metal chisels and saws, wooden mallets and wedges, and stone hammers strapped to wooden handles were the only tools Egyptian workers had to cut the millions of stone blocks needed to build each pyramid.

Before they began cutting the rock, the workers drew marks to out-line each block. Then with chisels and mallets they chipped small cracks into the stone. Next, the workers hammered wooden wedges into the cracks and soaked the area with water. As the water was absorbed by the dry wood, the wedges swelled and split the limestone rock. The Egyptians may have also heated the cracks and then cooled them sud-denly with water. The fast temperature change split the rock.

Once the gigantic blocks were cut, they had to be transported to the building site. To raise each block, the workers probably tied ropes of palm fiber around it and then tilted one side with a lever. The Egyptians may also have used a *weight arm* made of heavy timber. This tool had a central post and two arms, one short and one long. Workers slipped a sling under each block and then attached the sling to the tool's short arm. Small rocks placed on the long arm balanced the weight of the block. When the long arm was tipped, the block rose.

As soon as the massive block was lifted off the ground, a wooden sled was pushed underneath it. A team of workers pulled the sled out of the quarry along a path of logs—the logs kept the sled from sinking into the sand.

At the Building Site

As soon as the blocks were unloaded, masons cut them to the exact size needed for the pyramid. Workers cut away the larger bumps with saws or chisels and mallets. Then they smoothed the surface with rough stone or a piece of extremely hard rock.

Every surface of the block was tested with a *boning rod* to make sure it was perfectly level. The boning rod had three identical pegs, and a cord was attached to the tops of two pegs. Two workers rested these pegs on the stone and stretched the cord tightly. Another worker moved the third peg back and forth across the block's surface. If the surface was even, the third peg fit perfectly between the stone and the cord.

The workers used wooden right angles to make sure the corners were square. They knocked away extra rock with chisels or pieces of flint.

It must have taken days of backbreaking labor to make sure every block was exactly the right shape.

Finally, the workers dragged the stone blocks for the first layer into place. Ramps of mud and sand were built along the sides of the pyramids so that the blocks could be dragged to higher layers. Workers probably sprinkled water or oil over the stones to make them slide more easily. The blocks fit together so perfectly that no cement was needed. Not even a knife can be inserted between most blocks!

A surveyor checked that the corners of each layer were perfectly square. A *plumb line*—a cord attached to a pointed stone—was used to make sure that each layer rose at the correct angle. The cord was lowered until the stone just touched the earth. When it stopped swinging, it always made a right angle with the ground.

At the building site, the blocks were cut to the correct size and the surfaces were smoothed out. After making sure a block was perfectly square, workers dragged it up ramps of mud and sand. The block was then pushed into position.

The Egyptians placed a *capstone*—a pointed stone with a plug on the bottom—at the very top of every pyramid. The plug fit into a hole in the layer underneath. Once the capstone was in place, stoneworkers polished the outside of the pyramid. As they moved down toward the base, other workers removed the dirt ramps.

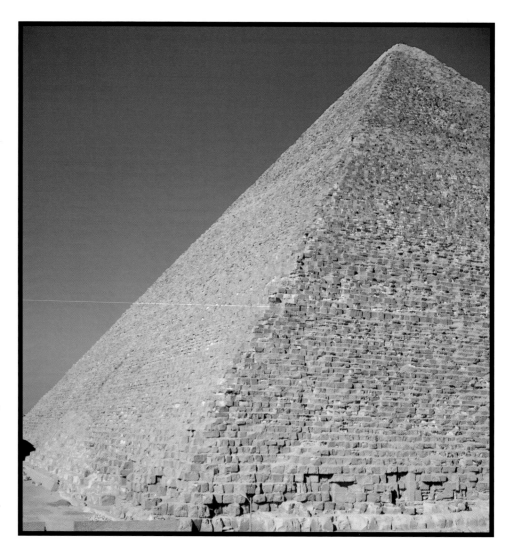

Thousands of years after they were built, Egypt's pyramids are still standing. Modern engineers and architects are amazed and fascinated by these monumental structures.

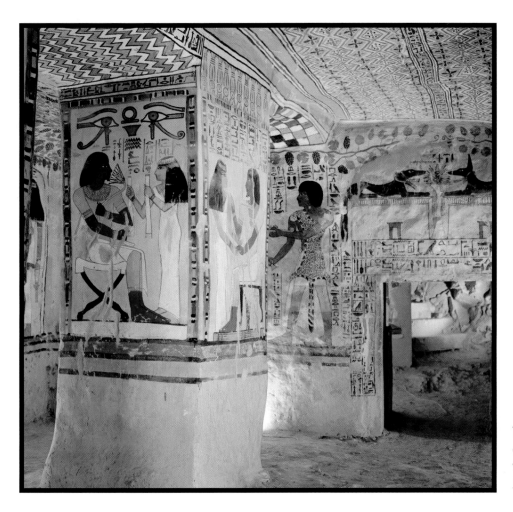

The inside walls of many tombs were covered with beautiful paintings.

The Pharaoh's Treasures

Pyramids contained treasures for the dead to use during their eternal life. Some tombs contain miniature statues of workers. The little figures—busy at tiny bakeries, butcher shops, and workrooms—were supposed to spare the dead from labor. Tomb paintings and a variety of *artifacts* provide important clues about the ancient Egyptians' lifestyle.

Limestone sculpture
of a servant grinding
grain

The pottery tells us that the Egyptians knew how to use a kiln to bake clay objects. The bricks reveal that the Egyptians knew how to sun-dry a mixture of mud and straw. (Our word "adobe" comes from the Egyptian word for brick.)

Tombs were also supplied with a variety of fine linen and wooden furniture. Egyptian women spun fibers of the flax plant into fine thread and wove it into cloth on flat looms shaped like bed frames. The weavers used sticks to pull the cross-threads. Carpenters built the wooden furniture with metal saws and hammers, chisels, and nails of copper or wood. They smoothed the wood with flat slabs of sandstone and sometimes glued expensive wood to cheaper material; this was the first *veneer.*

A chair recovered from Tutankhamen's tomb

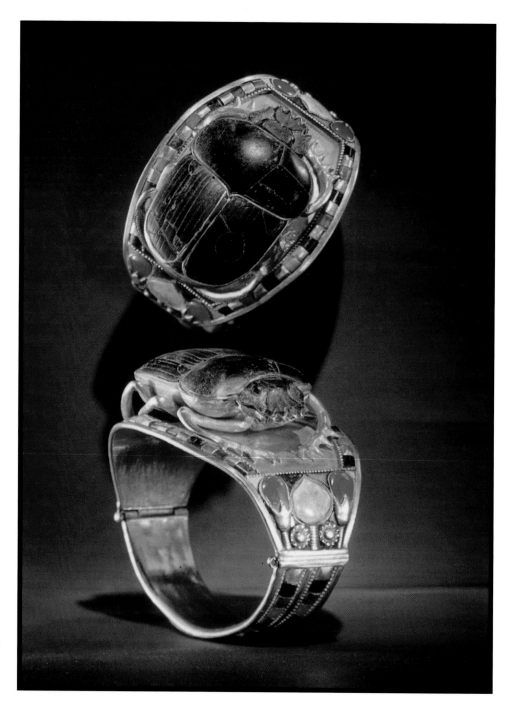

These bracelets were
found in the tomb of
the pharaoh
Tutankhamen.

Pharaoh Khufu had two full-sized boats in his tomb. The Egyptians were skilled boat-builders, and created the earliest known sail. Boats were made of reeds lashed together and, later, of wood. The Egyptians dug one of the first canals to bypass rapids, so they could sail farther up the Nile and obtain treasures for themselves and for their eternal tombs.

The Egyptians were fine glassmakers. They did not know how to blow glass, but they shaped it by twisting thin rods. They also filled bags with sand and dipped them into melted glass. When the glass hardened, the bags of sand were removed.

Egyptians fashioned jewelry from glass, metal, and *faience*—a material made from powdered stone. The Egyptians knew how to make bronze—a mixture of copper and tin—and they molded silver and gold into various shapes. A dagger made of iron from a meteorite was discovered in Pharaoh Tutankhamen's tomb.

chapter 3
Early Egyptian Mathematics

Egyptians used math to keep track
of how much grain they produced.

About 3,500 years ago, Ahmes the Moonborn wrote a book called *How to Obtain Information About All Things Mysterious and Dark.* The "mysterious and dark" subject matter was mathematics. Ahmes' book explained how to multiply and divide fractions and how to calculate the area of a circle, square, and triangle or the volume of some solids.

Although this arithmetic would be simple for most of today's fifth-graders, it was a great discovery to most Egyptians. The little math they did know was usually related to their jobs. Surveyors, for example, could measure a right angle, and traders could add the weights and values of their goods.

Mathematical theory was studied only by people who held high positions in Egyptian society. Government officials needed to know math to calculate taxes and keep track of land ownership. Priests used it to predict the actions of the Nile god Hapi.

As far back as 5,000 years ago, the Egyptians could predict how the Nile's flood would

A representation of Hapi, the god of the Nile

Nilometers, such as this one in Cairo, are used to record the Nile's yearly flood.

affect them. Using *nilometers*, stone gauges with lines to measure how much the river rose, the priests could determine whether there would be a good harvest. They always hoped for a nilometer reading of about 25 feet (7.6 m), which meant the Nile would bring just enough water for the crops. A higher water level meant dangerous flooding, and a lower mark on the nilometer meant a poor harvest.

Counting

Mathematics depends on a system of counting. Early Egyptians probably chipped notches on wood or stone to record the passing of time. Later, symbols were created to stand for different numbers. Like most number systems, the Egyptian method of counting gave special importance to the number ten and multiples of ten, probably because people have ten fingers.

1	I	10	∩ (head)
2	II	100	(coiled rope)
3	III	1,000	(flower)
4	IIII	10,000	(pointing finger)
5	III II	100,000	(tadpole)
6	III III	1,000,000	(surprised man)
7	III IIII		
8	IIII IIII		
9	IIII IIIII		

In the counting system we use today, the position of the number, or *place value*, is very important. To us, the *3* in *321* means three hundreds, while the *3* in *123* means three units. Place value didn't matter to the Egyptians because they used different symbols for hundreds, tens, and units. They had no symbol for zero, although a blank space was occasionally used to represent the lack of a number. This is how the ancient Egyptians wrote 1,492:

Without place value, arithmetic is very complicated. When we add 765 and 321, for example, we add the numbers one column at a time—5 + 1, 6 + 2, and 7 + 3—to arrive at 1,086. The Egyptians' numerical symbols could not be broken down into smaller values that were easier to handle.

The Egyptians understood only fractions that were "one part of" the whole, and had a special symbol that meant "one part of." Values like $\frac{1}{7}$ and $\frac{1}{10}$ made sense to them, but $\frac{3}{7}$, $\frac{6}{7}$, and $\frac{9}{10}$ did not. The only way they knew how to write three-sevenths was $\frac{1}{7} + \frac{1}{7} + \frac{1}{7}$ or $\frac{1}{4} + \frac{1}{7} + \frac{1}{28}$.

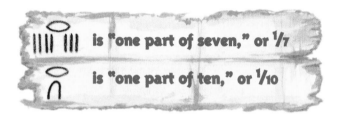

is "one part of seven," or $\frac{1}{7}$

is "one part of ten," or $\frac{1}{10}$

Measuring

The earliest Egyptian system of measurements was based on the body of the pharaoh. A *cubit* was the length of his forearm—from the elbow to the tip of his middle finger. The width of his palm and the width of four fingers held together were also used.

When measuring grain, the Egyptians used symbols based on the eye of the god Horus. A surveyor would draw Horus's eyebrow to represent the fraction $\frac{1}{8}$ or the eyeball to represent $\frac{1}{4}$.

The problem with this system was that all human bodies are different. Some people have fatter fingers, bigger hands, and longer arms than other people. The Egyptians soon realized that they needed a standard measurement system.

Official measuring sticks were created, although the old body-part names were kept. For example 1 cubit equaled 7 palms, and 1 palm equaled 4 digits (fingers). In the measuring systems we use today, 1 yard equals 3 feet and 1 foot equals 12 inches, 1 meter equals 100 centimeters and 1 centimeter equals 10 millimeters.

Egyptians created a system of weights based on a single grain of wheat. Later, standard stone weights were used.

Arithmetic

The Egyptians knew how to add and subtract. They could also multiply and divide, but their methods were very different from ours. To multiply 23 by 13, for example, the Egyptians made two columns of numbers. The first column always began with 1, and the second began with the number to be multiplied (in this case 23). Each line of the columns doubled the line before:

1	23
2	46
4	92
8	184.

Next, the Egyptians chose numbers from the first column that added up to the multiplier:

$$1 + 4 + 8 = 13.$$

Lastly, they added each number's partner:

$$23 + 92 + 184 = 299.$$

In other words, they added 1 × 23, 4 × 23, and 8 × 23. The answer was 13 × 23, or 299.

Division was also done with columns. To divide 48 by 8, for example, the columns began with 1 and 8 and doubled on each line:

1	8
2	16
4	32
8	64.

By trial and error the Egyptians would add the numbers in the second column to find numbers that totaled 48. In this case, 16 + 32 = 48. The answer to the division problem is the sum of their partners, 2 + 4, or 6. In effect, the Egyptians were calculating the answer to 16 ÷ 8 and 32 ÷ 8. If the two numbers in the second column could not be added to total the number being divided, the numbers that gave the closest total were used and the remainders were written as fractions.

Area, Angles, and Algebra

Because the Nile wiped out the boundary markers of each farmer's fields every year, surveyors had to be able to redraw the property lines. Surveyors, also called "rope stretchers," probably worked with a set of knotted ropes. For simple measurements, the surveyors laid out ropes in a straight line. Early on, the Egyptians discovered that a triangle measuring 3, 4, 5 or 5, 12, 13 would always include a right angle. By sighting with a right angle and constructing an imaginary triangle, surveyors could determine distances.

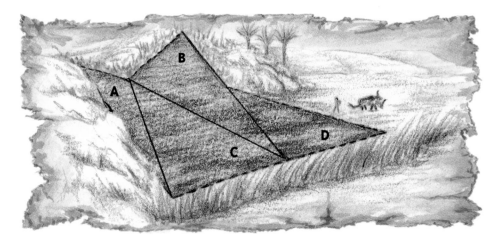

Egyptians measured the area of irregularly shaped fields by dividing it into triangles, finding the area of each triangle, and then adding all the areas together.

The amount of taxes a landowner paid was based on the area of each field, so government officials became skilled at computing the area of squares, rectangles, triangles, and circles. Most fields did not fit these shapes exactly, so irregular fields were divided into triangles. The area of the field in the figure above could be calculated by adding together the area of the triangles labeled A, B, C, and D.

The Egyptians even knew some basic *algebra*, a type of math you will probably learn in high school. In algebra, problems are often written in the form of *equations*, in which letters of the alphabet represent the unknown quantities. The goal of algebra is to figure out what number the letter stands for. For example, in the equation $2 \times x = 12$, the goal is to find out what number x stands for. In this case, x stands for the number 6 because $2 \times 6 = 12$.

Evidence for the development of algebra was found in an Egyptian document copied by Ahmes the Moonborn about 3,600 years ago. *Archaeologists* have also found ancient Egyptian scrolls containing problems with some unknown numbers.

37

chapter 4

Astronomy and Time

The Egyptians' earliest calendar was
based on the phases of the moon.

Early Egyptians probably measured time by the most obvious change in their lives—the flooding of the Nile. Before long, however, they turned to *astronomy*, the study of objects outside Earth's atmosphere.

The brightest object in our night sky is the moon. In just 29½ days the moon grows until it is a full round circle and then shrinks until it disappears completely. Each time a "new" moon appeared, the Egyptians began a new month. Twelve months were counted as 1 year. An Egyptian moon-year had 354 days. After several years, however, the Egyptians noticed that the Nile did not always flood during the same month. They could not use their calendar to predict accurately when the annual flood would occur.

The Egyptians solved this problem about 2,300 years ago. They noticed that Sirius, the brightest star in the sky, acted strangely. Every once in a while, the star vanished. When it reappeared, it was visible for just a few minutes at dawn. After that, Sirius stayed in the sky for a longer period of time each day, until it disappeared again. And Sirius always returned just before the Nile flooded.

Observing Sirius's movements allowed the Egyptians to predict the flooding of the Nile and prepare for the planting season. So the Egyptians made a new calendar based on Sirius. It was a good choice because Sirius' cycle is 365¼ days long—exactly the length of a year. (The length of a year is actually determined by the amount of time it takes Earth to revolve once around the sun.) With this new calendar, each month always came during the same season of the year.

The Egyptians subdivided their year into 12 months, each with 30 days, for a total of 360 days. So what happened to the other 5¼ days? The 5 days were added in as holidays and their origin was explained by a myth. According to this legend, the god Thoth had played a dice game with the moon and won some of its light. Thoth had then fashioned this light into the 5 extra days. This brought the yearly total to 365 days. Even though the Egyptian calendar was still one-fourth of a day short, it was the most accurate calendar in the ancient world.

The Egyptians also charted the movement of other stars across the sky. (Of course it is Earth that moves, not the stars, but this fact was not discovered until thousands of years later.) Egyptian astronomers tracked thirty-six specially chosen stars, called the "Indestructibles," with a forked stick and an attached cord. When the cord hung at a right angle to the ground, the astronomer could sight the stars through the forked stick and record their changing positions. The Egyptians eventually named the weeks of their calendar after the "Indestructibles."

The Egyptian astronomers grouped some stars into constellations named after familiar animals like crocodiles, oxen,

According to an Egyptian myth, Thoth, the god of wisdom and writing, won some of the moon's light in a dice game.

40

This painting on the ceiling of a
tomb includes information about the
movement of the stars and planets.

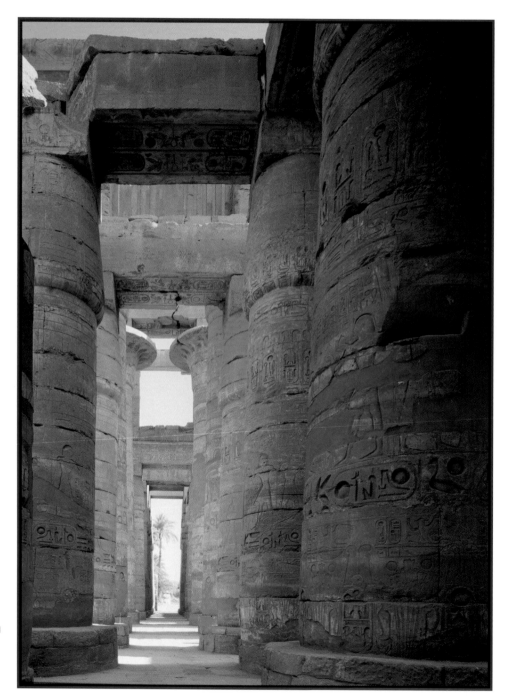

The Temple of Amon was completed during the rule of Ramses II.

and hippos. A group of stars that seemed to revolve around the North Pole and never set were called "The Imperishables." The Egyptians also observed Jupiter, Saturn, Venus, Mars, and perhaps Mercury. These planets were called "The Unwearied."

Astronomy and Architecture

The four sides of a pyramid always faced exactly north, south, east, and west. How did the architects manage to position the pyramids so precisely? It is possible that, before construction began, the architects built a tall circle of stone at the center of the site and asked a priest to mark the positions where a specific star rose in the evening and set in the morning. Halfway between these two marks was true north.

The ancient builders also positioned other structures according to the heavens. The Temple of Amon at Karnak has a long line of columns. An observer looking along this line at dawn on Midsummer Day will see the rising sun directly between the last two columns. At the pyramid of Khufu, the North Star can be sighted through an airshaft.

The Egyptians could also determine direction using the sun. They knew that the sun rises in the southeast in winter and in the northeast in summer. They marked the direction of the rising sun on Midsummer Day and Midwinter Day—the halfway point of each season. By halving the angle formed by these two lines, they found due east. A simpler, but less exact method, involved building a tall column. At noon, the shadow of the column points north. East and west can be found by crossing the shadow with a right-angle line.

Clocks and Timekeeping

The sun's shadow was also used to mark the passage of hours. The Egyptians' shadow clock had one flat arm and one upright arm. The upright arm was positioned to face due east at dawn. The upright arm cast a shadow on the flat arm. The longest shadow marked the sixth hour before noon; the shortest shadow marked midday. At that time, the clock was turned around. As the afternoon progressed, the shadow grew longer and longer.

The Egyptians also used water clocks. The simplest one was just a large bowl with a hole in the bottom. As the water flowed out of the bowl, hour lines became visible on the side of the bowl. The lines had to be carefully placed to allow for sloping sides of the bowl and the change in flow rate as the bowl empties. (A bowl filled to the top leaks more quickly than a bowl that is almost empty.) Another type of water clock counted hours as the water flowed into the bowl.

This shadow clock was used by Egyptians who lived more than 3,000 years ago.

44

A water clock
recovered from the
Karnak Temple

Egyptian hours were made by dividing both day and night into twelve equal parts. The length of a day changes with the seasons, and so does the length of one-twelfth of a day. In winter, days are shorter than in summer. As a result, the twelve winter-day hours were shorter than the twelve summer-day hours. The opposite is true of winter-night hours. Water clocks had markings for both summer and winter. The winter night was fourteen fingers of water tall, while the summer night was only twelve fingers tall.

chapter5

Ancient Egyptian Medicine

Ancient Egyptians ground leaves, stems, and roots to make remedies for a variety of illnesses.

46

When you are sick, you might visit a family doctor or a specialist. A pharaoh had the same choice. Among his doctors were the "Palace Eye Physician" and the "Palace Stomach-Bowel Physician." Chances are the pharaoh received good care—the Egyptians had the best medical knowledge in the ancient world.

Making a Mummy

The Egyptians believed that a preserved body could go on to another world with the spirit of the dead person. This religious idea may have inspired the Egyptians to *mummify* bodies—to preserve them forever.

Embalmers required 70 days to prepare a body for burial. They chanted prayers and spells as they wrapped each body.

Bronze knives like this one were used by Egyptian embalmers.

Because dry material is less likely to decay, the Egyptians removed as much water as possible from the body. First, a priest removed the heart, liver, and other organs. The body cavity and organs were washed with wine. (The alcohol in the wine is a natural germ killer.) The body and its organs were packed in natron (a type of salt) for 2 months and then treated with resin (a sealant) and wax. The organs were placed in jars and the body was wrapped in linen. Despite this careful process, however, the dry Egyptian air was what actually made mummification possible.

After a person's internal organs were removed, they were stored in canopic jars.

This engraving, which shows two men making an herbal remedy, is about 5,000 years old.

Early Druggists

Modern parents sometimes give castor oil to their children as a cure for an upset stomach. Thousand of years ago the Egyptians chewed castor berries for the same ailment. These berries were just one remedy in the ancient Egyptian "medicine cabinet." Drugs were also made from many other plants and spices such as anise, cumin, and poppy flowers. The Egyptians even made medicines of copper, sodium bicarbonate, and other minerals. Parts or all of various animals—birds, pigs, crocodiles, and ants—were also prescribed. Creams and ointments were created with goose grease, honey, or animal fat.

Poppies were used in a number of Egyptian remedies.

How effective were these remedies? Some were better than others. Patients with night blindness were probably helped by eating the liver their doctor prescribed. However, the treatment for nearsightedness (honey, lead, and water from a pig's eye injected into the patient's ear) was useless. Still, the Egyptians did discover a remarkable number of drugs.

Cranky babies were given pods of the poppy plant mixed with "fly dirt which is on the wall." Poppies supply opium, a calming drug. Hartshorn (powdered deer antler) was used to treat many ailments. Today doctors prescribe spirits of hartshorn—an ammonia mixture—for several conditions. Earaches were treated with a mixture of salt and hot wine. Today, eardrops contain alcohol and boric powder. The Egyptians also used acacia and honey as a form of birth control. When mixed, these two substances form lactic acid, an ingredient in some modern birth control products.

The First Medical Books

While mummification taught the Egyptians about the structure of the body's internal organs, the Egyptians also learned about medicine from the living. They noted symptoms and experimented with drugs and treatments. Successful healing methods were taught to new generations of doctors, often by means of papyrus scrolls. These were the world's first medical textbooks.

One ancient Egyptian scroll lists heart conditions and another discusses diseases of women and children. A "first aid" scroll explains how to treat a variety of injuries, and "recipe scrolls" give directions for making medicines. On a scroll, referred to as *The Book of Surgery*, forty-eight medical conditions are listed by body part from the head down. This scroll, which

Egyptian doctors kept track of remedies and procedures on papyrus scrolls. Many of these scrolls still exist today.

is about 3,550 years old, is actually a copy of another document written almost 1,000 years earlier.

The Book of Surgery includes instructions for examination and diagnosis of a wide variety of medical conditions. According to the scroll, some conditions are considered treatable and others as "not to be treated" because they are hopeless. In the case of a wound above the eyebrow, the doctor is directed to stitch the wound and place fresh meat on it. After the first day, a mixture of grease and honey is the prescribed treatment.

Egyptian doctors knew how to set broken bones. They sawed through the skull with copper tools to treat head wounds and opened the skin with straight knives similar to modern scalpels. They were among the first to use bandages and compresses. They also used several types of forceps, or grasping tools. They expected cuts to become infected (they had no antibiotics), but knew that they could tie the edges of a wound together to reduce scarring. One scroll even discusses skin grafts—transferring skin from one part of the body to another.

Hesi Re, a high official, is shown here holding a staff and scepter, which were considered symbols of authority.

Dentistry

Hesi Re, who lived about 4,600 years ago, was one of the world's first dentists. As the "Chief of Toothers and Physicians," he was probably a very busy man. Judging from mummies recovered from tombs, the teeth of ancient Egyptians were often infected or worn down to the gum line. This damage may have been caused by sand and dirt in the food they ate.

Most Egyptians ground their grain between stones and kept it in open storage bins where it probably picked up sand and dirt.

The first known set of "false" teeth

Luckily, the Egyptians knew how to fill cavities and treat infections. Archeologists have found a 3,800-year-old Egyptian jawbone with a hole under a molar. The jaw was probably pierced so that the pus from a dental infection could drain out. A 4,500-year-old Egyptian skull has the earliest known set of false teeth. Held together by gold wire, the false teeth appear to have been anchored to a hole drilled in another tooth.

Medical Mistakes

While Egyptian doctors could identify many of the body's organs, they did not always realize how the parts worked in living people. During mummification, for example, the brain was discarded because it was considered

During mummification, the corpse's skull was sawed in half, so the brain could be removed.

unimportant. Although the Egyptians knew that the pulse and heartbeat were related, they had only one word for muscles and blood vessels and believed that both were responsible for movement. They also thought that blood vessels carried many different substances—air, water, blood, semen, urine, and solid wastes.

The Egyptians mixed science, religion, and magic when they practiced medicine. A doctor would often recite spells over a clay statue, draw magic circles, or prescribe spells. Certain words had to be recited every few hours—just like doses of medicine! Many were prayers to the goddess Isis, who had once healed the god Osiris.

Sometimes doctors prescribed chants to encourage positive thinking. Someone with eye disease, for example, might say, "The crocodile is weak and powerless." According to Egyptian myth, the crocodile stole the eye of the sun. At other times the disease itself was addressed. A spell for the common cold told the "poison nose" and "son of poison nose" to flow out and begone. It's no wonder ancient Egyptians had no luck treating colds—modern medical science can't cure them either!

The ancient Egyptian goddess Isis, seated on a throne

chapter 6
What Ancient Egypt Gave Us

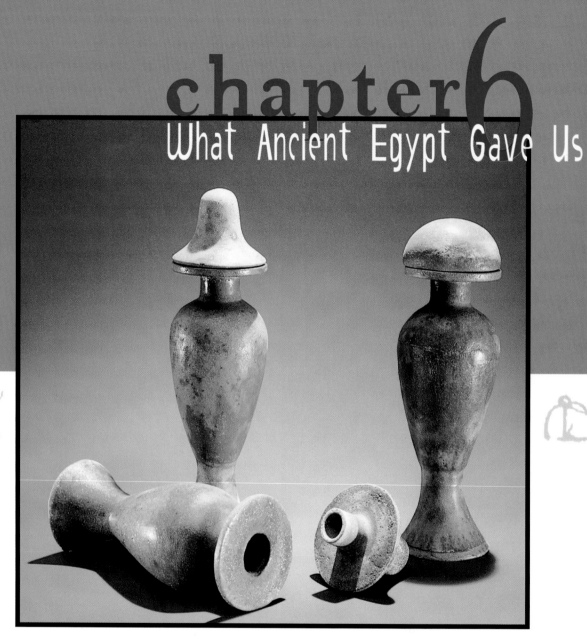

These small vases, which are made
of glass and faience, were found in
the tomb of Tutankhamen.

In Egypt the past is alive. The majestic pyramids are survivors of ancient times, as is the simple shaduf a farmer dips for water and the mud bricks that villagers set to bake in the sun. It is still possible to find flat looms, sun clocks, papyrus, and faience made in the 5,000-year-old way. These are only the obvious traces of the past. Many other achievements of the early Egyptians also appear in our modern world.

What is the most important contribution ancient Egypt has made to modern times? It may be time itself. Our sun-based calendar came to us from Egypt by way of Julius Caesar, who brought it to Rome about 2,050 years ago. So did our 24-hour days, although our winter and summer hours are always the same length.

The Egyptians also laid the foundations of geometry, a type of advanced math, with their formulas for calculating area and volume and their study of angles. Their practical engineering math was passed along to the Greeks when Alexander the Great conquered Egypt about 2,330 years ago. The Greeks extended this knowledge into the theories of math taught to schoolchildren today.

The scientific study of medicine also began in ancient Egypt. Their physicians handed down knowledge of anatomy, drugs, and surgery to later cultures. They also passed along an attitude. The ancient doctors were taught to observe, examine, diagnose, and prescribe treatment, just as doctors do today.

This detail of an Egyptian tomb painting shows a farmer plowing a field with oxen.

As pioneers in irrigation and agriculture, the ancient Egyptians were one of the first groups of people to build canals and reservoirs, to use a plow, to keep cattle, sheep, oxen, goats, and donkeys.

The form and craftsmanship of the pyramids probably inspired architects of later eras. The Egyptians invented many techniques for handling stone, and they were the first to use it in monumental structures. Until the Egyptians worked with this material, no one else in the world had even laid a slab of stone on top of two columns.

Recently an underground tomb containing almost 100 rooms was discovered. It will take decades to explore the tomb completely, and no one knows what wonders will be found. Yet even if no scientific artifacts appear, the Egyptians' achievements stand out. Their ideas and tools have been passed down through more than 100 centuries to shape modern science and modern civilization.

GLOSSARY

algebra—a form of arithmetic in which letters represent numbers.

archaeologist—a scientist who studies past human life and activities.

artifact—an object remaining from an ancient civilization.

astronomy—the study of objects outside Earth's atmosphere.

boning rod—a tool with three pegs of equal height, two connected by a cord and one loose. It was used to level stone.

caisson—a large tube-shaped structure used to build tunnels.

capstone—a pointed stone with a plug on the bottom. A capstone was placed at the very top of each pyramid.

cubit—a measure of length originally equal to the distance between the pharaoh's elbow and the tip of his middle finger.

equation—in algebra, a problem using letters to represent unknown values.

faience—a material made from powdered stone. It was used to make jewelry.

mummify—to enbalm or preserve.

nilometer—a stone gauge with lines used to measure the floodwaters of the Nile.

papyrus—a paperlike material made from reeds.

pharaoh—an Egyptian king.

place value—the value given to a digit as a result of its position in a number. In 71, the place value of 7 is tens. In 718, the place value of 7 is hundreds.

plumb line—a simple tool that can be used to establish a true vertical.

quarry—an open excavation site where the materials such as stone are dug out for use in construction or industry.

sarcophagus—a pharaoh's coffin.

shaduf—a weighted pole used by ancient Egyptians to raise water.

silt—a type of soil that contains a large quantity of crumbled sedimentary rock and a little bit of clay.

veneer—a thin layer of expensive wood laid over cheaper wood to produce furniture or other wooden items at a lower cost.

weight arm—a tool used by ancient Egyptians to move huge stones for the pyramids.

RESOURCES

Books

Defrates, Joanna. *What Do We Know About Egypt?* New York: Peter Bedrick Books, 1991.

Green, Robert. *Tutankhamun.* Danbury, CT: Franklin Watts, 1996.

Hart, George. *Ancient Egypt.* New York: Time-Life, The Nature Company Discovery Library, 1995.

Jessop, Joanne. *The X-Ray Picture Book of Big Buildings of the Ancient World.* London: Watts, 1992.

Kerr, Daisy. *Ancient Egyptians.* Danbury, CT: Franklin Watts, 1996.

Kondeatis, Christos and Sara Mitland. *Ancient Egypt Pack.* Boston: Bulfinch, Little Brown and Company, 1996.

Morley, Jacqueline. *How Would You Survive as an Ancient Egyptian?* New York: Franklin Watts, 1995.

Putnam, James. *Pyramid.* New York: Eyewitness, Knopf, 1994.

Tiano, Oliver. *Ramses II and Egypt.* New York: Henry Holt, 1995.

Internet Sites

Due to the changeable nature of the Internet, sites appear and disappear very quickly. The following resources offered useful information on ancient Egypt at the time of publication.

Welcome to Ancient Egypt provides information about the Sphynx, pyramids, the Nile, afterlife, hieroglyphics, Egyptian gods, and Tutankhamen. Its address is **http://www.geocities.com/Athens/Acropolis/3076/index.html**.

The Egyptian Museum is a great place to find out more about Egyptian mummies, sculptures, tomb equipment, written documents, and jewelry and other accessories. It can be reached at **http://www.idsc.gov.eg/culture/egy-mvs.htm.**

Egyptology Resources is a site set up by the Newton Institute at the University of Cambridge. It has information about upcoming conferences, exhibitions, seminars, and articles as well as e-mail addresses of egyptologists. The site also has links to many other related home pages. It's address is **http://www.newton.cam.ac.uk/egypt/**.

Exploring Ancient World Culture includes maps, timelines, essays, and images that describe ancient civilizations in India, China, Greece, and the Near East. It can be reached at **http://eawc.evansville.edu/index.htm**.

INDEX

ABOUT THE AUTHOR

Geraldine Woods is the author of more than thirty-five books for young people, many written with her husband Harold. She teaches English and directs the independent study program at the Horace Mann School in New York City. The Woodses have one son, Thomas, who is now in law school. Ms. Woods frequently visits the Egyptian section of the Metropolitan Museum of Art.